THE UNCERTAIN FUTURE

GORBACHEV'S EASTERN BLOC

THE UNCERTAIN FUTURE

GORBACHEV'S EASTERN BLOC

Edited by
Nicholas N. Kittrie
and
Ivan Volgyes

A PWPA Book

PARAGON HOUSE

New York

Published in the United States by
Professors World Peace Academy
481 8th Avenue
New York, New York 10001

Distributed by
Paragon House Publishers
90 Fifth Avenue
New York, New York 10011

A Professors World Peace Academy Book

The Professors World Peace Academy (PWPA) is an international association of professors, scholars, and academics from diverse backgrounds, devoted to issues concerning world peace. PWPA sustains a program of conferences and publications on topics in peace studies, area and cultural studies, national and international development, education, economics, and international relations.

Library of Congress Catalog-in-Publication Data

The Uncertain future
Gorbachev's Eastern Bloc
  "A PWPA book."
  Bibliography: p.
  Includes index.
   1. Europe, Eastern—Politics and government—1945–
2. Europe, Eastern—Foreign relations—1945–
I. Kittrie, Nicholas N.,   II. Volgyes, Ivan,
DJK50.U53.1988   947.085   88-12446
ISBN 0–943852–61–7
ISBN 0–943852–62–5 (pbk.)

Table of Contents

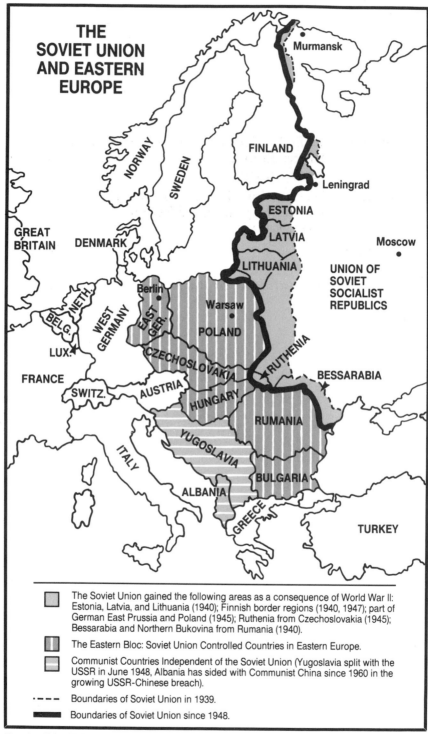

THE SOVIET UNION AND EASTERN EUROPE

NORWAY

SWEDEN

FINLAND

Murmansk

Leningrad

ESTONIA

LATVIA

LITHUANIA

Moscow

UNION OF SOVIET SOCIALIST REPUBLICS

GREAT BRITAIN

DENMARK

NETH.

BELG.

LUX.

WEST GERMANY

EAST GER.

Berlin

Warsaw

POLAND

RUTHENIA

BESSARABIA

FRANCE

SWITZ.

AUSTRIA

CZECHOSLOVAKIA

HUNGARY

RUMANIA

YUGOSLAVIA

ITALY

BULGARIA

ALBANIA

GREECE

TURKEY

The Soviet Union gained the following areas as a consequence of World War II: Estonia, Latvia, and Lithuania (1940); Finnish border regions (1940, 1947); part of German East Prussia and Poland (1945); Ruthenia from Czechoslovakia (1945); Bessarabia and Northern Bukovina from Rumania (1940).

The Eastern Bloc: Soviet Union Controlled Countries in Eastern Europe.

Communist Countries Independent of the Soviet Union (Yugoslavia split with the USSR in June 1948, Albania has sided with Communist China since 1960 in the growing USSR-Chinese breach).

‑ ‑ ‑ ‑   Boundaries of Soviet Union in 1939.

━━━   Boundaries of Soviet Union since 1948.

[Based on Richard F. Rosser, An Introduction to Soviet Foreign Policy (Englewood Cliffs: Prentice-Hall, Inc., 1969), p. 254]

THE UNDOING OF A MONOLITH

RESPONDING TO DIVERSITIES IN THE EASTERN BLOC

Nicholas N. Kittrie

N ow that the two competing superpowers have charted the course toward a new equilibrium in the relations between the communist East and the democratic West, the concerns as well as opportunities posed to Moscow's and Washington's allies by the restructured detente require serious and prompt attention. How will the old alliances withstand the hopefully benevolent winds of change? Many Western political commentators have already expressed concern about the impact of the mutual exchange of visits by President Reagan and Secretary General Gorbachev and euphoric pronouncements upon the resolve of America's NATO allies. The task of this volume, for counter-balance, is to explore the effect of these developments upon the nations held captive in the Soviet Union's Eastern Bloc. A region of Europe which geographically and historically has found itself squeezed between the march of the Ottoman Empire on the Southeast, Teutonic militarism in the Northwest, and Muscovite expansionism on the East, the Eastern Bloc finally has become part of Russia's expanded empire in the post-World War II era. The six countries of the Bloc (Bulgaria, Czechoslovakia, East Germany, Hungary, Poland, and Romania) cover a territory of 440,000 square miles (exceeding the combined size of France, West Germany, and Great Britain) and contain 115 million people (equaling the combined populations of France and West Germany). Militarily united under the Warsaw Pact, the nations of the Eastern Bloc claim a standing army of two and one-quarter million people and a potential reserve force of four and a half million soldiers, exceeding the comparable NATO armies. In battle tanks, artillery, antiaircraft guns, antitank weapons, surface-to-air missiles, armed helicopters, bombers, and interceptors/fighters, however, the Warsaw Pact forces far outnumber the resources of NATO.[1]

Since these nations have come under domestic communist rule as well as USSR's domination after the Red Army's march into Eastern Europe at the conclusion of World War II, there has been a persistent Soviet effort to turn Eastern Europe into a monolithic communist community. The early coalition governments—consisting of communist and noncommunist elements—were soon purged of the nonbelievers. No national political or economic deviations were permitted within the bloc. When the Poles and then the Czechs accepted the Western invitation to participate in the July 1947 conference to review the implementation of the Marshall Plan, Stalin vetoed the idea. No initiatives by Eastern Bloc countries or their leaders were to be tolerated. When Yugoslavia's Josip Tito proposed a Balkan federation, Stalin "was furious."[2] Under Stalin's rule, no departures were to be permitted from farm collectivization or from central planning. And even the slightest manifestation of political, economic, or cultural liberalization was deemed a threat to the well-being of the communist cause.

In 1948, the Cominform, founded a year earlier to bring about greater Eastern Bloc cohesion, unceremoniously expelled the independence-bound Yugoslavia and its leader, Marshall Tito. The Yugoslav leadership was charged with being imperialist agents, with operating a "purely Turkish terrorist regime," and with utilizing their "nationalist line" to turn the country into an "ordinary bourgeois republic."[3] In 1956, in the face of Hungarian efforts at liberalization, Soviet troops attacked and entered rebellious Budapest, resulting in a death toll of tens of thousands and in about 200,000 Hungarians fleeing the country. Again in 1968 the Soviet and Warsaw Pact forces, excepting Romania, ended the Czechoslovak effort under Alexander Dubcek to institute "democratic communism." Finally, in 1980, Poland's installation of martial law avoided the necessity for Soviet and Warsaw Pact intervention in order to suppress the liberal inroads made by the independent Solidarity movement.

One would expect the prospective thaw in East-West relations to greatly advance the movement towards greater domestic autonomy—political as well as economic—increasingly manifested throughout the region since the end of the Stalin era. The thaw is also likely to restore and enhance the forces of historical, cultural, and ethnic diversity within the Eastern Bloc. The region consists of a colorful assembly of ethnic backgrounds and histories. The Bulgarians, Czechs, Slovaks, and Poles are primarily Slavic in origin. Romanians, tracing their origins to the Roman conquest of the native Dacian kingdom in 106 A.D., are predominantly Latin in language and culture. The Hungarian origins go back to the Magyar invaders coming from the Orient, and the East Germans are derived from the Germanic tribes who fought against Julius Caesar in 53 B.C. and were consolidated into a German Empire by Charlemagne in the 8th century and again by Otto von Bismarck in 1871. In their religious persuasions, both before and after the coming of communism, the nations of the Eastern Bloc have ranged from the devoted Catholicism of Poland and Hungary to the Eastern Orthodoxy of Bulgaria and Romania, and the Protestantism of East Germany.

In the course of modern history the people of Eastern Europe have occasionally joined forces in their struggles against common enemies—be they the Ottoman or the

Austro-Hungarian empires. As often as not, however, they found themselves in conflict with each other and on different sides of the trenches in the aftermath of the Balkan Wars, during World War I, and World War II. Four of the Eastern Bloc nations—Bulgaria, East Germany, Hungary, and Romania—joined the Axis forces of Adolf Hitler and Benito Mussolini in World War II. No wonder, therefore, that Winston Churchill and Franklin D. Roosevelt were unwittingly willing to permit the communist subjugation of these defeated Axis nations as part of the reparations accorded the Soviet Union for its human and material sufferings during the world war. Not only did the Allied leaders concede the Soviet need for friendly regimes on its borders, but they also approved the economic exploitation of these former German satellites for the rebuilding of the Soviet economy.

Despite all efforts by Stalin and his successors to impose the Leninist-Stalinist model on Eastern Europe—including forced industrialization, the collectivization of agriculture, and the centralization of the economy—local diversities could not be totally suppressed. On the contrary, for purposes of domestic survival and to dispel the domestic impression of subservience to Moscow, many of the region's communist leaders had assumed an ultranationalistic stance.

The more than forty years of actual living under the Marxist-Leninist dogma and its promise of greater social, economic, and political justice eventually have produced in the region a wide range of experiments as well as varied results. In increasing measure, national characteristics and historical forces have begun to manifest themselves. "The countries of the Warsaw Pact can no longer be regarded as 'Stalinist peas in a pod'," recently asserted Thomas W. Simons, Jr., United States Deputy Assistant Secretary of State for European Affairs.[4] There has been growing economic diversification within the region—from tokens of private production and marketing to fullblown second economies. There has been a resurgence of national traditions and political culture within the different countries. There has been a growing revitalization of religious experiences and institutions. There has also been a weakening of the stifling economic links between the nations of the Eastern Bloc and the Soviet Union. In its own unrelenting surge towards technological advancement, the Soviet Union has come to rely less on Eastern Bloc raw materials and low-quality consumer goods. Increasingly, the Eastern Bloc must sell its products in the West and in Third World countries. Moreover, much as the Soviet Union is looking to the West for improved technology, the Eastern Bloc is also seeking to acquire from the West the technologies which are not readily available from their old master, the Soviet Union. The balance of trade between the Eastern Bloc, the Soviet Union, the West, and the Third World reflects these new changing realities. Increasingly, Western Europe and the United States have assumed the roles of major trading partners with several Eastern Bloc nations.

Now that in the name of *glasnost'* and *perestroika*, Mikhail Gorbachev appears to be encouraging less rigid and more experimental approaches to socialistic society and economics in his own country, the Eastern Bloc nations may likewise be expected to be relieved of the old pressure to follow the doctrinaire dictates of an over-zealous Moscow. Moreover, the State Department's Thomas W. Simons suggests that, overall, the "Soviet perception of reduced cold war tensions" may make Eastern Bloc countries "less important as pawns in the East-West struggle." Hence he foresees reduced Soviet sensitivity towards the directions and destinies of the Eastern Bloc.

Karl Radek, one of Stalin's chief spokesmen on international affairs, wrote as far back as January, 1934, in the American journal *Foreign Affairs:* "Foreign policy is a function of domestic policy. It solves problems which result from the development of a given society, a given state, under definite historical conditions. . . . Its aims are. . . shaped by the economic and political structure of changing forms of society."[5] Given the currently weakened state of the economies of the Eastern Bloc countries, given their technological deficiences and needs, given their people's striving for more consumer goods and for a greater degree of cultural and political freedom, and finally, projecting a lessening of Soviet dominance—how long can the entrenched domestic and foreign policies of these nations lag behind? Past experiences with governmental responses to rising expectations in the Eastern Bloc should make one cautious. Not always have these expectations met progressive changes. Stricter enforcement of the status quo and even retrogression have often been the lamented outcome. Yet there is strong evidence that the time might now be right for dramatic and lasting changes in the Eastern Bloc's domestic as well as foreign policies. How will the United States and its Western allies respond to this opportunity?

To this observer the Eastern Bloc, due to its distinct socioeconomic heritage, seems to offer more suitable and better opportunities for change than those that exist in the Soviet Union. Not only are the nations of Eastern Europe distinct from each other and not the same "peas in a pod," but whatever pod they do share might be considered radically different from that of the Soviets. Russia, beginning with its early history and throughout its empire, has known little more than political and economic oppression and despotism. Writing in 1965, R. V. Burks pointed out in *The Dynamics of Communism in Eastern Europe:* "For the Russian and Asian cultures there is, in the realm of government, virtually no alternative to political despotism."[6] But many of the nations of Eastern Europe have known better and have striven for more. Despite the existence of corrupt bureaucracies, fixed elections, coups d'état, and oppressive regimes, the liberal tradition has had deep roots in Eastern Europe. Hungary has had a limited parliamentary system since the Middle Ages. Poland, in 1988, lagging only one year behind the United States, is celebrating the bicentennial of its own constitution. "The people of eastern europe, in contrast to those of Russia and Asia," claims Burks, have, therefore, been "well aware of alternatives to authoritarian government, and never more aware than after a generation of rule by authoritarian others, first Nazis, then communists."[7]

NICHOLAS N. KITTRIE

This volume has undertaken to record and realistically review the historical as well as contemporary forces within the Eastern Bloc countries. We have sought to assess both existing realities and aspirations for the future. It is hoped that this effort might contribute to the formation of a more creative and pro-active rather than reactive American policy towards the Eastern Bloc, a policy which will also place greater emphasis on the dynamics and opportunities in each of the region's distinct countries. In setting out to refine the American policy towards the region, and its specific nations two self-evident measuring sticks must continue as our guidelines: one, the measure of distinctiveness and independence manifested by each Eastern Bloc country towards the foreign policy of the Soviet Union, and, second, the degree of domestic liberty permitted by each country in the realms of politics, society, religion, and economics.

NOTES

This book benefitted from a conference sponsored by the Professors World Peace Academy held in Washington, D.C., December 18, 1987. There the authors met to discuss and improve their chapters. The editors wish to express their gratitude to the Academy and to Dr. Gordon Anderson, the Academy's Secretary-General, and the staff, for their dedication and wholehearted support for this project.

1. Molly Moore, "INF Treaty Raises Apprehensions within NATO," *The Washington Times*, December 5, 1987, p. A10, col. 1. The Warsaw Pact nations are reported to have 52,200 battletanks compared to NATO's 22,000; 46,500 artillery pieces compared to NATO's 13,700; and 4,930 interceptors/fighters compared to NATO's 899.
2. Richard F. Rosser, *An Introduction to Soviet Foreign Policy*, (Englewood, N.J.: Prentice-Hall, 1969), p. 255.
3. *Ibid.*, p. 256.
4. "Emerging Economies in the Eastern Bloc," *The Wilson Center Reports* (December, 1987), p. 1.
5. Quoted in Richard F. Rosser, *op. cit.*, p. 16.
6. R.V. Burks, *The Dynamics of Communism in Eastern Europe* (Princeton: Princeton University Press, 1965), p. 197.
7. Burks, *op. cit.*, pp. 198-9.

ONE

FIRE AND WATER

POLITICAL REFORM
IN EASTERN EUROPE

Bennett Kovrig

Few faiths in history spread as rapidly and dramatically as did Marxism-Leninism. A unique amalgam of spurious science, naive egalitarianism, and dictatorial politics, it raised the hopes of toiling masses and captured the imagination of intellectuals eager for the power to realize utopia. The simple notion that private property lies at the root of exploitation and oppression served to justify a political revolution that concentrated power to an unprecedented extent in the hands of a small elite. The vanguard party appropriated the state and all instruments of social reproduction, destroyed its real and alleged enemies, and thereafter claimed to rule with the consensual support of a seamless socialist society. The new political order presented itself as historically preordained, inherently progressive, and therefore essentially and unquestionably legitimate. Its ultimate triumph over capitalism and political alternatives, notably liberal democracy, was claimed to be equally preordained. Communism and capitalism, in the typical observation of Erich Honecker, were as different and incompatible as fire and water.

This orthodox vision of the nature and promise of Marxism-Leninism has spawned many variants ranging from Stalinism to Yugoslav-style self-management, each claiming for itself ideological and historical validity. The building of socialism required tactical flexibility and adaptability, but the ruling party retained the exclusive right to define the changing parameters of "real existing socialism." And yet, belying its promise, the formula for the pursuit of humanistic objectives by the concentration of political power has registered a failure of historic proportions. To be sure, some elements that are essential to Marxism and that fall under the rubric of social justice have conquered the world in the guise of the welfare state. But the record of Marxist economics and Leninist politics is so dismal that their appeal to Western intellectuals and workers has largely dissipated, while in the East true believers and power-holders rule over disillusioned and restless subjects.

That Marxism-Leninism is in a state of crisis can be seen even in the pages of *Izvestia*, where a commentator recently acknowledged that because of "reversals, contradictions, crises, and stagnation" the Soviet Union had failed to create a socialist model worthy of emulation.[1] The capacity of despotic oligarchies to survive and reproduce must not be underrated, and it is equally ahistorical to be optimistic about their ability to engineer fundamental political reforms. The crisis may be terminal, but Gorbachev and some of his counterparts in Eastern Europe are evidently intent on altering some hitherto sacred elements of Marxist-Leninist economics, and even politics, in a desperate attempt to save socialism from the dustbin of history.

The failure that the more clear-eyed communist leaders are disposed to acknowledge lies in the realm of the economy, where state ownership and central planning have nurtured low productivity, technological backwardness, endemic shortage, and stagnation. From Cuba to China, from Yugoslavia to the Soviet Union, socialism has failed to deliver more than an equality of poverty. Socialist revolutions succeeded in redistributing existing wealth (and rewarding the new ruling elite), but despite forced savings and heavy investment, the objective of sustained and balanced growth and modernization has not been met. Past attempts at structural reform did produce some successes, notably in the covert privatization and marketization of agriculture in Hungary and China. However, with the exception of East Germany, which derives a huge advantage from its special relationship with the Federal Republic, none of the socialist economic variants has fostered the productivity and technological innovation necessary to narrow the gap separating them from the free market economies.

This enquiry addresses the political consequences of the failure of socialist economics rather than the complex causes of that failure, although economics and politics are inseparable in the theory and practice of socialism. Since the historic promise of socialism was essentially economic, conjuring up not only equality but material wealth for all, its failure undermines both the ideology's and the ruling parties' claim to popular legitimacy. That the new socialist man with his Marxist faith remains a rare and endangered species in Eastern Europe is a fact that causes acute political (if not necessarily ideological) discomfort to the regimes, for it confirms not only the failure of decades of indoctrination and socialization but also of the socialist economy. When Ferenc Havasi, a member of the Hungarian party's Politburo, observed in a speech at Chatham House that "Marxism is identified with a minority point of view in our country," one is surprised not by the message but by the medium.[2] Rather more significant was the publication in *Komsomolskaya Pravda* of the results of a poll among Soviet youth showing that over 30 percent did not believe in communism, while barely half professed belief without reservations. Communism, said a Komsomol member, is a fairy tale.[3] Political apathy and alienation represent the fundamental challenge to any reform of Marxism-Leninism.

"A new reading is needed of the theoretical legacy of our predecessors," said Gorbachev before a gathering of communists and other leftists in Moscow on November 4, 1987.[4] Indeed, in the Soviet Union and its dependencies the irreducible requisite of Marxist economics is being redefined as the predominance of social (read state) property. Central planning and the central allocation of resources and setting of prices are under attack. Decentralization, a more flexible price structure, and privatization are in vogue. Restructuring, or *perestroika*, aims to revitalize the economy by tapping the invisible incentives of the market, but as Politburo member Alexander Yakovlev observed, "many minefields lie in its path," for the forces of "stagnation and conservatism have so far only surrendered their first fortifications."[5]

The obstacles are indeed formidable, for they are deeply rooted in the political and social culture of the Soviet Union. The instinct for self-preservation of the political elite, the party apparat, and the state bureaucracy is inimical to the risks of innovation. Managers in industry and agriculture are not eager to exchange the security offered by the classical command model for the uncertainties of the market. Workers guaranteed a standard of living, albeit low, fear unpredictable prices, wage differentiation, and unemployment. Only in intellectual circles has Gorbachev's "new thinking" aroused instant enthusiasm, and for reasons that have little to do with economics. Abel Aganbegyan, Gorbachev's outspoken economic adviser, foresees the reduction in the number of centrally-set prices from 500,000 (out of 24 million officially determined prices) to 1,000 by the end of 1990, and a trebling of productivity.[6] Western experts are skeptical. Partial marketization, particularly in light of the performance of the more radical Hungarian economic reform, offers little assurance of improved productivity. It is easy to cite Marx in defense of wage differentiation ("from each according to his ability, to each according to his work," until socialism is superseded by the perfect state of communism); it is quite another matter to alter the rigidities of Soviet society.

Determined to forestall the economic decline of the Soviet Union, Gorbachev is promoting his economic restructuring with the political devices of *glasnost'* (transparency) and *demokratizacya* (democratization). These are clearly meant to be the handmaidens of *perestroika* and not primary and independent objectives, although to Western audiences even the cautious

Yegor Ligachev will insist that democratization is the "key link" of restructuring.[7] The Soviet reformers realize that turning their economy around will be difficult and painful, requiring the collaboration of the elites and middle classes and the—at least passive—support of the working masses. Political reform is therefore the Leninist regime's instrument of mobilization and legitimation, and not a design for its fundamental transformation. The intelligentsia is to be wooed with *glasnost'*, which sanctions a greater but uncertain degree of free debate and artistic license. Democratization aims to increase the popular sense of political participation by such innovations as multi-candidate local elections and the participation of workers in the selection of managers.

Nothing in Gorbachev's vision of reform threatens the integrity of single-party rule. Even though the fundamental flaw of the Soviet system is more political than economic, the Leninist legacy remains the keystone without which the entire edifice would collapse, and no Soviet leader dares envisage such a historic surrender. The Gorbachevian concept of political reform aims, in Seweryn Bialer's excellent analysis, at "inverted democracy," that is, at modest expansion of participatory democracy at the microsocietal level while leaving the macroinstitutional level essentially intact. This, observes Bialer, is the reverse of what historical experience shows to be the prerequisite of modernization.[8] As long as the party apparat and the state bureaucracy retain the monopoly of ideological and administrative authority, free from public accountability and institutional checks and balances, the creative potential of authentic democracy cannot be tested in the Soviet Union.

The reforms may nevertheless generate new political tensions in the system. Trimming the mandate and size of the state bureaucracy will not proceed without resistance. Bureaucrats and apparatchiks may not welcome the proposed autonomy of enterprise managers and farmers, and the embryo of a civil society nurtured by *glasnost'* and grassroots democratization could grow to challenge the discipline of Leninism. Gorbachev realizes that economic reform demands modification in the behavior of communists who are used to issuing "strings of orders," and he has made vague references to the need for democratization and "socialist pluralism."[9] There can be little doubt, however, that many party members share the late Konstantin Chernenko's view that "practice shows that where 'pluralism' flourishes it leads only to the loss of the party's fighting efficiency, to the erosion of its ideological foundations."[10] Innovation so far is limited to local elections by secret ballot with, in a few instances, a choice of candidates. A poll conducted after last summer's trial run indicated that 77 percent of the respondents favored the new system, and further improvements are under consideration for ensuring real competition on issues among candidates.[11]

Even Soviet observers concede that the ground is not fertile for participatory democracy: the absence of democratic experience, and the patriarchal tradition that easily accommodated Stalin's personality cult are obstacles as formidable as the conservatism of the entrenched apparat.[12] Also illustrative is the fate of a draft law on referendum. The right to hold referenda was enshrined in both the Stalin and the 1977 constitutions, and work on a draft law began after its reiteration, but the eventual draft addressed only "nationwide discussions." Such experiments in direct democracy, particularly after the Polish referendum fiasco in November 1987, evidently carry too many risks for socialist regimes. And yet, as the reformist editor of *Ogonyok*, Vitaly Korotich, observed, it is "impossible to take the next steps (toward economic reform) under totalitarianism"; democracy, he averred, means "free discussion around every problem."[13] The public airing of such questions is, of course, a remarkable departure from established Soviet practice. A Russian philosopher, Gennady Batygin, wrote in the weekly *Novoye Vremya* that individual human interests held "absolute priority over the interests of states, classes, nations and ideology." He defined democracy as the recognition of each individual as a sovereign person and the protection of individual opinions.[14] No wonder that conservative forces are alarmed and that amidst the talk of restructuring, *Pravda* will warn that "playing into democracy may result in catastrophe" and that since the party's leading role is entrenched in the constitution, party committees have the right to recommend candidates for official posts.[15] Grassroots democracy and *glasnost'* have already generated a wide range of discussion clubs (notably the Russian nationalist "Pamyat") and local nationalist protests from Riga to Alma Ata. Most Soviet citizens may be accustomed to the party's monopoly of power, but the winds of socialist pluralism threaten to stir up social turbulence not seen since the October revolution.

The Gorbachevian vision of *perestroika* has a bearing on Eastern Europe, if only because the revitalization of the Soviet economy needs that region's resources and may be held back by the burden of an economically stagnating empire. Reflecting on the crises in Hungary in 1956, in Czechoslovakia in 1968, and in Poland in 1956 and since 1980, Gorbachev does not blame socialism. He blames "miscalculations by the ruling parties."[16] He intimates therefore that restructuring, openness, and democratization should be emulated throughout the region while insisting that the several ruling parties are independent and free to choose their own roads to modernization. In his speech on the 70th anniversary of the October Revolution, Gorbachev invited concern for the general cause of socialism but allowed that "we have become convinced that unity does not mean being identical or uniform. We have also become convinced that socialism does not, and cannot, have a model against which all [socialist systems] are compared."[17]

The Kremlin's new mixture of reformism and permissiveness is a complex stimulus for regimes struggling with economic crisis and social discontent. The stimuli from other outposts of socialism are equally unsettling. The Chinese have decollectivized agriculture, are experimenting with decentralized planning and the market, and now appear intent on depoliticizing government. Observing that the party had become a "hotbed of bureaucracy," Chinese party secretary Zhao Ziyang has called upon that organization to get out of day-to-day government and limit its role to "supervision and guidance."[18] At the same time that the Chinese are divesting themselves of the last vestiges of Maoism, Yugoslavia is in the throes of the agony of Titoism. The legacy of worker self-management and regional autonomy has brought the country to the brink of bankruptcy and anarchy. In Djilas's summation, "self-management without a free market economy, and that without political pluralism, cannot be made to work; it is one auxiliary Utopia among many that communists resort to when practical life repudiates the principal Utopia of communism itself."[19] As the international communist movement becomes ever more pluralized, casuistic appeals to Marxism-Leninism lose their last shreds of credibility. Lacking a model of successful socialism, and uncertain about the fate of *perestroika*, the East European ruling parties are like swimmers unable to see the other shore and uncertain whether to tread water or adopt a fast stroke.

The mandatory qualifier for every existing and proposed political variant in Eastern Europe is the word "socialist." Socialist morality, socialist market, socialist culture, socialist legality, and socialist democracy are ritualistic formulas whose common denominator is claimed to be some elusively distinctive humanism free of capitalist sin. Particularly in the case of socialist democracy, the positive, socialist dimension escapes most East Europeans even if they do not share the view of a Polish dissident that the difference between democracy and socialist democracy is analogous to that between a chair and an electric chair. It is clear enough that in "real existing socialism," socialist democracy can take despotic form. How socialist democracy can accommodate social and political pluralism without converting itself into Western-style pluralistic democracy is a theoretical and practical problem that is receiving unprecedented attention in contemporary Eastern Europe.

Marxism-Leninism remains the exclusive state religion, but since the departure of its infallible interpreters, Stalin and Mao, it has served to legitimize a proliferation of roads to socialism. The Leninist party's leading role is one of the few immutable tenets, and even that is now subject to cautious reconsideration. The question is posed: ought the party's exercise of power be monopolistic or merely hegemonistic? The debate is informed by redefinitions of the nature of socialist society. The socialist revolutions eliminated the economic basis of class differentiation and antagonism, and in time the advent of a classless society was officially proclaimed. The primacy of the industrial proletariat, whose vanguard the party claims to be, lost some of its practical significance as farmers and the intelligentsia were absorbed into a class-free workers' state. The fiction of an undifferentiated socialist society, possessed of coherent interests articulated by the ruling party, began to give way by the early 1960s to a more realistic acknowledgement that even under socialism a multiplicity of social strata existed, as did group interests distinct from both individual interests and the great collective interest. The social changes induced by economic modernization accentuated the pluralistic nature of East European societies, posing a tough challenge to single-party regimes in quest of authentic legitimacy.

The diverse legitimation strategies of the East European parties can only be adumbrated here, and only in a few cases do they reflect a disposition to political reform. In East Germany and Romania, the most and least prosperous countries of the region, there is no sign of openness and democratization, or even of any inclination to follow the Soviet lead in economic restructuring. Both Honecker and Ceausescu profess to be satisfied with their own version of economic reform. In fact, the East Germans have created a relatively successful variant of the command economy, characterized by huge industrial combines. The dissenting voices of various religious and ecological groups and of writers chafing under censorship are occasionally heard, young people have publicly hailed Gorbachev, and some still risk their life to flee across the infamous wall, but the ruling party shows no sign of willingness to relax its control over a naturally disciplined and comparatively affluent population. Relations with West Germany rank high in official and popular interest, and the regime's dedication to demarcation and separate nation-building precludes experimentation with popular democracy.

In Romania, the despotic rule of the Ceausescu clan has driven the country into penury and despair. The leadership has tried to legitimize its Stalinist and totalitarian rule internally, by fostering nationalism, and externally, by a foreign policy occasionally at variance with Warsaw Pact orthodoxy. Economic decline undermined the appeal of nationalism, which had as its most negative manifestation the ruthless pursuit of repressive and assimilationist policies toward the large Hungarian and German minorities. The regime's appalling record on human rights gradually dissipated the credit it had earned with its diplomacy, turning Romania into an international pariah (even within the Soviet bloc) and driving the U.S. Congress to demand suspension of its most-favored-nation tariff privilege. The rare open expression of popular discontent has been met with temporary concessions and severe reprisals by the dreaded Securitate. Ceausescu's determination to trim the country's foreign debt by reducing domestic consumption and essential imports has depressed the standard of living and debilitated industry.

Romanian history (outside Transylvania) has not nurtured the autonomous impulses of a civil society, a factor that facilitates tyranny, although economic distress has provoked a few strikes and riots, the most serious in Brasov in November 1987. That event prompted an unprecedented public warning from a party veteran, Silviu Brucan, that the workers would no longer tolerate being treated like obedient servants and that mass repression would only precipitate a rupture between the party and the working class similar to that in Poland.[20] Brucan had just published, in the West, a treatise on the reforms necessary to adapt socialism to the scientific-technological revolution of the late twentieth century. He argues that "although change will have to start from the economic end, it must necessarily involve social relations, and ultimately the political system and the Communist party itself." His key proposal is "party pluralism," or the legalization of factions and their representation in the Central Committee, as the necessary condition of democracy. (Factionalism, of course, has been proscribed in the Soviet and derivative parties since 1921.) Brucan also advocates the separation of power between the executive, legislative, and judicial branches of government and an open electoral process. The party, in Brucan's schema, remains the sole political organization.[21]

In perpetuating the historically worst features of Marxism-Leninism, including the cult of personality, Ceausescu has alienated not only the mass of his subjects but also his less despotic allies, including the Soviet Union. The symptoms of monarchical megalomania displayed by the "genius of the Carpathians"—his proclaimed infallibility, monumental building projects, disregard for human suffering, statesmanlike posturings—suggest that political reform, even of the Marxist-Leninist sort, will have to await his natural demise. In Romania, Ceausescu told the national party conference on December 14, 1987, democratization means increasing the party's role, not decreasing it.[22]

The Czechoslovakian political culture bears the richest tradition of organized pluralism as well as of democratic socialism. The revolution from above of the Prague Spring promised to reinvigorate these latent tendencies, and Dubcek's "socialism with a human face" heralded the political and even institutional legitimation of pluralism in some hypothetical adaptation of Marxism-Leninism. The Kremlin's alarm at this forerunner of *glasnost'* led to the second Prague coup in twenty years, this time with the visible rather than just an implied threat of violence.

Haunted by the specter of 1968, the restoration regime of Gustav Husak preserved one reform—the federal structure accommodating Slovakian nationalism—but otherwise branded as anathema all liberalization evocative of the Prague Spring. This conservative immobilism is being put to the test by Gorbachev's "new political thinking," which bears embarrassing similarity to the reformist notions of 1968. Husak's embarrassment must have been aggravated by the popular display of admiration for Gorbachev on the occasion of the latter's visit to Prague and by the report that the disgraced Dubcek sent his best wishes to the Kremlin on the 1987 anniversary of the Bolshevik revolution.

The Prague regime has drafted a minimalist version of economic *perestroika*, sanctioned experiments in the choice of enterprise managers by an elected workers' council, and provided for the more competitive selection of cadres, but there is no suggestion that the party might lower its profile. Moreover, far from emulating Moscow's *glasnost'*, the regime has stepped up harassment of the peaceable and politically moderate Charter 77 dissident group. The replacement of Husak as general secretary by the conservative apparatchik Milos Jakes is not likely to lead to the "democratization of public and political life" evoked in Gorbachev's congratulatory telegram.[23] In Prague, as in East Berlin and Bucharest, political reform is absent from the official agenda.

"Deeds, deeds, and only deeds" is the ubiquitous slogan on the walls of Sofia. Bulgaria has been tinkering with economic reform since the 1970s, to little apparent effect. But under Gorbachev's impetus, the trickle turned into a flood of proposed changes in the course of 1987. At the July plenum of the Central Committee, the doyen of East European leaders, Todor Zhivkov, criticized bureaucratic inertia, mismanagement and inefficiency, and called for the restructuring of central, regional, and local government and for *glasnost'* in the media. The scope of reform was expanded at the November plenum to encompass the party, the electoral system, the legal system, and the price and wage structure of the economy. The proposals ostensibly aim at decentralization and "self-government." The party, said Zhivkov, should "devolve its extrinsic state and economic activities" and "not usurp the functions of other bodies (nor) supersede the elected bodies of self-government." He reportedly assured the plenum that Gorbachev's restructuring is an "irreversible process."[24] The mass media needed radical change to free them from "paternalism"; the party daily, *Rabotnichesko Delo*, ought to comment on, and if necessary oppose, the work of the Central Committee.[25] Legal reform should make the judiciary impervious to political pressure. Positions of responsibility should be opened to capable nonparty members. The party would no longer use "administrative methods" to get its way.

In the economic sphere, the regime is considering the currently fashionable remedies of trimming central administration and devolving responsibility to the enterprises, giving workers a say in the choice of managers, linking prices to market forces, converting the state agro-industrial complexes into associations of "work teams," and allowing greater wage differentiation. Also envisaged are changes in ownership law transferring the state's "anonymous property" to the workers.[26] Zhivkov's reformist zeal has yet to be tested in implementation, but he has evidently hitched Bulgaria to the Gorbachev bandwagon.

Apart from the chaotic restructuring of public administration, the government has introduced a bill providing for multiple candidacies in local and national elections, although the party and the *Fatherland Front* will continue to play a leading role in the choice of candidates. Zhivkov has also called for regular national and local referenda. It is too early to tell whether these measures represent significant democratization of a hitherto thoroughly authoritarian political system, and the press so far has paid only token tribute to *glasnost'*. In July the *Fatherland Front* daily published the view of a Bulgarian philosopher, that "every monopoly, whether in the material or intellectual sphere, entails a limitation or loss of liberty and leads to social stagnation"; without political pluralism, he warned, "spontaneous" explosions of unrest could occur.[27] The same newspaper later carried an interview with Lech Walesa, quoting his opinion that "without pluralism in three areas—politics, society, and economic life—no system can work well." The interviewer asked rhetorically what guaranteed the preservation of socialism in such a system.[28] Bulgaria's delicate flirtation with pluralism will presumably not overstep the mark set in Moscow. For all the talk of self-government, there was no open discussion of the political issues and options before Zhivkov revealed the reform package.

The political climate in Poland remains poisoned by the challenge of Solidarity and the response, martial law, in 1980-81. The crushing foreign debt and a faltering economy contribute to the social malaise confronting the regime of General Jaruzelski. The three great failed revolutions in communist Eastern Europe had taken diverse forms. Hungary in 1956 went through a violent revolution from above and below. Czechoslovakia's experience in 1968 represented essentially a revolution from above. Solidarity was a massive revolution from below. The Hungarians tried to discard Marxism-Leninism, whereas the Czechs and Poles ostensibly aimed to modify its practice. It took Kadar a decade to forge a new social contract with his people. Jakes and Jaruzelski have yet to devise a viable compromise. The Polish regime rules over a profoundly alienated society characterized by an unconcealed oppositional subculture that draws its inspiration from Solidarity, nationalism, and the Roman Catholic church.

Kadar's alliance policy of the 1960s held out the promise of economic modernization and cultural tolerance to win popular support for his regime. Poland already enjoys the most liberal cultural environment in the region, while in the economic sphere Jaruzelski can only offer prolonged austerity, not a propitious circumstance for a regime in quest of popular legitimacy. The general is an enthusiastic Gorbachevite, but in the words of a Solidarity leader, "he does not know how to realize *glasnost*', or political opening, in Poland without Solidarity, and he is not willing to try it with Solidarity because he is afraid of losing control of the country."[29] His attempts to break this political deadlock have so far brought little reward. The Consultative Council, which was meant to draw non-party notables into an advisory relationship, enjoys marginal political influence and no public recognition. The official "Patriotic Movement for National Rebirth" (PRON) is equally impotent. Meanwhile, along with a multitude of other opposition groups (including the more radical "Fighting Solidarity"), the officially banned Solidarity survives both underground and in public life. Its legitimacy is sustained by regular policy statements and the international recognition given to Lech Walesa, whose foreign visitors have included Vice President Bush.

The regime in October announced a reorganization of the government, including the trimming of the central bureaucracy, and an economic recovery program encompassing some decentralization, expansion of the private sector, and the phasing in of market principles, notably in the form of reduced subsidies and steep price hikes. The party's leading bodies meanwhile engaged in heated debate over a program for the development of "socialist self-government." The original draft asserted that the party "does not demand a monopoly for ruling" and anticipated a "socialist opposition" consisting of the two small "allied" parties (the Democratic and Peasant parties), presumably acting with greater freedom than hitherto, and of legally sanctioned political discussion clubs. The program also advocated strengthening local government, amendment of the electoral law to allow more than two candidates and dropping the preferential candidate ballot format, a second chamber of the Sejm (parliament) possibly composed of representatives of local governments, and equal access for nonparty members to managerial posts. This "further democratization of political life" had limits, warned Jaruzelski: "We are clearly drawing the line between our changes and those which would debilitate the state and dismantle socialism."[30] Criticized from opposite perspectives by party conservatives and opposition spokesmen, and technically rejected in the subsequent national referendum, the political reform proposals face an uncertain future.

The Polish regime's practice of *glasnost'* is schizophrenic. It tolerates the technically illegal manifestations of a pervasive oppositional subculture, including over four hundred underground periodicals. It has sanctioned the appearance of an independent magazine of political comment, *Res Publica*. Meanwhile, the main official publishing house has instituted a system of bonuses to reward journalists for toeing the party line.[31] The authorities have displayed great reluctance to register independent associations. A few local "economic associations," conceived to aid private enterprise, have been sanctioned, and a church foundation for channeling foreign aid to private farmers received official approval. The grudging concessions to "socialist pluralism" did not extend to the reestablishment of the old Polish Socialist Party, attempted by a group of opposition activists on November 15, 1987. Although no Polish law bans the formation of political parties, police broke up the founding meeting, and the government spokesman declared that since their intention was to "harm the process of democratization in Poland," the party would "not be tolerated but treated as an illegal group."[32] The shifting sands of civil rights in Poland will put to the test the ombudsman appointed a few days after this event.

The national referendum conducted on November 29 was a landmark event in postwar East Europe. Since the manipulated votes of the takeover period, only one nationwide plebiscite had been held in the region, in Romania in November 1986, when 99.99 percent of the voters approved a cut in defense spending. The Jaruzelski regime asked Poles to endorse a radical economic cure, including huge price increases, and "the Polish model of a deep democratization of political life, the objective of which is to consolidate self-government, to broaden the rights of citizens and to increase citizens' participation in governing the country." Although no one apart from diehard conservative communists disagreed with the need for reform, Solidarity dismissed the exercise as an affront to the dignity of Poles and called for a boycott, while the church pointedly refrained from comment. The regime's campaign for support was remarkably candid, for it included details on the proposed price increases as well as assurances that the reforms would proceed regardless of the outcome of the referendum. The threshold of approval was set at 51 percent of eligible (rather than actual) voters, apparently a leftover provision from an early draft that would have allowed citizens' groups to call referenda. In the end, the government's tactics backfired. Only two-thirds of the electorate voted, and roughly the same proportion of the ballots cast endorsed the two propositions, falling short of the required threshold.

The outcome of the referendum could technically be regarded as a vote of no confidence in the government, which announced lamely that it would proceed with a modified reform program. The cynical paternalism characteristic of socialist regimes was displayed by the government spokesman: "The Sejm by announcing the referendum gave its power to the public. The public failed to act decisively and so has returned the power to the Sejm."[33] Paradoxically, both party conservatives and opposition forces felt vindicated by the results. Yet for the first time an East European regime had allowed its policies to be tested in a free and publicly reported vote. Since the leading role of the party is beyond question, a vote of no confidence has no predictable consequences in a socialist system. Still, a precedent has been set that, despite the outcome, may inspire communist and other reformers.

In Hungary, misgivings about the viability of Marxism-Leninism abound even in the public media. The country that experienced the most radical economic reform in the Soviet sphere is now engaged in extraordinarily wide-ranging and open debate on the shortcomings of the political system and possible remedies. Part of the impetus, at least in party circles, comes from a deepening economic crisis. The hybrid model of market socialism, launched in 1968, registered some successes, notably in the spheres of agriculture and consumer goods. But a multitude of negative factors—-bureaucratic obstruction, political caution induced in part by Soviet apprehensions and a domestic egalitarian backlash, incompetent management, and the wasteful misuse of massive foreign credits—impeded the healthy development of market forces to the point that by 1987 the country found itself on the brink of bankruptcy. The government's remedy is, inevitably, a heavy dose of austerity, and it is the attendant social tensions that are driving the leadership to consider political reform as well.

Kadar's alliance policy entailed a certain depoliticization of everyday life. He acknowledged the stratified nature of even socialist society but offered little institutional outlet for the multiplicity of interests. Sectoral organizations, such as the National Council of Trade Unions, the Chamber of Commerce, or the National Association of Producers' Cooperatives, were consulted on economic matters and occasionally won concessions to their interests, but this embryonic corporatist model operated in secrecy, without public accountability, and with little regard for the nominal sovereignty and representative function of parliament. Multiple candidacies for parliamentary seats have been permitted since 1966, and in

1985 they were made mandatory. Despite much manipulation from the center, some 70 "spontaneously-nominated" candidates ran for election, and 45 became deputies. It took another two years, and an economic crisis, for a relatively open debate to be sanctioned in the National Assembly on the introduction of income tax and value-added tax, and for the passing of a minor amendment to the government bill.

The problem of political reform has been addressed over the past year by working groups of the Central Committee, by the Patriotic People's Front and other mass organizations, and by opposition groups as well. These explorations are symptomatic of the decomposition of the Kadarist social contract, of a crisis of legitimacy that affects the party leadership as well as the political system in which the party lays claim to a permanent and leading role. Their common denominator is the observation, conceded even in official circles, that the regime has made a mess of the economic reform and has failed to deal with a multitude of social needs and ills. In a speech to the National Assembly, Kadar offhandedly accepted some responsibility for the crisis and allowed that restructuring of the economy required political reform as well:

> "We have a one-party system—this is how it happened historically. But obviously some things have slowly altered— the various state, social and economic institutions and organizations have become more autonomous. Perhaps they are not autonomous enough, but this is the direction we have taken and will follow. With regard to the political structure, the Central Committee has put on its agenda a review of the leading role of the party."[34]

The debate on ideology in Hungary is addressing hitherto taboo topics, such as the problem of legitimation. The socialist states, observes Jozsef Bayer, a senior member of the party's Institute for Social Science, have developed national variations of Marxism, thereby fostering in practice that which they officially deny, the pluralization of Marxism.[35] The contradictions and tensions generated by economic change have intruded into the most sensitive ideological area, that of the political system's ability to cope with conflicts of interest. The party is intent on reforming the system, and there is consensus on the need for a better mechanism to articulate, reconcile, and aggregate social demands, to develop alternate policies, and ensure social control. Some advocate minor modifications to the existing system, others argue that only Western-type pluralism, a multi-party system, can do the job. Between the poles of the monolithic-bureaucratic system of Stalinist times (writes Bayer, citing Gyorgy Lukacs) and of the manipulative pluralism of bourgeois democracy lies a form of socialist democracy based on the old concepts of councils and social self-management.[36]

The excessive linkage of ideology and daily politics, argues Bayer, is dysfunctional in that it transforms a government crisis into a political crisis, and the latter into a legitimacy crisis of the entire system. One practical consequence is that many have come to identify Marxism-Leninism with complacency and conservatism. The remedy, according to the "new political thinking," is to diffuse the burden of legitimation by decentralizing decision-making and expanding forms of self-management. The old style of forced consensus (codified within the party in the ban on factionalism) makes it impossible to accept the basic rules of the system and at the same time dissent from all or part of the dominant ideology. This suppression of dissent and latent pluralism has a disorienting and demoralizing effect and erodes the hegemony of the ideology. The need, then, is for a system of institutional and legal guarantees for democratic openness and debate, for predictable "rules of the game" consistent with the hegemony rather than the monopoly of socialist ideology.[37]

Officially sanctioned free debate will liberate Marxists from the "moral defensive," and although it is bound to have some negative consequences, the party can set the limits through its direct and indirect control of the mass media and education. The legitimation of the ideology and system can thus be pursued in a rational and democratic fashion. There is an ominous generational challenge to legitimacy, concludes Bayer, for a growing number of young people are hostile to Marxism, distrust authority, and believe that the modernizing capability of socialism is inferior to that of liberal democracy.[38]

Party resolutions dating back to 1971 have called for greater devolution of responsibility to state organs, but the Politburo concluded in October 1986 that the results were insufficient and launched a massive two-year research program on reform of the political mechanism. The general thrust is toward a new division of authority and labor, decentralization, and greater "socialist democracy." What is in question is not the principle of the party's leading role but its practice. In that practice, the party has gone beyond the setting of broad guidelines to interfere directly in the process of government and administration. This pattern is reinforced by the inclination of state agencies to bypass the government and seek party rulings on matters within their purview, on the assumption that the party is the sole arbiter of conflicting interests. There exists also an excessive duplication of work on policy development in the party and government apparatus, conducted in excessive secrecy. The tentative solution is a clearer separation of the powers of party and state, allowing the government greater latitude to legislate and administer on the basis of the party's general political guidance.[39]

One officially endorsed remedy is the invigoration of a parliament that is constitutionally sovereign (subject to the leading role of the party) but in practice has functioned as a purely symbolic ratifier of policy issuing from the overlapping elites of party and state. Indeed, most rules in Hungary take the form of decrees rather than of parliamentary bills. The problem is to define a role for parliament that is neither formalistic nor unpredictably "parliamentaristic," i.e., threatening the party's political primacy. The ideas for reform advanced in the relevant working group include longer sessions, more committee work, votes of no confidence, secret votes on personnel matters, and a parliamentary agency for the auditing of public expenditure. A more active role for the recently created Constitutional Law Council is also envisaged.[40]

A related issue is the role of the Presidential Council, which is a creation of parliament that serves both as the collective head of state and as a surrogate for the National Assembly by virtue of its unlimited power to issue decrees. It is proposed that the Presidential Council's rule-making powers be circumscribed and its draft degrees submitted to standing committees of parliament. With regard to the Council of Ministers, or Cabinet, and the ministries, a certain streamlining is envisaged whereby the party's guidance would be conveyed to government departments primarily through the Council, transforming the latter into a "responsible political government," while the ministries would acquire greater autonomy in the implementation of policy.[41]

The review of the political structure could not ignore the electoral system, the latest version of which was tested in the 1985 elections. That experience showed mixed results, including a systematic and covert operation from the center to set quotas (for women, for social groups) and to manipulate the nominations, and attempts by dissidents to exploit the opportunity for spontaneous nominations. (The party's pressures and manipulations were excoriated in the controversial recent film *Valasztasok* [Elections].) Hailed by some officials as the first real election in socialist Hungary, the event alarmed conservative communists as bearing the seeds of anarchy. Only minor modifications are envisaged by the party-sponsored working group, such as the earlier public identification of candidates enjoying official sponsorship prior to the nomination meetings, and nomination to the national list (which accounts for 35 seats in parliament) by various mass organizations in addition to the Patriotic People's Front. The neo-corporatist tendency of this last proposal is also evident in the suggestion that such institutionalized interest groups as the Chamber of Commerce and the National Council of Trade Unions be brought under the aegis of the Presidential Council and serve as equal partners (rather than subordinates) of the government in the preparation of policy decisions.[42]

The public debate on political reform encompasses politicians and academic experts as well as opposition groups, their only common denominator being the necessity of some reform and the imperative (denied by only a few dissidents) of accommodating the leading role of the party. Thus the political scientist Attila Agh evokes Gramsci in calling for transition from the monolithic-monopolistic to the hegemonistic exercise of power so that the "democratic energy of a civil society can be released."[43] Reflecting on a related problem, the current prime minister and Politburo member Karoly Grosz complained that "collectivism dilutes individual responsibility."[44] The scope of the debate has been broadened by the party's own, admitted, sense of ideological uncertainty. As Janos Berecz, the party's chief ideologue, conceded in a speech to the Central Committee on November 11, the "capacity of capitalism to renew itself ... has proved to be considerably stronger than we thought"; at the same time, many elements of the image of socialism propagated by the party are "contradicted by reality," and "cracks have appeared in the party's ideological unity." Socialism, he said, must be able to transcend its past self and advance toward social self-management and self-government.[45]

Such key political institutions as the trade unions and the Communist Youth League have joined the chorus of critics, acknowledging that their traditional mobilizing function has left their nominal constituencies unrepresented. Decentralization and authentic interest representation are the common themes of their advocacy.[46] The boldest urgings for political reform in leading circles have come from the secretary-general of the Patriotic People's Front, Imre Pozsgay, who at the Lakitelek meeting of reformist intellectuals on September 27 called for escape from "enlightened absolutism" in the direction of humanized political relations, public accountability of party and government, national referenda, and the clarification of the relationship of party and state, which in its present bureaucratic form degrades the party. At other times he has argued that the predominance of state property is economically counterproductive, that greater institutional guarantees for pluralism were necessary, and that in the long run even the question of new parties may be raised.[47] Authentic political pluralism signifies of course individual and group autonomy, and this, observed a professor of constitutional law, necessitates revision of the party's own role. Multiple candidacies, writes the same authority, are as meaningless as single candidacies in elections unless they reflect valid social differences.[48]

The most comprehensive program for political reform was drafted by the political scientist Mihaly Bihari for the Patriotic People's Front.[49] Its arguments and recommendations go only marginally beyond those that have been publicly aired. The first step in becoming a democrat, says Bihari (quoting the late populist scholar Istvan Bibo) is not to be afraid. He calls upon a reformist party to exploit to the fullest the freedom of action allowed by international (read Soviet) and domestic circumstances. Accepting the leading role of the party as an unalterable principle, he envisages a political structure in which the party exercises its dominant, hegemonic role by political rather than administrative means. In this radically decentralized system, the authority of the party and other institutions should be delineated by law, with a clear separation of powers. The government should be responsible to parliament, the latter should become an authentic legislative body, and like-minded deputies should be free to form parliamentary "fractions." This artful symbiosis of Marxism-Leninism and pluralism entails the restoration of authentic constitutionalism and the fundamental transformation of the official political culture.

Perhaps the most remarkable feature of the reform debate in Hungary is that the programmatic contributions of the democratic opposition are consistent in spirit if not detail with the more official proposals. "Social Contract," the document drafted by three leading opposition intellectuals, is strikingly similar to Bihari's version[50] They, too, display reluctant realism with respect to the party:

> The "leading role" of the party is, in actual fact, a limitation of the sovereignty of the people; this, however, must be accepted as being the guarantee towards the Soviet Union that the Hungarian state will satisfy its obligations in its external policy and will ensure the perpetuation of its social political

system. This special role of the Party, however, does not exclude the progress of the country's political system towards more constitutional forms, including a pluralism enshrined in law, provided that the Communist Party becomes a constitutionally regulated part of the State's legal framework.

This guarantee, according to "Social Contract," could be provided either by the device of a head of state, independent from parliament, and nominated by the party, or by some "Law on the party" defining the Central Committee's constitutional powers, which would include veto power on foreign policy and a limited *nomenklatura* authority. As the dissident writer Istvan Csurka put it, "a multiparty system is against the rules of the big empire. We have to create something else."[51]

Having tested with mixed results the reformability of socialist economics, Hungary may be progressively testing the political reformability of Marxism-Leninism. The regime is evidently seeking some new political formula that can insulate the party from immediate responsibility for the hardships besetting the Hungarian people, alleviate some inefficiencies of the economic system, and neutralize pluralistic pressures that might otherwise conspire to present a radical challenge to its legitimacy. The openness of the debate on political and economic reform has its critics in the party, and the depth of latent popular opposition was vividly displayed recently in questions addressed by coal miners to party secretary Janos Berecz. The questions (and his evasive answers) were published in a provincial party paper. They included: Why were the incompetent leaders responsible for wasting $15 billion of foreign credits not called to account? Why were people first informed about leadership changes by foreign radio (i.e., Radio Free Europe)? Why were the socialist countries sinking into poverty while nonaligned Finland and Austria were prospering? And finally, if the party and government were confident of enjoying public trust, why did they not sanction free elections under international supervision?[52]

Unqualified democracy signifies majority rule, a condition that the East European parties claim to satisfy without ever testing it. There is every indication that after forty years of socialism, only a small fraction of their electorates would vote for the communist party if given a free choice. For instance, independent sociologists in Czechoslovakia conducted a secret survey in 1986 and found that barely 14 percent would vote for the communists.[53] At the same time, some of the communist elites have come to the realization that economic rationality and its potential benefits cannot be realized with constant political and bureaucratic meddling, and that a depoliticization of the economic sphere is inseparable from a greater tolerance of pluralism. The East European systems are in a state of political and economic exhaustion, and while the totalitarian state can preserve a semblance of stability even amidst stagnation, most communists find that prospect ideologically unpalatable.

In their quest for economic salvation, the parties prefer to resort to cosmetic measures, such as reorganizing and trimming the central administration, and to half-hearted concessions to market forces. When impelled to go further into the murky waters of political reform, they try to coopt the intelligentsia with material rewards and a dose of cultural freedom, and to mobilize political support with controlled experiments in grassroots participation. What such palliatives cannot alter is the fundamental power relationship between the party and the people—a relationship characterized by a Hungarian dissident as "Mengeleism," endless experimentation by irresponsible communists on helpless human subjects.

The attempt to redefine Leninism in order to accommodate pluralism, that is, a sharing of power, can be easily dismissed as squaring the circle. Political pluralism means choice within limits set by consensus, or social contract, and not by a self-appointed elite. To be sure, most of the East European systems have transcended the monolithic Stalinist model and display a measure of bureaucratic pluralism, a contest of interests within the administrative structure of the state. But the broad plurality of interests in the society at large does not enjoy institutional channels and legal guarantees for the free articulation of its choices. The party alone thus bears the multiple burden of identifying, reconciling, and satisfying the growing diversity of social interests, of acting as its own opposition while proscribing factionalism, of asserting the legitimacy of its rule while disclaiming responsibility for misgovernment. Communism's real failure, observes Zbigniew Brzezinski, "lies in its inability to transcend the phase of industrialization, to move from the industrial era into the post-industrial world." That step "requires a solution to the problem of participation," and "genuine participation is incompatible with the rule of a Leninist-type party." The party, then, is the "fatal flaw."[54]

Yet even if Marxism-Leninism is fundamentally incompatible with the open society of liberal democracy, the prospect of its gradual and limited pluralization is theoretically conceivable and may be practically realizable. Single-party pluralism is an oxymoron only if political pluralism is held to be an absolute state that obtains solely in multi-party systems. The party's claim to moral authority and legitimacy may be analogous to that of a philosopher-king, but there is a world of difference between absolute and constitutional monarchy, for in the latter a civil society and its representative institutions can exercise a wide range of choice. Djilas is ambivalent regarding the prospect of pluralized socialism, offering on the one hand the axiom that the disease of communism cannot be mitigated by excising or diluting some of its elements, and on the other hand allowing that "anything that dilutes a generically bad political system must be welcome."[55] Constitutional communism, defined as the acceptance by the party of legal constraints, of a separation of powers, of a structure of interest representation that provides for authentic political participation, and of freedom of expression, could nurture a civil society better equipped to cope with the daunting task of modernization in Eastern Europe.

The seismic faultline of socialism runs down Eastern Europe, where national traditions, pluralistic pressures, and the wretched record of "real existing socialism" conspire to threaten the stability of the regimes. It is in Eastern Europe that revolutions have shaken the Marxist-Leninist edifice, and it is in Eastern Europe that the capacity of the system for politi-

cal self-reform is most likely to be tested. The momentary disposition of some communists to explore political alternatives
could easily founder on the shoals of the distrust of freely expressed popular choice that characterizes a profoundly
authoritarian and paternalistic dogma. The ultimate arbiter of
change remains, of course, the Soviet Union. A new social contract along the lines that emerge from the debate in Hungary
nevertheless could win a reprieve for socialism. Given the
tenuous base of their legitimacy, communists may well recall
the fate of the sorcerer's apprentice and fear releasing incalculable social forces that could eventually overwhelm them. The
figurehead role of a constitutional monarch will appeal to
neither the true believer nor the power-seeker. But even if a
moderately pluralized model of socialism does not create a permanent new state of political equilibrium, it is rationally
preferable to the doldrums of despotism and the danger of
bloody revolution.

NOTES

1. Aleksandr Bovin in *Izvestia*, July 11, 1987.
2. *East European Markets*, October 30, 1987, p. 5.
3. *The Times* (London), September 30, 1987.
4. Tass, November 4, 1987.
5. *Pravda*, December 3, 1987.
6. *The Economist*, November 28, 1987.
7. *Le Monde*, December 3, 1987.
8. Seweryn Bialer, "Gorbachev's Move," *Foreign Policy*, No. 68, Fall 1987, pp. 63-65
9. Tass, November 20, 1987.
10. K. Chernenko in *Kommunist*, No. April 6, 1982, quoted in Timothy J. Colton, *The Dilemma of Reform in the Soviet Union* (New York: Council on Foreign Relations, 1984), p. 60.
11. *The Guardian*, October 16, 1987.
12. These points were made by the *Literaturnaya Gazeta* commentator Fyodor M. Burlatsky on Radio Prague, September 8, 1987.
13. *Washington Times*, November 17, 1987.
14. Reuter, October 20, 1987.
15. Yuri Makhrin in *Pravda*, November 16, 1987.
16. Mikhail Gorbachev, *Perestroika: New Thinking for Our Country and the World* (New York: Harper & Row, 1987), p. 163.
17. Tass, November 2, 1987.
18. *People's Daily* (Beijing), November 26, 1987.
19. Milovan Djilas and George Urban, "New Utopias for Old," a conversation in seven parts, unpublished, 1987, p. 54.
20. *The Independent*, November 28, 1987.
21. Silviu Brucan, *World Socialism at the Crossroads: An Insider's View* (New York: Praeger, 1987), pp. vii, 140-146.
22. Radio Bucharest, December 14, 1987.
23. Tass, December 17, 1987.

24. Associated Press, November 13, 1987.
25. Reuter, November 20, 1987.
26. *The Independent,* November 16, 1987.
27. Vasil Prodanov in *Otechestven Front,* July 24, 1987.
28. *Otechestven Front,* December 4, 1987.
29. Bronislaw Geremek quoted in the *Washington Post,* September 18, 1987. The magnitude of popular discontent with the regime and its austerity policies was revealed by a government-commissioned opinion poll conducted on November 19, 1987, i.e., before the referendum but after the announcement of the proposed price increases. Over three-quarters of the respondents expressed wholly negative opinions about the government and saw the likelihood of social conflict. (*Polityka,* 9 January 1988, and *The Washington Post,* January 7, 1988.)
30. Associated Press, November 25, 1987.
31. Reuter, November 9, 1987.
32. Reuter, November 17, 1987.
33. Jerzy Urban quoted in *The Times* (London), December 2, 1987.
34. *Nepszabadsag,* September 17, 1987.
35. Jozsef Bayer, "A mai ideologiai problemak ertelmezeserol (On the Interpretation of Current Ideological Problems)," *Tarsadalmi Szemle,* No. 11, November 1987, p. 44.
36. *Ibid.,* pp. 45-46.
37. *Ibid.,* pp. 46-47.
38. *Ibid.,* pp. 50-51.
39. *Nepszabadsag,* November 24, 1987.
40. *Nepszabadsag,* November 25, 1987.
41. *Nepszabadsag,* November 26-27, 1987.
42. *Nepszabadsag,* November 26, 1987.
43. Attila Agh, "Politikai reform es civil tarsadalom (Political Reform and Civil Society)," *Magyar Tudomany,* October 1987, pp. 777, 786.
44. *Magyar Nemzet,* November 28, 1987.
45. *Nepszabadsag,* November 14, 1987.

46. On trade union attitudes, see *Nepszava*, 1 December 1987; on the Communist Youth League, *Magyar Ifjusag*, October 2, 1987, and *Dunantuli Naplo*, October 20, 1987. See also the roundtable discussion "A part es a tarsadalmi szervezetek (The Party and the Social Organizations)," *Partelet*, October 1987, pp. 30-40.
47. *Heti Vilaggazdasag*, October 24, 1987; *New York Times*, October 25, 1987; *Hufvudstadsbladet* (Swedish-language daily, Finland), November 21, 1987.
48. Interview with Dr. Peter Schmidt, *Uj Tukor*, October 11, 1987; Peter Schmidt, "Kotelezo tobbes jeloles az 1985-os kepviselovalasztasok tukreben (Compulsory Multiple Nominations in the Light of the 1985 Elections)," *Tarsadalmi Szemle*, October 1987, pp. 48-57.
49. Mihaly Bihari, "Reform es demokracia," unpublished, August 1987.
50. Ferenc Koszeg, Janos Kis, Ottilia Solt, "Tarsadalmi szerzodes: A politikai kibontakozas feltetelei," *Beszelo* (samizdat), June 1987, reproduced as "A Social Contract: Conditions for a Political Renewal," *East European Reporter*, Vol. 3, No.1, 1987.
51. *Baltimore Sun*, November 21, 1987.
52. *Dunantuli Naplo*, September 12, 1987.
53. Reuter, December 1, 1987.
54. Zbigniew Brzezinski, "The Crisis of Communism: The Paradox of Political Participation," *The Washington Quarterly*, Vol. 10, No. 4, August 1987, pp. 168, 172.
55. Djilas, *loc. cit.,* pp., 50, 59.

TWO

IDEOLOGY DISABUSED

COMMUNISM WITHOUT A FACE IN EASTERN EUROPE

Andrzej Korbonski

I shall begin this essay by apologizing to Marx and Engels and by hypothesizing that toward the end of the 1980s, "a specter is haunting Europe—the specter of [anti-]communism." It will be the purpose of this paper to try and discover whether this hypothesis has any validity, whether we are dealing with a short-lived transitional phenomenon, or whether, at best, it represents wishful thinking on the part of professional communist-haters.

A number of caveats are in order, in no particular order of importance. To begin with, I shall confine my analysis to Eastern Europe which I shall define as being composed of seven countries—the so-called "East European Six" (Bulgaria, Czechoslovakia, East Germany, Hungary, Poland, and Romania), plus Yugoslavia.

At first glance this constraint makes sense since it will allow me to focus on only communist-ruled states and to trace the demise of traditional Marxist-Leninist ideology. On the other hand, it is in the non-communist polities of Western Europe that the bankruptcy of Marxism-Leninism has recently become most visible. A simple comparison of the political situation in such countries as France, Greece, and Italy in the second half of the 1940s and today, some forty years later, is most revealing.

It is often forgotten today that the communists occupied key positions in the French and Italian governments as late as 1947 and that Greek communists were conducting what appeared to be a reasonably successful civil war in an attempt to overturn the "Stalin-Churchill" wartime deal which assigned Greece to the British sphere of influence. To be sure, the communists were ultimately ousted from the governments in Paris and Rome, and General Markos was also defeated in his bid for power in Athens, but both the PCF and PCI continued for quite a while as major actors in their respective political arenas.

After all, even such an astute observer of the international political scene as Henry Kissinger appeared quite concerned about *appertura a sinistra* and the historical compromise in Italy. The rise of Eurocommunism in the late 1960s and early 1970s appeared to provide a persuasive testimony to the continuing vitality and attractiveness of Marxism-Leninism in its new reincarnation, especially when the French and Italian parties were joined by the resurrected Spanish Communist Party. As it turned out, Eurocommunism proved to be a flash in the pan rather than a truly revisionist movement, but at least it could be argued that by its willingness to experiment and to search for new solutions, Marxism-Leninism was far from dead. Even in West Germany, hitherto impeccably opposed to any legitimation of communist activities, the legalization of the *Deutsche Kommunistische Partei* and growing leftist leanings of an important segment of the SPD, manifested the persistent dynamism of communist ideology. The fear of a potential communist takeover in Portugal by a pro-Stalinist party provided still another indicator. After all, only seven years ago, the newly-elected President Francois Mitterrand invited four members of the French Communist Party to join his cabinet, suggesting that the communists at the beginning of the 1980s still represented a potent political force in France.

It is hard to believe today that all this happened less than 15 years ago. To be sure, since then an astute observer of the West European political scene would have noticed a rightward trend in several countries, most prominently in Britain, West Germany and, more recently, France. If one adds the United States and Canada, the triumph of the moderate right and the collapse of the left appeared complete. It is not the purpose of this essay to analyze the reasons for the seeming collapse of the West European left. However, if one assumes that such a striking bankruptcy of Marxism-Leninism has indeed occurred in the West, it stands to reason that a similar demise has most likely set in across the demarcation line in Eastern Europe, even though none of the ruling oligarchies in the region would be willing to admit it, at least not yet. What follows is an attempt to survey the ideological scene in Eastern Europe and to answer the question posed earlier, to wit, has the Marxist-Leninist creed eroded completely in the region?

THE IDEOLOGICAL SCENE IN EASTERN EUROPE: THE LAST THREE DECADES

Much has been written by both East and West about the role of Marxist-Leninist ideology in the communist systems of Eastern Europe, and I do not intend to repeat familiar arguments.[1] However, since it is also my objective to trace the evolution of the official doctrine from the mid-1950s until its present collapse, it is necessary to provide, even if only rudimentary, a basis for comparison, starting with a brief description of the ideological scene in the region around the time of the death of Stalin in 1953, which is still a most convenient marker for various analyses of the East European situation.

It must be kept in mind that with the notable exception of Yugoslavia, the rest of Eastern Europe in the spring of 1953 was still very much a part of the monolithic Stalinist empire with all its corollaries. One of them was the fact that the official Stalinist doctrine, based on the principle of "one road to socialism," represented an obligatory religion which tolerated no dissent. In light of the future developments on the ideological scene, it must also be remembered that Stalinism was imposed on Eastern Europe from the outside as part of a Soviet conquest; that it was never popularly accepted or legitimated; and that it remained an alien implant in the East European body politic and society at large.

It is worth noting that even the native East European communists, who otherwise welcomed the Soviet intervention, had serious doubts about the utility of transplanting the Soviet brand of communism to East European soil. Some of them, such as Gomulka in Poland, tried their best to limit the ill-effects of the ideological transplantation, but to no avail, especially after the proclamation of the doctrine of "one road to socialism."

As is well known, the only East European leader who succeeded in retaining a considerable degree of independence from the Soviet Union was Marshal Tito of Yugoslavia, who subsequently managed to offer to the world his own "Titoist" or "national-communist" model that was to serve as an alternative to Stalinism. Tito's major achievements notwithstanding, it will become clear below that his "model"—hailed throughout the world by both communist and non-communist as a major positive innovation that would revitalize international communism—turned out to be ultimately as much of a fraud as other "experiments" or "innovations" perpetrated by other communist leaders.

One additional point needs to be emphasized. So far, I have discussed Stalinism in its "domestic" context, regulating and governing the internal political and economic decisions within each member of the Soviet colonial empire. There was, however, another "international" aspect of Stalinism, which implied that "one road" applied not only to the domestic but also to the foreign arena and that the East European satellites were also obliged to follow Soviet foreign policy to a tee.

While the widespread belief in the immutable character of the Stalinist system, held strongly by the East European *apparatchiki* and Western political scientists, assumed that no radical changes were likely to follow in the wake of Stalin's death, actual history proved otherwise. Here it ought to be noticed that the initial changes, both ideological and political, originated not in Eastern Europe but in the Soviet Union. Of course, for various reasons that need not be discussed here, the changes echoed most loudly in Hungary and Poland. But, despite the fact that both the bloodily suppressed Hungarian revolt and the bloodless Polish turnover were hailed, as glorious examples of a serious challenge to communist doctrine, by the Hungarian freedom fighters and Polish peasants and intellectuals within a year, in November 1957, it became apparent that the Soviet empire in Eastern Europe survived essentially unscathed at the cost of minor ideological concessions. The fact that these minor concessions were viewed by many Western specialists as a major surrender by Moscow, reflecting fundamental revisions in communist ideology and behavior, must have amused the successive occupants of the Kremlin. In Eastern Europe the gains of the "Polish October" also proved ephemeral—more of a cruel joke perpetrated on the gullible Polish society than a domestic reform claimed by Gomulka and his clique—and the same was true for Kadar in Hungary, who could not even save Imre Nagy from execution in 1958. Perhaps the only truly significant gain of the *annus mirabilis* in 1956 was the Kremlin's endorsement of the principle of "many roads to socialism" which, on the one hand, seemed to have given the individual East European countries license to behave in a somewhat deviant manner, and on the other hand, allowed the USSR to retain its status of *primus inter pares* within the alliance, and to experiment with its dualistic policy vis-a-vis Eastern Europe, oscillating between the emphasis on cohesion and on viability.[2]

The 1960s and 1970s witnessed the increasingly idiosyncratic nature of Soviet policy toward its allies. The two decades saw the defection of Albania, the declaration of economic independence by Romania, the proclamation of "Socialism with a human face" and the "Prague Spring" in Czechoslovakia, the growing violence and anticommunist opposition in Poland—all accompanied by attempts at economic reforms in several of the countries in the region. It was becoming clear to all, except perhaps for the ruling oligarchies in the individual countries, that on the eve of the 1980s communist

Eastern Europe was entering a serious crisis and that the only disagreement concerned its depth and the rulers' ability to solve it. There was a consensus that it was a systemic crisis in all its ramifications: political, economic, strategic-military, and ideological.

The prediction of a major systemic upheaval appeared to come true in the summer of 1980 with the birth of the independent labor union "Solidarity" in Poland. Even though the democratic experiment in Poland lasted for only 18 months and has not spread to other countries in the region, it was perhaps the clearest proof of a progressive paralysis affecting communist systems which seemed unable to deal with the growing malaise. The common explanation of the obvious immobilism in Eastern Europe put the blame on Moscow. As long as the Kremlin rulers remained oblivious to the crisis, not only in Eastern Europe but also in the Soviet Union itself, the chances of successful remedial action were nil. The signals out of Moscow were not encouraging: Brezhnev's attitude toward the Polish crisis spoke for itself and he also appeared to be quite pleased with his own stewardship of the Soviet state over the last 18 years; Andropov offered some promise but did not live long enough to fulfill it; Chernenko was obviously Brezhnev's clone and as such did not offer any promise. Mercifully, he expired after barely a year.

Chernenko's successor, Mikhail Gorbachev, was an unknown quantity in Eastern Europe and no one really knew what to expect of him. If there was any speculation about him in the region, it was that he was likely to be more like Andropov rather than Chernenko, but no individual East European leader appeared ready and willing to stick his neck out and to embrace Gorbachev with open arms.

It soon became obvious that the caution exercised by the East Europeans was well taken. Within a year or so, Gorbachev embarked on a major campaign, criticizing the Soviet domestic system, in terms that had never been used before—even by the sharpest critics of the regime. Although the target of the criticism was the Soviet political and economic system, and even though the Kremlin ostensibly disavowed any intention of insisting that the junior allies follow the contemplated reforms in the USSR, the East European leaders, some of whom have been in charge of their respective countries for more than three decades, knew only too well that the signals emanating from Moscow could not be entirely ignored.

Moreover, if the Soviet system until the mid-1980s managed to escape serious criticism by its successive leaders at least since Khrushchev, this was not the case with Eastern Europe. While the outcome of the various criticisms, reforms, and challenges to the established order in the individual countries was, at best, mixed, at least the attempts at overhauling the existing system suggested that even the ruling oligarchy in Eastern Europe was having second thoughts about the system it inherited from its predecessors. Interestingly enough, until now, the impetus for change usually originated in the individual East European countries and it has been the Kremlin which, more often than not, manipulated the threshold that the reformers dared not to cross. This time the reverse was true: the process of reform was ignited in the Kremlin and it was most of the East European leaders who tried hard to dampen it.

It may be argued that one of the reasons behind the lukewarm reception accorded Gorbachev's reforms throughout most of Eastern Europe was the fact that many East European countries in the mid 1980s were facing a serious systemic crisis and there was a growing fear among the respective leaders that an additional reformist push from Moscow might propel their political and economic system on a downward path to a real debacle, similar to that experienced in Poland at the beginning of the 1980s.

EASTERN EUROPE
AT THE END OF THE EIGHTIES

The basic question underlying the discussion in this section is whether the seven East European countries should still be considered as Marxist-Leninist or communist regimes. A corollary question is: if these polities no longer fall under the communist rubric, what rubric do they fall under, and when did they cease belonging to that category?

Anyone trying to answer these questions is faced with three major dilemmas: the first one deals with the proper definition of communism; the second one concerns the choice of the most useful approach to, or method of, analysis of communist systems; and the third one deals with the question of selecting a model, or ideal type, best suited for the investigation of the seven countries in the region.

The record shows that we had no difficulty defining communism up until the post-World War II period or as long as the Soviet Union remained the only communist-ruled country in the world. Today, according to my calculations, there are 18 countries throughout the world ruled by the Communist Party and the question is whether there is a single model that can serve as an analytical tool in the investigation of all 18 states.[3]

An argument can be made that until the middle of the 1950s, the so-called totalitarian system served its purpose admirably, both East and West. However, after 1956, Western scholars for the next twenty-odd years became deeply involved in discovering a model that would best explain what has been happening in international communism, and especially in communist Eastern Europe. It should not surprise anyone, therefore, that in the twenty-year period, 1956-1976, Western scholars suggested no less than ten separate models, including, of course, the original totalitarian model associated with Carl Friedrich and Zbigniew Brzezinski.[4]

I would submit that this rather long list reflects both the process of change in the region as well as the presence of a fertile imagination on the part of Western Kremlinologists.[5] Many of the theories, approaches, and paradigms evoke considerable nostalgia, especially when the model happens to be called "bureaucratic"[6] and the theory is that of "convergence."[7] But of course, there were others: "administered society" or "totalitarianism without terror,"[8] "transformation or degeneration,"[9] the "group theory" approach,[10] "institutional pluralism,"[11] and, last but certainly not least, the "developmental" model.[12]

This proliferation of explanatory devices makes it virtually impossible to select a model that would adequately serve our purposes. Because of that, I decided to utilize parts of the conventional totalitarian model which I view as representing the communist universals. These particular four components are:

1) the leading role of the party;
2) the party's control over means of coercion—police and military;
3) the party's control over means of communication;
4) the party's control over the economy.

These may be said to compromise what some analysts see as the historical experience of the Soviet Union which, as the first communist state, provided a reference point for its East European allies. To put it differently, these four characteristics may indeed be seen as "communist universals," applicable across the wide spectrum of communist countries in Eastern Europe.[13]

The problem is, however, that several of these "universals" are not universally applicable and, in fact, have not been universally adopted by several of Moscow's allies. Let us look, for example, at the Leninist conception of the party with its emphasis on the party's monopoly of political and economic decision making. It may be argued that in at least three out of the seven East European countries, the ruling party lost its privileged position some time ago and there are no indications that the existing situation is likely to change soon and revert to its ideal state. Thus, in Poland it may be said that the partial surrender of power and authority by the party took place about thirty years ago with the release of the Primate of the Polish Catholic Church from prison. Stefan Wyszynski, who soon thereafter assumed the co-leadership of the Polish state with Wladyslaw Gomulka, initiated a three-decade long rule by the cardinal and the party secretary. In the most recent period the party was further undermined by the workers, only to be completely ousted and replaced by General Jaruzelski and the Polish military in December 1981. Despite attempts to reinstate traditional party hegemony, the resulting changes appeared largely cosmetic and the party continued to play a secondary role.

The other two countries in question have been Romania and Yugoslavia. In the former, President Nicolae Ceausescu suc-

ceeded in subordinating the party to his own personal rule—
together with the military, the police, and the government
bureaucracy—and the chances of an early return to traditional
communist norms appear slim. In Yugoslavia, it may be argued
that the Leninist conception of the party disintegrated in the
early 1950s with the creation of the League of Communists of
Yugoslavia (LCY) and with the workers council which de facto
greatly weakened, if not entirely destroyed, the party's unity
and ability to rule. While the Communist Party in the remaining four countries (Bulgaria, Czechoslovakia, East Germany,
and Hungary) seemed to approximate the traditional model,
there were growing signs that (with apologies to Walter
Bagehot) the party was becoming a part of the "dignified"
rather than the "efficient" government structure.

What about the party's control over the means of coercion?
This has always been one of the least credible component parts
of the totalitarian syndrome. At the height of Stalinism, the
reverse tended to be true and it was more often the secret police
controlling the party than the other way around. Subsequently,
the steady decline in the power of the secret police arrested the
trend, only to be reversed once again when the military in some
countries slowly but surely began to increase its polemical clout,
overshadowing first the police, and then the party.

As pointed out above, the military is firmly in control in
Poland, it appears to share the power with other institutions in
Romania, and is becoming quite conspicuous in Yugoslavia,
where it is probably the only true national (read Yugoslav)
force capable of maintaining and/or restraining order in
Kosovo and elsewhere, if necessary. The military is obviously
less conspicuous in the remaining countries which, of course,
does not mean that they could not be quickly mobilized for a
specific purpose, including staging a coup against the party.
Hence, the second variable of the totalitarian model shows
signs of growing wear and tear.

Is the party in Eastern Europe still in command of the
countries' respective systems of communication? The answer is
both yes and no. The birth of organized political opposition in
several countries in the region since the mid-1970s was in-

variably closely tied to the appearance of clandestine publications. In some countries, such as Poland, the sheer number of underground publications is staggering and one may speculate that the authorities simply gave up their efforts to suppress the so-called "second circulation" which *ipso facto* acquired a semi-legal status in the country. The presence of illegal publications in Czechoslovakia is also very noticeable and the situation in Yugoslavia is different in that the official party press seems to enjoy considerable freedom, which it often utilizes to criticize the government. As a result it is difficult to talk about the strict party control of the media in Yugoslavia and the same is becoming true for Poland. Elsewhere in the region the party still clings strongly to this prerogative, remembering only too well what happens when the censors simply walk off their jobs, as in Czechoslovakia in 1968, or when the party press assumes the leadership of the official opposition, as in Hungary and Poland in 1956. In light of the continuing strong emphasis on *glasnost'* radiating from Moscow it may not be long before the East European diehards will have to revise their attitude and allow greater freedom for the media.

Finally, what about the party's control of the economy? This is, by far, the most complicated, albeit the most interesting, aspect of communist rule in Eastern Europe, and as such it deserves special attention.

In theory, governmental control over the economy has rested on two pillars: the state ownership of the means of production and the central economic planning system. The former was intended to eliminate whatever capitalism existed in Eastern Europe and the latter represented simply an extension of the Stalinist model to Moscow's satellites, aiming at gradual destruction of the market economy and giving priority to planners' preferences. This was the theory; in practice, however, things appeared considerably different.

The first exception to the rule was, of course, Yugoslavia. As part of creating a Titoist model to serve as an alternative to Stalinism, a major effort was launched to eliminate certain basic features of the Soviet model, such as agricultural collectivization and comprehensive central planning and to introduce new economic institutions, such as the workers' councils. But there were other significant departures from the Stalinist model, especially in the farm sector and also in the industrial and service sectors. It almost appeared as if Stalin, who clearly insisted on political *Gleichschaltung* in the region, was much less concerned with absolute economic conformity. The same seemed true for his immediate successor, Khrushchev, who not only did not object to some radical departures from Stalinist norms, such as decollectivization in Poland, but appeared interested in, and even encouraged, the early discussions about revamping the economic systems in Czechoslovakia, East Germany, and Poland.

The existing literature on economic reforms in Eastern Europe is by now so large that I will not even attempt to summarize the various arguments. From the point of view of this essay the two most important features of economic reforms in the different countries included decentralization, and reprivatization, both of which greatly affected the party's control of the economic systems. While the breadth and depth of reforms varied from country to country, one common epiphenomenon has been the impressive growth of both the legal and illegal private sectors, the latter known variously under the labels of "second economy" or "parallel market." Again, significant inter-country differences exist, with Hungary and Poland considerably ahead of the rest in terms of the extent of privatization.

To conclude this part of the argument, it is clear that only one East European country—Bulgaria—seems to fulfill satisfactorily the four conditions listed above. Czechoslovakia and East Germany come close but they show serious cracks in their armor: political opposition poses a growing challenge to the absolute party monopoly of power, and after a long period of somnolence, the Catholic and Protestant churches are beginning to show signs of life. Also the Czechoslovak and East German youth are no longer willing to tolerate the ideological straitjacket, thus creating a potentially serious problem for the authorities who until recently were used to dealing with a rather docile younger generation.

The next logical question to be answered is: if six out of the seven East European countries are not communist states or "developed socialist societies," what are they?

IS THERE ANYTHING LEFT OF MARXISM-LENINISM IN EASTERN EUROPE?

My immediate gut reaction to the question is—not very much. I tried to demonstrate above that few if any of the countries in the region fulfill the basic four requirements of communist statehood. To be sure, various institutions in many of these states still have the same name as twenty or thirty years ago, although their functions have changed significantly. Much of the rhetoric still sounds the same as before and many of the old symbols still exist. However, calling the East European countries Marxist-Leninist or communist would be a serious misnomer.

I would argue that rather than being Marxist-Leninist, the East European countries resemble more closely the traditional, conventional, authoritarian, one-party regimes that could be compared to Franco's Spain, the Greece of the colonels, Portugal on the eve of the "Carnation Revolution," and several Latin American and Middle Eastern countries—rather than to their erstwhile model, the Soviet Union.

This image of Eastern Europe is hardly new. Already some years ago, John Kautsky hypothesized that there was really little if any difference between communist and developing and/or modernizing societies,[14] and I joined him in postulating a similar hypothesis, focusing on Eastern Europe.[15] Other scholars, including Melvin Croan, thought in parallel terms, raising the question of whether "Mexico was the future of Eastern Europe?"[16]

Although the above hypothesis caused considerable interest, ultimately the feeling was that communist states were different from developing countries because of their emphasis on the role of Marxist-Leninist ideology. Arguments to the contrary were not taken seriously and, at least in the discipline of political science, the formal distinction between communist and developing polities was maintained assiduously, at least during the American Political Science Association's annual conventions. Moreover, some of the pronouncements and actions by Moscow, such as the "Brezhnev Doctrine," the respective interventions in Czechoslovakia and Afghanistan, and the threat of similar military action in Poland in 1980-81, implied that ideology was far from dead and that it could be resurrected whenever necessary.

The widely observed progressive demise of Marxist-Leninist systems throughout the world did not escape the attention of some of America's most renowned experts on communism. Thus, Kissinger discussed the "End of a Communist Illusion," in terms of economic inefficiency perpetuated by central planning[17], while Brzezinski blamed the ills of communist political systems on the absence of channels for meaningful popular participation.[18] Neither of the two mentioned the presence and impact of an official ideology as a contributory factor to the bankruptcy of East European communism.

And yet it seems to me that it is the changing popular perception of Marxism-Leninism that, in the final analysis, has been largely responsible for the difficulty encountered by the East European communist states. Although many people recognized from the start the inherent contradictions within the ruling ideology, it was the positive side-effects of the political system imposed on Eastern Europe after 1945 that persuaded significant popular majorities to accept the new political order and even to grant it some legitimacy. I have in mind the welfare or safety net aspects such as land reform, full employment, equal access, educational opportunity, rapid upward mobility, and other similar phenomena. Those groups which benefited from these aspects were willing to forgive and/or ignore the darker sides of the system—absence of democracy, violations of human rights, and restrictions on personal liberty.

By hindsight, we know that at some point the bubble burst and the beautiful dream came to an end. I do not intend to discuss the reasons for the failure of the communist systems: suffice it to say that the upward sloping curves ultimately flattened and began to turn downward. This meant a slowdown in mobility, lower rates of growth, and reduced consumption—

which in turn necessitated economic reforms that signalled further hardships such as closing inefficient factories, threat of unemployment, inflation, and general reduction in living standards.

This caused the upheaval in Poland in 1980-81, during which the Polish working class finally declared the communist system illegitimate, hoping against hope to replace it with something of its own creation. The record shows that the Polish workers not only failed to change the existing system in their own country but also failed to spread their message to their counterparts in the rest of Eastern Europe. The fact that the Czechoslovakian and East German workers reacted with considerable hostility to events in Poland provided convincing testimony to the total destruction of the traditional Marxist myth of international class solidarity that was replaced by narrow parochialism and stimulated by old-fashioned nationalism. The fact that Czech steel plants had difficulty in fulfilling their plans because the striking Polish miners did not deliver their promised quotas of hard coal angered the Czechs who refused to pay any atention to what had been happening across the border.

But this is only a part of the whole picture. It is a well known fact that in Hungary the chief opposition to economic reforms now comes not from the Communist Party but from the population, parts of which find themselves under the subsistence level. In Yugoslavia, which once hoped to synthesize of the best features of capitalism and communism, the inflation rate in 1987 was 200 percent, unemployment reached 17 percent, and corruption in the government resembled that in the Third World. In Poland, economic anarchy was rapidly producing two nations—the rich and the poor—with the apparent blessing of the party and the military, and the situation in Romania, the *anus mundi*, has reached the stage where the majority of the population would most likely greet the Soviets as liberators.

Whatever it is, it is clearly neither Marxism-Leninism, nor communism, nor "developed socialism," nor "socialism with a human face." Neither is it enlightened absolutism, which I dare

say most East Europeans would gladly welcome. What exists is neither enlightened nor absolutist. It is communism without a face, most of whose rulers do not even have the courage to admit that the system has failed. It is this refusal to acknowledge the errors and to assume the responsibility for the mistakes which is so characteristic of the current systems. Instead, the ruling oligarchies proclaim their innocence and blame the people for causing the crisis. The inevitable outcome is that the chasm between the rulers and the ruled keeps widening, as does the gap between Eastern Europe and the rest of the world. The former is decaying while the latter is developing, and it is only a matter of time before Eastern Europe becomes a part of the Fourth World, alas, with its leaders remaining loyal to the disabused legacy of faceless communist ideology.

NOTES

1. See, for example, Sarah M. Terry, "Theories of Socialist Development in Soviet-East European Relations," in Sarah M. Terry, ed., *Soviet Policy in Eastern Europe* (New Haven and London: Yale University Press, 1984), pp. 221-253.
2. For the definition of the concepts of "cohesion" and "coexistence," see James F. Brown, *Relations Between the Soviet Union and Its East European Allies: A Survey.* R-1742-PR (Santa Monica, CA: The Rand Corporation, 1975).
3. According to my own calculations, in 1988 there are nine communist-ruled countries in Europe, six in Asia, two in Africa, and one in Latin America.
4. Carl J. Friedrich and Zbigniew A. Brzezinski, *Totalitarian Dictatorship and Autocracy* (New York: Praeger, 1962), pp. 9-10.
5. For an interesting summary, see William Taubman, "The Change to Change in Communist Systems: Modernization, Postmodernization, and Soviet Politics," in Henry W. Morton and Rudolf L. Tokes, eds., *Soviet Politics and Society in the 1970s* (New York: The Free Press, 1974), pp. 369-394.
6. Alfred G. Meyer, "USSR, Incorporated," *Slavic Review,* Vol. 20, No. 3, October 1961, pp. 369-376.
7. Zbigniew Brzezinski and Samuel P. Huntington, *Political Power: USA/USSR* (New York: The Viking Press, 1963), pp. 419-436; and Alfred G. Meyer, "Theories of Convergence," in Chalmers Johnson, ed., *Change in Communist Systems* (Stanford, CA: Stanford University Press, 1970), pp. 313-341.
8. Allen Kassof, "The Administered Society: Totalitarianism Without Terror," *World Politics,* Vol. 16, No. 4, July 1964, pp. 558-575.
9. Zbigniew Brzezinski, "The Soviet Political System: Transformation or Degeneration," *Problems of Com-*

munism, Vol. 15, No. 1, January-February 1966, pp. 1-15.
10. H. Gordon Skilling, "Interest Groups and Communist Politics," *World Politics*, Vol.18, No. 3, March 1966, pp. 435-451.
11. Jerry F. Hough, "The Soviet System: Petrification or Pluralism," *Problems of Communism*, Vol. 21, No. 2, March-April 1972, pp. 42
12. John H. Kautsky, "Comparative Communism versus Comparative Politics," *Studies in Comparative Communism*, Vol. 6, Nos. 1-2, Spring-Summer 1973, pp. 135-70.
13. Archie Brown, "Eastern Europe: 1968, 1978, 1998," *Daedalus*, Winter 1979, pp. 151-174.
14. Kautsky, "Comparative Communism versus Comparative Politics," pp. 140-142.
15. Andrzej Korbonski, "The Prospects for Change in Eastern Europe," *Slavic Review*, Vol. 33, No. 2, June 1974, pp. 219-239 and 253-258.
16. Melvin Croan, "Is Mexico the Future of East Europe: Institutional Adaptability and Political Change in Comparative Perspective," in Samuel P. Huntington and Clement H. Moore, eds., *Authoritarian Politics in Modern Society* (New York: Basic Books, 1970), pp. 451-483.
17. Henry Kissinger, "End of a Communist Illusion," *Washington Post*, October 25,1987.
18. Zbigniew Brzezinski, "The Paradox of Political Participation," *The Washington Quarterly*, Autumn 1987, pp. 167-174.

THREE

THE GREAT MALAISE
ECONOMIC CRISIS
IN EASTERN EUROPE

Jan S. Prybyla

Recent Western literature on Eastern Europe is dominated by titles such as: "The Polish Road to the Abyss;" "Hungary: Before the Storm Breaks;" "Romanian Economic Performance During the First Half of 1987: Mr. Ceausescu's Irrational Policies Are Driving the Economy to Ruin;" "Bulgaria's Odd Reforms;" and "Political Drifting, An Economy in Chaos Prevails in Yugoslavia." The only bright spot in an otherwise black firmament is East Germany and the brightness is due mainly to that country's special relationship with, and significant financial help from, capitalist West Germany.[1] Mikhail Gorbachev, whose own economy is not in good shape, has complained that the Soviets sell the East Europeans good oil in exchange for "stuff that mostly belongs to the trash can." East Europe, says one observer, is "a debt-ridden, energy-short, energy-expensive region with stagnant economies, declining markets, dispirited populations, restive youth, and ageing leaders."[2] There is a perceptible drift toward Third World status. Unlike some Western governmental analyses which attribute the East European economic malaise primarily to domestic policy mistakes and exogenous causes (the two oil shocks, steep rise in interest rates on international markets, devaluation of the U.S. dollar against other hard currencies), the East Europeans, with insight gained through erosion of their modest living standards, blame the system. "Have we reached full communism yet," they ask, "or is it going to get worse?" The malaise is distributed democratically among the socialist countries, affecting every variant of the centrally planned system, from Stalinist Romania (gulag communism) to "liberal" Hungary (goulash communism). What then are the symptoms of this malaise?

SYMPTOMS OF THE MALAISE

A Stasticical Warning

Economists like to quantify. That is all right as far as it goes, except that it does not go far where communist regimes are concerned. Communist regimes regard economic statistics as a political weapon of the state. They lie. The situation is better today than it was in Stalin's time and it varies among countries (Mao simply stopped publishing figures), but it is not good. Three examples:

In the February 13, 1987 issue of *PlanEcon Report*, Jan Vanous examines the serious deterioration since 1985 (about the time of Gorbachev's accession) of Soviet statistical reporting from earlier unexemplary standards of veracity. He observes that, at the very least, we are witnessing a fundamental breakdown of the Soviet statistical system involving the construction of "political" key economic aggregates, and a clumsy attempt at economic disinformation—uncritically accepted by the Western media in their euphoria about Gorbachev's reforms. In 1986, for example, the officially reported growth of Soviet net material product was 3.6 percent, when, in fact, it was at best 0.8 percent, that is, one-fifth, of the official figure. The 7th Bulgarian Five-Year Plan (1975-79) projected growth of services to the population of between 400 and 500 percent. In 1980, at the 12th party congress, it was reported that actual growth had been only 50 percent. However, Bulgaria's statistical yearbook *(Statisticheski Godishnik)* covering the relevant years and circulated in only 2,500 copies among the planners and selected economists, showed that the increase had been 9.45 percent (note the double digits)—a "shocking discrepancy," as one commentator put it.[3] In Romania the planned growth of net material product (NMP) for 1987 was 7.7 percent (7.3 percent growth officially reported for 1986). Adjusting for exaggeration and suppressed inflation, the growth in 1987 was likely to be under 1 percent, putting the aggregate output of the economy 3 percent below 1986.[4]

The official figures cited below must, therefore, be seen in this context of a well documented socialist propensity for statistical manipulation and distortion.

Growth of Product

Table 1 gives the official data for national income (net material product, socialist definition) produced from 1951 (where available) through 1986. It reveals decline/stagnation of the growth rate beginning in the early to mid-1970s. Growth of product (irrespective, it should be noted, of the product's quality, assortment, or destination) has always been a matter of the utmost concern and pride for the socialist centrally planned economies, and by far the most important objective of the system. Moreover, one of the claimed advantages of central planning is the planners' supposed ability to take risks, chaos, and randomness out of the economy and, through resort to scientific methods and rational projection, assure continuous smooth growth and forever banish the capitalist business cycle. Table 1 suggests that this is far from being the case.

Retail Trade Turnover

In the last analysis an economy is only as good as its ability to cater to the needs of the final consumer. Retail trade turnover is a rough measure of this test, although it abstracts from the quality of the goods turned over, many of which in Eastern Europe are substandard and in short supply. Table 2 shows developments on that front, with decline/stagnation setting in during the mid-1970s.

What Table 2 does not reveal directly are, among others, the twenty year wait (on the average) for a new apartment in Poland and that based on the most optimistic assumption Poland might regain its modest 1979 standard of living by 1990, as well as long lines for low quality basics everywhere, high prices for consumer goods above the basics, severe food shortages (including bread rationing in Romania), the closing, on and off, of Romanian restaurants at 6 p.m., the limitation of TV programming to a few short hours a day, and the banning of private cars and taxis from the streets of Bucharest after four decades of socialist construction. In the USSR—the *matushka* of the system—a decree, marking the 40th anniversary of the defeat of Nazi Germany, stipulated that one had to be a veteran of World War II to get a new telephone installed.

Factor Productivity

The product growth achieved in the past has been of the "extensive" type, due to the addition of factors of production embodying known technology, particularly capital and labor. The East European economies have not been successful in moving toward "intensive" growth, that is, growth fueled by improvements in the productivity factors. Available figures indicate sharp reductions of labor productivity in all East European economies beginning in the mid-1970s.[5] This has been disappointing in view of the effort made by most East European countries in the 1970s—during the era of détente—to import (legally and illegally) advanced technology from the capitalist West in the expectation that such technological infusion would result in substantial factor productivity enhancement and transition to intensive, that is, "modern," growth. The attempt to break the back of the technology/productivity problem by large-scale imports of technologically progressive hardware and engineering know-how from the West has contributed to the emergence of heavy East European indebtedness on convertible currency accounts (Table 3).

HARD CURRENCY DEBT

More than 80 percent of the East European hard currency debt of about $100 billion is long-term, the remainder being short-term (two years or less). More than 80 percent of the debt is held by Western commercial banks, the balance by Western governments or creditors whose loans are insured by their governments. About 60 percent of the debt is owed to Western European commercial banks and governments (20 percent for West Germany). The U.S. commercial bank share has declined dramatically since 1981 (due mainly to market-related causes).[6] Overall, the U.S. share at the end of 1986 stood at about 15 percent. Half the East European debt is denominated in U.S. dollars, 20 percent in German marks, and 10 percent in Swiss francs.[7]

Repayment of the debt has put a lot of strain on the East European economies despite successive reschedulings and the stretching-out of repayment periods (Table 4). The most severe hardship has been experienced by Romania which has adopted a policy of accelerated forced repayment without regard to the consequences on the domestic economy. The cost to the Romanian economy has been described as "horrendous."[8] Growth of the Polish debt since 1982 has been due entirely to accumulating interest on the unpaid (in fact, defaulted) portion of the debt. Increases in the Hungarian and Bulgarian debts in 1986 were caused by new borrowing. Since half the debt is denominated in U.S. dollars, the depreciation of the dollar against other hard currencies has added to East Europe's debt burden—several hundred million dollars in the case of Romania alone. Not only does repayment of the debt affect current consumption, but it takes resources away from investment which, in the absence of intensive growth, is needed at least to maintain extensive product growth (Table 5). Foreign exchange shortages in all East European countries, with the possible exception of East Germany (where the situation is better, due to West German assistance), will hamper the

East European countries importing the replacements and spare parts for machinery and equipment that had been imported from the West in the 1970s, and will further erode East Europe's already small share of world trade and its participation in the rapidly emerging international division of labor. It will strengthen the economically retarding inward orientation of the bloc and increase the dependence of the debtor countries on the Soviet Union.

Investment

What Table 5 does not show is the resource waste resulting from capital being immobilized in unfinished construction projects and from inordinately long construction cycles. In Czechoslovakia, for example, at the end of the 1970s, one-fifth of the country's capital funds were tied up in 30,000 unfinished industrial projects. In this, as in other respects, Czechoslovakia has been in step with the USSR where in 1985 the industrial enterprise inventory showed 436.5 billion roubles' worth of unused assets.[9]

Anticipating our discussion of the systemic roots of East Europe's economic malaise, it is appropriate at this point to note that past and present investment in the region has been singularly wrongheaded. Imitating the pattern adopted by the Soviet Union, the East European countries, without exception, concentrated their investments on import substitution industries emphasizing energy-intensive intermediate product-producing industries, iron and steel, machine tools, chemicals, and extractive industries. This has had two unfortunate consequences. The first is more resource waste. The small East European countries (in sharp contrast with the "four dragon" East Asian market economies) failed to participate in the benefits from international specialization that has become particularly vigorous and important in the 1970s and 1980s. The result of this "underspecialization" has been the production of too many intermediate and final products that are too expensive by international standards. In addition to foregoing the cost-saving advantages of international specialization through attempts at national autarky, firms in the East European countries have sought to become self-sufficient by producing virtually all the inputs needed for their planned output (with which managerial incentives are positively correlated), and this because of (a) the well known systemic condition of chronic shortages and unreliability of delivery schedules, and (b) the absence of negative correlation between managerial rewards and input costs in the system. And so the East European centrally planned economies are doubly underspecialized: externally they fail to participate in the worldwide division of labor; internally they unwittingly compel each enterprise to become self-reliant, thus breaking the equivalence between size of firm and scale of production. In East Europe large scale usually means high cost, as each country ignores international comparative advantage and each firm tries to become self-sufficient. This twofold under-specialization (as Jan Winiecki calls it) is not a simple policy mistake.[10] The policy is an inevitable consequence of the system. Even if the East Europeans decide to import (better and cheaper) products presently produced at home and to abandon enterprise autarky, they would not know which goods to buy abroad (and in exchange for what) because of the lack of correspondence between their internal prices and world market prices and the nonscarcity nature of their (allocatively irrational) domestic price system.

The second consequence of copying the Soviet investment blueprint is the vulnerability of East Europe's highly energy-intensive industrial structure to fluctuations in world primary energy prices.

Energy

East Europe is deficient in primary energy (except for Polish coal). Dependence on energy imports has been accentuated by the already mentioned Soviet-type industrial investment pattern, the wasteful use of energy in obsolete plants (at least 40 percent above the energy use levels of comparable Western factories, but perhaps as much as 80 percent), the relatively little attention given to the exhaustion of indigenous oil sources in Romania and even less attention to the effect on energy conservation measures, conversion in the 1960s and early 1970s of much industry to oil when oil was cheap, and the expense of nuclear energy development which has also become politically expensive since the Chernobyl disaster of April 1986. Electric power outages are common (with disastrous effects on the newly installed computers), as is underutilization of plant and equipment and disruption of the production process due to recurrent shortfalls in energy supply. Given their hard currency indebtedness, the East European countries are obliged to procure the bulk of their oil and natural gas from the Soviet Union, which, after a period of comparatively liberal pricing of its oil to its East European customers under the lagged COMECON formula, has raised prices and insists on better quality manufactured goods and foods in exchange for good grade oil and natural gas. Between 1971 and 1981 the price of Soviet oil to Eastern Europe increased five times. During the same period oil consumption in Eastern Europe doubled. Despite this, Soviet oil prices to Eastern Europe are believed to be below Soviet marginal production costs estimated at between 27-34 roubles per barrel in 1986 and sold to East Europe at around 24 roubles a barrel.[11] (More on this later). There has been a reduction since 1980 in the net volume of Soviet oil exports to socialist countries and an increase in natural gas sales (the increase is due, to a degree, to the plentiful availability of gas in the USSR and demand limitations on Soviet gas exports to Western Europe). (Table 6)

Ecological Damage

Emphasis on the development of energy-intensive smokestack industries, the preoccupation with maximizing output growth irrespective of cost (including externalities), the general sloppiness and bureaucratization of industrial safety services, the fact that government is simultaneously producer and polluter, and the shift since 1980 in Poland, East Germany, and Czechoslovakia to high sulfur content brown coal to generate energy have produced in Eastern Europe one of the world's more advanced ecological disaster areas. In East

Germany, it is reported, 90 percent of the trees are sick, dying, or dead, the worst damage being in the Erzgebirge on the East German-Czech border. Poland faces a critical shortage of clean water. Half the country's water supply is so polluted that it cannot be used for anything at all. Only 1 percent of the water is clean enough to drink. Temporary water shortages affect 120 cities and 10,000 smaller towns. In Prague mothers are counseled not to give their babies water even after boiling it. Pollution damage in Poland is estimated to be costing the country about 10 percent of its gross national product. Environmental-related causes are thought to be responsible in large measure for the sharp rise in mortality rates in Poland, Hungary, and Bulgaria. In the industrialized regions of Bohemia life expectancy is 10 years shorter than in the rest of Czechoslovakia. A 1985 report issued by the Polish Academy of Sciences notes an "appalling increase" in the number of retarded children in industrialized Upper Silesia. It used to be one of the tenets of Marxist dogma that environmental destruction is a systemic byproduct of capitalism's blind pursuit of profit, and that it cannot occur under socialism where man and nature live in harmony. There are still some in the GDR who blame acid rain on the West, deny the existence of environmental degradation, or (like one Czech party official) attribute it to "nonsocialist individuals still surviving in the country."[12] However, by and large, the realization is beginning to sink in that the ecological catastrophe is in large measure system-related, and that the system in this instance is socialism. Just as the causes are in great part systemic, so possible remedies are impeded by the system. Environmental groups are seen as subversive of the party's exclusive right to rule, cleaning-up operations which require advanced pollution abatement equipment, available only in the West, cannot proceed because there is no foreign exchange to purchase such equipment and, where pollution controls are in place, they are often suspended when output falls short of the plan, or simply to save money. In most East European countries, environmental policy, says one reporter, "consists largely of praying for strong winds."[13]

Rouble Trouble

It has been argued earlier that the East European countries, in sharp contrast with the up-and-coming, market-oriented, export-promoting East Asian NICs (newly industrialized countries), missed the boat in the 1960s and 1970s by failing to join the emerging world trade and financial community. Instead, they engaged in what Winiecki calls the "twofold underspecialization" at the national and firm levels, a costly exercise in autarky which has excluded them from the great currents of technological innovation and grounded them in an economic ghetto.

There is a third dimension to East Europe's underspecialization-cum-autarky, and that is the heavy trade involvement in the Council of Mutual Economic Assistance (CMEA), an arrangement invented and imposed on Eastern Europe by the Soviets in the late 1940s. The CMEA, as Holzman points out, is "the most restrictive, autarkic trading group in recent history," representing in effect a third—international—level of autarky/underspecialization.[14] The East European countries were compelled to enter this quasi customs union out of military and political considerations formulated by the USSR. For the East European countries, entry into the CMEA involved losses due to (a) trade diversion away from traditional West European markets and toward the USSR and the Soviet bloc (the same happened in China between 1950 and 1960), and (b) trade destruction.

Trade diversion meant redirection of trade toward countries that were not well suited to trade with each other. Costs arose from the unavailability within CMEA of certain products or their availability at standards of inferior quality compared with similar products obtainable outside the CMEA. Losses from trade destruction resulted from the need to produce at home, at higher cost, many goods previously imported, or to sacrifice altogether the consumption of goods either unavailable within the CMEA or priced beyond reach. The costs of (a) and (b) were higher for the East European countries than for the USSR because of the East European countries' higher trade participation ratios. Trade diversion toward the "socialist world market," as it was once called, entailed a restructuring of domestic industries in every CMEA member country to fit the import needs of other members. This, as Holzman notes:

> has often been difficult and costly to accomplish and has resulted in every nation getting lower quality goods through trade. Moreover, since production for export, particularly in the machinery and equipment area, is geared to lower quality markets than would otherwise be the case, and to lesser competitive pressures, there is little incentive to quality improvement.[15]

Trade diversion also entailed a shift to more primitive bilateral, barter-type exchanges, away from multilateralism, and toward the demonetization of intrasocialist trade relations—the international equivalent of the Stalinist trend toward the "natural" (demonetized) domestic economy controlled by planners through physical-administrative levers rather than scarcity prices.

The longer-term result of the restructuring of East European industry and trade has been that the East European countries have had to import oil, natural gas, and many raw materials from the Soviet Union ("hard" goods) in exchange for manufactures—both producer and consumer goods—of a poor quality and technical sophistication ("soft" goods). To partly compensate Eastern Europe for the losses sustained through forced participation in CMEA, to keep the alliance together, and to keep popular unrest at bay, the USSR has over the years accepted, within the CMEA, terms of trade unfavorable to itself. It has sold, and continues to sell, to Eastern Europe oil, gas, and raw materials at less than world prices and purchases East European manufactures at higher than world prices. This amounts to implicit subsidization by the USSR of East European trade within the CMEA, which the current Soviet leadership appears to be increasingly uncomfortable and irritated with. Pressures are being put on the East European countries to participate in the financing of investments in the USSR's domestic extractive industries, supply labor for construction projects, upgrade the quality of exported manufactures (leaving the defective goods for home consumption), and to add "hard" goods, such as food, to exports destined for the Soviet Union.[16]

Technological Lag

The massive importation of advanced Western technology in the 1970s (Czechoslovakia excepted) did not produce the anticipated breakthrough in and diffusion of engineering and business techniques (business know-how) in Eastern Europe. This is a serious problem, one which seems to demand an institutional restructuring of the centrally planned economy attended by far-reaching changes in that economy's political culture.[17]

Inflation

One of the claims of the centrally planned system, as it used to compare itself with capitalism, was the stability of the socialist general price level (absence of inflation). This stability has always been statistical and illusory due to the fact that the price level was set and frozen by the planners and could not change without administrative permission. Since the death of Stalin, prices of basic necessities (including staple foods, some items of clothing, residential rents, and public transportation) have been heavily subsidized by the governments from their state budget to keep official state retail prices low. In Poland, for example, total budgetary expenditure on price subsidies rose from 96.2 billion zlotys in 1970 to 745 billion zlotys in 1982, while in the same period price subsidies on foodstuffs alone went up from 7.5 billion zlotys to 211 billion zlotys.[18] However, despite the overt statistical price stability, suppressed inflation existed in all socialist countries at all times, which manifested itself in goods shortages, long lines outside stores, bribery, massive theft, and a bloated black market.[19] In more recent years this hidden inflation has come out of hiding as governments tried to reduce their subsidy burden. In Yugoslavia the inflation rate in 1987 was 130 percent, up from 90 percent the year before. In Poland, between 1980 and 1986, food prices rose 500 percent (wages between 100 and 200 percent). In Hungary the inflation rate in 1987 was at least 20 percent [20]. One of the side effects of openly rising prices has been the emergence of labor unrest, most clearly articulated in Poland, but present also in other countries. In Yugoslavia in the first quarter of 1987, there were 70 strikes involving more than 10,000 workers.[21]

Breakdown of Central Planning

While Western economists debate whether systemic collapse can occur, and if so, how to identify it in econometric terms, the central planning system in a number of countries of Eastern Europe (e.g., Poland, Romania, Czechoslovakia) has, in fact, broken down in the sense that crisis management through ad hoc decrees has replaced planners' directives; those sectors of the economy which perform according to plan (e.g., the military and public security economies) do so by working according to rules totally different from those that govern the putatively planned civilian sector;[22] a very large amount of civilian economic activity takes place underground, in the "second" or "alternative" economy, in accordance with black market rules; and the mass of population—the labor force included—is alienated from the system, apathetic, going its own way, brought to heel increasingly by state police action. It is not an exaggeration to say that more and more East European economies are becoming unresponsive to central direction. The alienation from the system of much of the youth and large sections of the intelligentsia and the working class translates itself, in economic terms—proximately through the near-non-convertibility of money into consumer goods—into problems described as ones of "labor discipline": unresponsiveness of the labor force to material and other incentives, sloth, absenteeism, theft of materials and time, cynicism, apathy, corruption, and an acquired dislike for work. Under the socialist policy of full employment, everyone has a job but no one works, and so the wage is really unemployment compensation paid on the job. Matters become different when the same workers, after collecting "sleeping money" at their official place of employment, massively, assiduously, and ingeniously engage in income-generating activities in the parallel-market-economy. The dynamism of the socialist system's private legal, semilegal, and illegal sectors is well documented.[23] Although primarily a redistributive phenomenon—albeit of vast dimensions—the second economy generates a significant proportion of extra national income in all East European countries and, more importantly, in real terms this income is composed of goods and services (especially the latter) that people actually want. In that sense the shadow economy improves the citizens' material well-being and retards the centrally planned economy's process of degenerative collapse. It contributes at the same time to moral disequilibrium in that people are compelled to pursue illicit activities because the system does not operate in accordance with its proclaimed principles and does not deliver on its promises. In this context dissimulation and cynicism become a way of life.

Sociologically, alienation manifests itself in alcoholism that in some countries (e.g., Poland) reaches epidemic proportions, juvenile delinquency, nihilism, drug abuse, and vandalism—some of which, even though not well documented by the authorities, are endemic. While not system-specific these social ills are certainly system-related and are not, as the agitprop analysis would have it, exclusively the products of a capitalist society smuggled into the socialist world as part of socialism's quite relative opening-up to the West.

CAUSES OF MALAISE

The standard reaction of communist authorities to the troubling problems that beset their economies has been to attribute them to policy mistakes, or the "wrong style of work" as the official explanation has it. Of the many elements that make up this wrong style of work, "bureaucratism" has been cited as the most important, frequent, and pervasive. Policy mistakes can be remedied by policy adjustments, that is repair and parts replacement interventions which leave the structure of the system and its operating principles (economic philosophy) untouched. In addition to planners' (and the Communist Party's) policy mistakes, economic problems are traced to extraneous factors over which the planners have little or no control. These range from bad weather to fluctuations in interest rates on the world capitalist market.

That this diagnosis and the policy adjustment remedies which flow from it are at best only partially relevant, that they do not go to the heart of the problem, and that they fail to identify the fundamental causes of the malaise have been, I think, amply demonstrated by the continuing and deepening East European and Soviet crisis and the socialist universality of it. Neither conservative nor the bolder (Hungarian-type) "liberal" adjustments of the basic Stalinist administrative command model have brought the anticipated and needed improvements to the centrally planned system's afflicted areas. This is so because the causes of the economic malaise are inherent in the system and can be remedied only by restructuring the system. Such restructuring, or real "reform", cannot stop halfway, at some theoretical midpoint of "market socialism" or "socialist market."[24] The only reformist road open to socialist central planning is the road of marketization and privatization of property rights (economic, as distinct from administrative, decentralization). I agree with Birman that it is very true that the (centrally planned) economy is extremely inefficient, and that in this sense it has colossal reserves. But to use the reserves, you need another economic system [25].

I have dealt with this issue and the systemic origins of socialism's economic problems in my *Market and Plan Under Socialism: The Bird in the Cage* (Stanford, CA: Hoover Institution Press, 1987) and in several essays to which the reader is referred. There is no need here to restate the argument in its manifold detail. The following points merely summarize the analysis.

1. The centrally planned system of administrative command, in both its original Stalinist form and its revisionist reincarnations, lacks a spontaneous mechanism that would automatically and on an ongoing basis (a) indicate what needs

to be done in society, and (b) reconcile microprivate and macropublic interests in the process of doing it. The market, equipped with private property rights, does just that. It does it through a combination of voluntariness and tolerable (not perfect) competitiveness of transactions that capture the scarcity relationships arising from cost and utility (supply/demand) conditions in the system and resolve conflict at a relatively "low" buyer-seller level. Voluntary competitive buying-selling transactions do more than reconcile buyer-seller conflict: the consummation of each and every transaction in such a setting represents the harmonization of private and public interest as both sides gain from the exchange. Exchange and harmonization of interests occur in the context of the rule of law—not of acts, rules, and decrees alone, but of legal order. The legal order adds to economic exchanges and the possession of property by private parties, a crucial contractual dimension guaranteed and protected by society.

The centrally planned system of administrative command lacks not only the coordinating and harmonizing mechanism of the market and the right of private property as the basic and dominant form of ownership, but it is devoid of the concept and reality of the rule of law. Like statistics, law in the system serves the purposes of the monoparty government. It is a tool rather than a principle that everyone, the state included, must observe. The absence of voluntariness, competitiveness (market), private property as the dominant ownership form, and of legal order results in the emergence of a hierarchically structured economy and polity, ruled by decree of the power holders—involuntary and adversarial. All economic relationships become *ipso facto* political and are arbitrated by political-administrative fiat. The involuntary nature of economic relationships in the system (mandated output targets and input coefficients, fixed prices, assigned customers) makes a state of war of transactions in which one party is seen as losing unless it resorts to elaborate game playing, deception, or political connections (*blat*).

The alienation so manifest in East European societies, the apathy and sloth—what Soviet economist Tatyana Zaslavskaya calls "the conspicuous and general tendency of passivity"[26]—the paralysis of the centrally planned economy's motivational subsystem, the widespread private appropriation of public property by those in and out of power, are due in very large measure to the absence of the market as the economy's basic coordinating and conflict-resolving institution and to the presence of laws without rule of law. The ripple effect is felt in the important area of factor productivity and technological innovation. While the market by itself is not exemplary in handling externalities, governments in market economies can and do correct externality problems through fiscal intervention in the market and by affecting the cost of private property. In the centrally planned economy, as we have noted, the unitary nature of property, the tautness of the plan, the overriding importance of output norms, and adversarial bureaucratic relationships among the agents, make governmental action in behalf of the environment weak and ineffective.

2. The tautness of the plan is a substitute for market competition. When inputs are made very scarce relative to mandated outputs—as they are in all centrally planned economies—firm managers, workers, and others are presumably subject to great pressure to perform at their peak. This has proved to be faulty reasoning. An economy of chronic shortages—of both producer and consumer goods—encourages cheating (especially on quality and assortment), has disincentive effects on effort, since money incomes (or profits of enterprises) are not readily convertible into goods, and encourages enterprises to integrate vertically (underspecialization of firms) thus promoting resource waste and aggravating goods shortages. The most prominent failure of the centrally planned system is its ability to produce scarcity as its principal output. It is an economy that ignores the user of goods, philosophically and in practice. A system of shortages (permanent sellers' "market") is one under constant strain. It accentuates the confrontational and adversarial buyer-seller relationship and makes more elusive the resolution of private

and social conflict through political intervention. In the context of a socialist full employment policy, it fuels inflation and spills over into a black market of gigantic proportions. The most original feature of Hungary's post-1968 "New Economic Mechanism" has been the co-opting by the planned sector of the vast underground market economy.

3. The information system of central planning is comprised of physical/technical indicators and administratively determined prices that bear little if any relation to cost and utility, supply and demand, and relative scarcities prevailing in the economy. In these circumstances the system is structurally suboptimal, unable to indicate the trade-off costs of possible alternative courses of action (without, that is, costly and elaborate, and ultimately not very practical and effective, mathematical modeling). The system is, therefore, inefficient in a static sense. Even mere internal consistency of decisions is arrived at randomly, if at all. Applied to investment, static resource misallocation translates into dynamic inefficiency. Shortages are accentuated; factor productivity suffers; growth is expensive and suboptimal. The absence of reliable indicators of relative scarcities extends to the centrally planned economies' external trade and payments relations. Phony exchange rates and currency inconvertibility make it difficult for planners to decide what should be imported in exchange for what. The system turns inward and reverts to primitive barter.

4. To overcome its technological lag, the centrally planned system resorts to hard currency loans intended to finance imports of state-of-the-art technology from the capitalist West. The assumption is that technology is systemically neutral, and that it can be successfully grafted onto the body of the plan. This, too, is wrong. Engineering and business technologies, especially in the revolutionary sphere of information, are not systemically and culturally neutral. They require for their effectiveness the free dissemination, to every agent, of accurate information about relative costs and utilities in the system. Central planning, however, regards such information as privileged, not to say secret, and—more importantly—it generates, as a matter of course, defective and misleading in-

formation. Expenditures on advanced foreign technology, not to mention the ingenuity that goes into economic espionage, are therefore, by and large, yet another instance of resource waste. They help the mistaken policy of import substitution and accumulate mountains of hard currency debt.

5. Satellite status and the adoption of the Soviet model of central planning have compounded East Europe's problems by imprisoning the East European countries in the "natural" barter economy of the CMEA at substantial and rising cost in terms of benefits foregone from the expanding international division of labor.

CONCLUSION

The symptoms of the great economic malaise of Eastern Europe are, among others: decline of product growth, neglect of consumption, stagnation of factor productivity, huge hard currency debts, flagging investment, energy shortages, ecological damage, underspecialization, technological lag, inflation, and alienation. The malaise is due primarily to systemic reasons; to structural defects in the system of central administrative command planning, imposed on Eastern Europe by the Soviet Union in the 1940s and tinkered with ever since: a lot in Hungary; not at all in Romania. The malaise can only be removed by systemic reform, that is, by replacing central planning with a market system and private property rights. Intermediate solutions of the "market socialism" type will not work.

Table 1

AVERAGE ANNUAL GROWTH RATE OF NATIONAL INCOME
(NET MATERIAL PRODUCT–NMP) PRODUCED IN EASTERN EUROPE
1951-1986
OFFICIAL DATA
(Percent)

	1951-55	1956-60	1961-65	1966-70	1971-75	1976-80	1981-85	1986
Bulgaria				8.5	7.8	6.1	3.7	6.9
Czechoslovakia	8.1	7.0	2.0	6.9	5.7	3.7	1.8	3.4
German Democratic Republic (GDR)	13.1	7.2	3.5	5.2	5.4	4.1	4.4	4.3
Hungary	5.7	5.9	4.1	6.8	6.3	2.8	1.4	0.5
Poland	8.6	6.6	6.2	6.0	9.8	1.2	-0.8	5.0
Romania	13.9	6.9	9.0	5.7	11.2	7.3	4.4	7.3
Yugoslavia[1]	5.1	7.8	6.8	5.8	5.9	5.6	0.6	3.6

Sources: Country statistical yearbooks; U.S. Department of Agriculture, *Eastern Europe, Situation and Outlook* Report (Washington, D.C.: June 1987), p. 30; *PlanEcon Reports*, various issues.

1 Gross material product (GMP)

Table 2

AVERAGE ANNUAL GROWTH RATE OF RETAIL TRADE TURNOVER
IN EASTERN EUROPE
1951-1986
OFFICIAL DATA
(Percent)

	1951-55	1956-60	1961-65	1966-70	1971-75	1976-80	1981-85	1986
Bulgaria						2.9[1]	3.7	4.4
Czechoslovakia	7.5	6.5	3.3	6.3	5.2	1.7	1.0	2.0
German Democratic Republic (GDR)	12.8	7.3	2.6	4.6	5.0	4.1	2.5	4.4
Hungary	4.7	9.1	5.3	9.0	6.5	2.4	1.3	
Poland	6.7	9.3	5.7	6.2	10.3	3.4	-1.4	
Romania	13.1	9.0	10.1	8.3	8.1	7.7	1.7	2.1
Yugoslavia	7.1	10.9	9.5	8.1	5.9	4.6	-2.1	

Sources: Country statistical yearbooks; *PlanEcon Reports*, various issues.

1 1977-80

Note: While retail trade turnover is a good proxy for personal consumption levels, this is not so in Romania. The Romanian figures appear to be completely fraudulent. See *PlanEcon Report*, Vol. II, No. 46, November 14, 1986, pp. 4, 6.

Table 3

GROSS AND NET HARD CURRENCY DEBT OF EASTERN EUROPE
1971 AND 1980-1986

(Billion U.S. dollars)

		1971	1980	1981	1982	1983	1984	1985	1986
Bulgaria	G	0.7	3.5	3.1	2.8	2.6	2.2	3.2	4.7
	N	N.A.	2.8	2.2	1.7	1.4	0.8	0.9	3.4
Czechoslovakia	G	0.5	4.9	4.5	4.0	3.7	3.6	3.8	4.4
	N	N.A.	3.7	3.4	3.3	2.8	2.6	2.8	3.2
German Democratic	G	1.4	14.1	14.9	13.0	12.7	12.2	14.0	15.3
Republic(GDR)	N	N.A.	11.6	12.3	10.7	9.0	7.6	7.4	7.8
Hungary	G	1.1	9.1	8.7	7.7	8.3	8.8	11.8	15.1
	N	N.A.	5.5	7.0	6.6	6.8	6.7	8.8	12.0
Poland	G	1.1	25.0	25.4	24.8	27.5	26.8	30.2	33.5
	N	N.A.	24.4	24.7	23.8	26.4	25.3	28.6	31.2
Romania	G	1.2	9.4	10.2	9.8	8.9	7.1	6.6	6.0
	N	N.A.	9.1	9.8	9.4	8.8	6.4	6.4	5.5
Yugoslavia	G	3.2	17.4	19.0	18.5	18.8	18.8	19.2	19.4
	N	N.A.	14.0	16.3	16.8	17.6	17.7	18.1 ،	17.9
TOTAL	G	8.2	83.4	85.8	80.6	82.5	79.5	88.8	98.4
	N	N.A.	71.1	75.7	72.3	72.8	67.1	73.0	81.0

Sources: Francis Urban, "East European External Debt: Its Effects on Production and Trade Prospects," *Eastern Europe, Situation and Outlook Report* (Washington, D.C.: U.S. Department of Agriculture, June 1987), Table A, p. 27.

Notes: G = gross
N = net

Table 4

BURDEN OF NET HARD CURRENCY DEBT IN EASTERN EUROPE
1985

	Debt per capita	Debt service ratio (2)	Ratio of debt to exports (3)
	U.S. Dollars (1)	Percent	Percent
Bulgaria	100	14	76
Czechoslovakia	181	31	74
GDR	443	26	144
Hungary	827	70	259
Poland	768	109	506
Romania	282	26	96
Yugoslavia	783	45	81

Source: As in Table 3.

(1) Net debt divided by mid-year population.
(2) The ratio of interest plus debt repayments to the sum of hard-currency non-socialist merchandise exports and the net balance of invisibles.
(3) Gross debt to hard-currency non-socialist exports.

Table 5

GROSS CAPITAL INVESTMENT IN EASTERN EUROPE
1971-1986
(Annual Rate percent)

	1971-75	1976-80	1981	1982	1983	1984	1985	1986
Bulgaria	12.9	0.1	14.8	-3.3	-3.6	2.8	1.9	8.9
Czechoslovakia	8.4	1.4	-21.7	-3.6	-7.2	1.5	1.3	3.0
German Democratic Republic (GDR)	2.9	3.0	-3.4	-19.9	-1.9	3.3	2.3	5.0
Hungary	8.1	-2.0	-8.6	-12.4	-20.4	-0.4	0.2	5.1
Poland	18.1	-11.8	-27.6	-6.6	4.9	5.0	3.5	N.A.
Romania	N.A.	6.6	-22.1	-4.3	2.0	3.4	1.6	1.2
Yugoslavia	5.5	5.4	0.5	-4.0	5.7	-9.4	-10.0	N.A.

Source: As in Table 3.

N.A. = Not Available

Table 6

ANNUAL PERCENTAGE INCREASE OR DECREASE IN SOVIET OIL AND NATURAL GAS EXPORTS TO SOCIALIST COUNTRIES
(Percent)

	1981	1982	1983	1984	1985	1986
Oil	-0.45	-6.13	-0.32	1.87	-1.48	3.56*
Natural gas	20.47	-4.17	-3.17	7.56	4.86	6.44

Source: Based on data in *PlanEcon Report*, Vol. 3, No. 3, January 21, 1987, Table 1, p. 5.

* Most of the increase in 1986 consisted of oil deliveries to Romania in a hard currency barter for food, raw materials, and oil equipment priced at prevailing world market prices.

NOTES

1. Jan. S. Prybyla, "The GDR in COMECON: Does the GDR Economy Demonstrate that Orthodox Central Planning is Viable and Has a Future?" *Comparative Strategy*, Vol. 7, No. 1, 1988, pp. 39-49; Thomas A. Baylis, "East Germany's Economic Model," *Current History*, Vol. 86, No. 523, November 1987, pp. 377-381, 393-394; Irwin L. Collier, (ed.), "Symposium on the German Democratic Republic," *Comparative Economic Studies*, Vol. 24, No. 2, Summer 1987, pp. 1-70.
2. Michael Kraus, "Soviet Policy Toward East Europe," *Current History*, Vol. 86, No. 523, November 1987, p. 353.
3. Alex Alexiev, "Demystifying Bulgaria," *Problems of Communism*, Vol. 34, No. 5, September-October 1985, p. 92.
4. *PlanEcon Report*, Vol. 3, No. 43, October 22, 1987, p. 1. The *Report* (Vol. 2, No. 10, March 10, 1986, p. 1) notes that "virtually every piece of data on the growth of Romanian output, consumption, and investment is inflated upwards by 3-5 percentage points."
5. Thad P. Alton, "East European GNPs: Origins of Product, Final Uses, Rates of Growth, and International Comparisons," in Joint Economic Committee, U.S. Congress, *East European Economies: Slow Growth in the 1980s* (Washington, D.C.: U.S. Government Printing Office, 1985), Table 23, pp. 123-124.
6. *PlanEcon Report*, Vol. 3, Nos. 18-19, May 7, 1987.
7. Francis Urban, "The East European External Debt: Its Effects on Production and Trade Prospects," *Eastern Europe, Situation and Outlook Report* (Washington, D.C.: U.S. Department of Agriculture, June 1987), p. 27.
8. *PlanEcon Report*, Vol. 3, No. 43, October 22, 1987, p. 4.
9. *Problems of Communism*, Vol. 36, No. 4, July-August 1987, p. 88, note 2.
10. Jan Winiecki (Institute of Management, Polish Academy of Sciences), "The Overgrown Industrial Sector in Soviet-

Type Economies: Explanations, Evidence, Consequences," *Comparative Economic Studies*, Vol. 18, No. 4, Winter 1987, pp. 25-28.

11. *PlanEcon Report*, Vol. 3, No. 3, January 21, 1987, p. 2.

12. Above data from James Bovard, "A Silent Spring in Eastern Europe," *The New York Times*, April 26, 1987. On the environmental crisis in Czechoslovakia: Michael Kraus, "Czechoslovakia in the 1980's," *Current History*, Vol. 84, No. 505, November 1985, pp. 375-376, 392.

13. James Bovard, "A Silent Spring in Eastern Europe."

14. Franklyn D. Holzman, "The Significance of Soviet Subsidies to Eastern Europe," *Comparative Economic Studies*, Vol. 28, No. 1, Spring 1986, p. 64. The trade diversion/trade destruction argument outlined below, follows Holzman's reasoning (pp. 54-65). See also his "COMECON: A Trade Destroying Customs Union?" *Journal of Comparative Economics*, Vol. 9, No. 4, December 1985, pp. 410-423.

15. Holzman, p. 55.

16. A somewhat different explanation of these implicit Soviet trade subsidies is given by Michael Marrese and Jan Vanous in their *Soviet Subsidization of Trade with Eastern Europe* (Berkeley: University of California, Institute of International Studies, 1983), and *idem.*, "Unconventional Gains from Trade," *Journal of Comparative Economics*, Vol. 7, No. 4, December 1983, pp. 382-399. Some 15,000 East European workers were used in building the 1,600 miles-long gas pipeline from the Urals into Czechoslovakia (6,000 Poles, 5,000 East Germans, and 4,000 Hungarians, Bulgarians, Czechs and Slovaks). Romania and Bulgaria contributed equipment. *The New York Times*, May 16, 1979, p. A11. Polish credits amounting to 900 billion zlotys (1986-2000) were reportedly to be used for three projects: construction of a gas pipeline from the USSR to Warsaw; the Yamburg gas pipeline; and a coal gasification plant in the USSR. Zdzislaw M. Rurarz, "Poland Gives Credit Where It's Due: to Russia," *The Wall Street Journal*, June 19, 1985, p. 31; Frederick

Kempe, "To Dismay of Some Comecon Members, Soviets are Firm on Tighter Trade Ties," *The Wall Street Journal*, June 19, 1985, p. 31.

17. Philip Joseph, (ed.), *Adaptability to New Technologies of the USSR and East European Countries* (Brussels: NATO Colloquium, 1985).

18. P.T. Wanless, "Sales Taxes and Price Subsidies in Poland, 1970-1982," *The ACES Bulletin*, Vol. 26, No. 2-3, Summer-Fall 1984, Table 7, p. 55, and Table 8, p. 56.

19. The existence of suppressed inflation under central planning has been questioned by Richard Portes. Portes' contention has been rejected at one point as "absurd" by Hungarian economist Janos Kornai and disputed by Jan Winiecki in his "Portes Ante Portas: A Critique of the Revisionist Interpretation of Inflation Under Central Planning," *Comparative Economic Studies*, Vol. 27, No. 2, Summer 1985, pp. 25-51.

20. *Current History*, Vol. 86, No. 523, November 1987, pp. 372, 374.

21. *The New York Times*, March 21, 1987, pp. 1, 5.

22. Jan S. Prybyla, "The Soviet-Type Economy: Strong or Weak?" *Issues & Studies*, Vol. 22. No. 11, November 1986, pp. 80-96. In Poland, 70 percent of industrial production has in the past been exempted from reformist experimentation, so as not to disrupt supplies for the military.

23. Gregory Grossman, *The Second Economy in the USSR and Eastern Europe: A Bibliography* (Berkeley, CA, and Durham, NC: Berkeley-Duke Occasional Papers on the Second Economy of the USSR), Paper No. 1, September 1985. Updated and revised in Paper No. 9, April 1987.

24. Many East European and, since *glasnost'*, a growing number of Soviet economists publicly agree with this assessment. See, for example, "Letter from Candidate of Economic Sciences, L. Popkova," *Novy Mir* (Moscow), No. 5, May 1987, pp. 239-240, 241.

25. Igor Birman, "The Soviet Economy: Alternative Views," *Russia*, No. 12, 1986, p. 70.

26. Bohdan Nahaylo, "A Heretic's Star Rises Under Glasnost'," *The Wall Street Journal*, October 14, 1987, p. 30.

FOUR

HUMAN RIGHTS AND WRONGS

DISSENT AND REPRESSION IN EASTERN EUROPE

Robert Sharlet

The winds of change are blowing across Eastern Europe from the East. Moscow's ambitious domestic reform program is putting the East European regimes under pressure to amend and revise not just their policies on the official systems, but their policies bearing on what I have conceptualized as the indigenous "contra-systems"[1] as well. Gorbachev's themes of "restructuring," "democratization," and "*glasnost*" are intended to apply not only to East European planning, industrial administration, and local elections, but these ideas will have implications for how the contra-behaviors of political, religious, and ethnic dissent are handled as well.

Several general statements are in order before we proceed:

1. Indeed, Gorbachev publicly promised the East European leaders that the USSR would not impose its reform model on them, but half of his six points on the "new thinking" on Soviet-East European relations provide substantial loopholes

through which cross-system pressures can flow. I am referring to the points on the shared "concern for the general cause of socialism," the need for mutual respect and appreciation for each other's achievements and experience, and the expectation of "voluntary and varied cooperation" within the European communist community.[2]

2. The Soviets are likely to give higher priority to economic over political, social, and cultural reforms within Eastern Europe. The fate of their own economic restructuring will be partly dependent on interfacing relationships within COMECON.

3. In turn, the individual East European states are differentially positioned to resist, accommodate, accelerate, or even outstrip Soviet pressures for reform:

A. Two states, Albania and Yugoslavia, are not within the orbit of direct Soviet influence. Albania, of course, is just beginning tentatively to enter the first phase of de-Stalinization, while in some aspects of the reform program, Yugoslavia preceded the USSR years ago.

B. The "resistors" include the GDR, CSSR, and Romania, but among them there are different attitudes toward resistance. The GDR leadership claims to have anticipated certain aspects of economic reform. The Czechoslovak regime is tactfully resisting the full menu of Soviet ideas, but diplomatically selecting specific features, "cafeteria-style" (the less destabilizing economic package), and deferring implementation for several years. Romania appears to be the most intransigent on all points of Gorbachev's reform program.

C. Bulgaria tends to be accommodating the pace of Soviet reform, although confining it largely to the official system.

D. Poland, whose internal crisis is most severe, is accelerating the full range of Soviet reforms with regard to both the official and the contra systems. Given the scope of Poland's problems, the regime has nothing to lose by stepping up the tempo of reform.

E. Finally, Hungary which pioneered (along with Yugoslavia) market socialism is forging ahead, well beyond the present scope of Soviet reform, especially in terms of the economic system.

Although the familiar Soviet-type system has been operative throughout Eastern Europe for decades (except in Yugoslavia since the early fifties), the actual rules of governance, especially pertaining to contra-phenomena, have varied widely over time and across political space. There are several reasons for these variations:

1. Stalin's death in 1953 cut short the Stalinization process in Eastern Europe; hence, the communist parties of the region did not in all cases effectively complete the social penetration and politicization of their respective societies.

2. The subsequent transition to de-Stalinization (from a few years to over a decade) permitted the resurgence of contra phenomena (e.g. an independent intellectual tradition) which had gone dormant in the face of Stalinization, but remained undisrupted due to incomplete party penetration.

3. The collective memory, and vestigial traces of and closer proximity to Western models of political, social, and cultural behavior, especially the West European model of a civil society independent of the state, has provided alternatives to official reality.

RISE OF THE CONTRA SYSTEM IN EASTERN EUROPE

The contra-system is a metaphor I created to depict a largely invisible constellation of loosely interrelated attitudes, beliefs, behaviors, and activities which are for the most part contrary to the official norms, values, customs, and rules of a communist system. As such, it includes such diverse but interconnected phenomena as a youth counterculture and a parallel culture, both antithetical to the accepted canon of popular and high culture respectively; a sprawling, mainly illegal, market-driven second economy which varies in complexity inversely with the scarcity of consumer goods and services in a given country; the hidden and elusive core contra-value of privatism which is counterposed to social collectivism, a central tenet of the official political culture; and the more familiar triad of dissent—political, religious, and ethnic which are formally proscribed under the prevailing law of the land in the East European communist systems.

The thrust of the contra-system as a whole is toward enhancement of the quality of life for the individual in its economic, social, religious, cultural and, to some extent, political dimensions rather than fundamental change in the East European communist systems. In this sense, then, the contra-system is primarily a fragmented, inchoate, grassroots effort by many millions of ordinary citizens to informalize and humanize their authoritarian, overly-centralized, rigidly bureaucratic, and scarcity-ridden national systems for the private purpose of making them more responsive to their personal needs and yearnings, both material and spiritual.

The regimes of Eastern Europe have not witnessed the emergence of contra-systems impassively. Official reactions fall within a four-fold framework for social control which has evolved in the post-Stalin period.[3] In this scheme, a party's most benign control mechanism is mass *pacification through consumption*. Post-1968 Czechoslovakia is the epitome of this method. In the more scarcity-ridden societies, even the second economy is allowed to play a *subrosa* and unacknowledged role in consumption-improvement. For the social elite, the humanistic and technological intelligentsia, a variation on sating the material appetite of the mass public is *repressive tolerance*,[4] a technique for corralling intellectuals within the illusion of independent thought. No country has practiced this control device more subtly and effectively than Hungary with its "para-opposition"[5] quietly going about its business within Miklos Haraszti's "velvet prison."[6]

For those East European citizens who slip through the regimes' first two finely-sewn nets unpacified or unappeased (the numbers are not large), the next line of defense of the status quo is *differentiated political justice*. This is so called because unlike the Stalin era where there was a rough equality before political justice, the successor regimes have crafted quite an array of juridical and extra-juridical means for contending with a wide variety of possible challenges to authority. These instruments include political trials, criminal trials as crypto-political trials, forced expatriation, psychiatric internment, "official hooliganism," and, last but not least, an entire universe of arbitrary bureaucratic deprivations.[7] Unlike the Stalin era, one usually has to do something deemed contrary to warrant one or a combination of these punishments.

If all else fails and public order breaks down, the ultimate line of defense—*suppression through main force*—is invoked by the authorities to save the day and even, sometimes, the regime itself. Troops were called in three times during 1981 alone. In the spring, the Yugoslav army restored order in the strife-ridden ethnic-Albanian Kosovo province;[8] during the autumn, special Romanian secret police troops reportedly put down allegedly violent strikes in the Oltenian coal-mining region of Motru;[9] and, of course, in December of 1981 the Polish army and police carried out a well-planned coup against the militant, but peaceful, independent trade union Solidarity.[10]

Obviously, the strength and extent of the contra-system varies from country to country depending upon the durability of pre-communist culture, the depth of communist social transformation, the ethnic and religious makeup of society, the degree of consumer scarcity, the extent of exposure to Western influences, and the level of official tolerance/intolerance of the various contra-phenomena. Thus, at one extreme Poland, especially since the imposition of martial law, has the most sophisticated and highly-developed contra-system, while Bulgaria's appears to be a less-developed version.

In terms of the aforementioned variables, pre-communist Polish culture endured, party social penetration was shallow, Catholicism enjoyed special historical legitimacy, scarcity is acute, Western influences are strong, and official tolerance of the contra-system is relatively high due to the post-1981 stalemate between regime and society. Conversely, prerevolutionary Bulgaria was historically pro-Russian, party penetration was effective, ethnically the population was relatively homogeneous and the church historically weak *vis-à-vis* the crown, the food supply is adequate, Western influences minimal, and official tolerance of contra-phenomena relatively low.

Apropos of the question of official tolerance/intolerance of a contra-system in any given society, the answer can actually be quite complicated. To deal with the different contra phenomena within the broad social control framework previously discussed, the regimes have developed a more specific set of policies designed to fine-tune the response to individual contra-phenomena. These responses in effect, form a policy continuum between the polar positions of tolerance and intolerance. The policy responses are: (a)Corrective accommodation, (b)Cooptation, (c)Coexistence, and (d)Containment.

Corrective accommodation proceeds gradually, incrementally, and, often imperceptibly. It is a common policy response to the parallel high culture. Over time, a regime may, via its control over censorship, marginally enlarge the parameters of permissible artistic expression so that parts of the contra-culture are accommodated in the process. This is a continuous process in most regimes as yesterday's literary rebels become today's literary lions. In Poland, the thriving business of underground literature is pushing the state publishing industry to be more adventurous in order to compete for the *zloty* of the book-buying public.[11] In the USSR, Gorbachev's cultural *glasnost'* is beginning to accommodate "parallel" literature of both the present and the past. Witness reports that Pasternak's *Dr. Zhivago*, one of the earliest *samizdat* novels, is being published in a mainline official literary journal in 1988.

Accommodation, however, does not mean the withering away of the alternate culture. More often than not, it is a slow, cautious policy response which usually leaves a cadre of artists, both establishment and nonestablishment types, impatient with the pace of accommodation and still inclined to try out new forms and themes in the parallel culture.

Cooptation is a more deliberate, observable shift as a policy response to contra-phenomena. Basically, it is the regime's way of saying if we can't beat it, let's join it and coopt it. Usually, after fruitlessly resisting the youth counterculture, most East European regimes have begun trying to coopt the less offensive parts of it within the official youth program. Often the response is too little, too late, as the international youth culture, of which the East European youth would like to think themselves a part, marches on to new music, new fads, or new styles. So while certain rock music is now becoming acceptable on the state's concert stages, heavy metal groups are not. While selected Western rock stars may tour the East, music fans in Czechoslovakia and the Soviet Union are discouraged from making the late John Lennon of Beatles' fame a hero-martyr.[12]

Cooptation is also used to respond to illegal moonlighting in the service sector. Poland originally led the way in decriminalizing, and hence coopting, service moonlighting. Hungary later followed suit, and in 1987 the USSR entered the era of the legal moonlighter.[13]

Coexistence is a policy response of omission rather than commission. It is an act of passive resignation to and tacit acceptance of a contra-phenomenon by a party-state. In effect, the leadership adopts the attitude if we can't stop it, we'd better learn to live or coexist with it. In the European communist states, coexistence is a common political response to much of the burgeoning off-the-books second economies which involve several millions of illegal "producers," diverters, and speculators and tens of millions of "consumers." This phenomenon seems to have grown exponentially throughout much of the region in the long Brezhnev era. While the authorities, with varying degrees of commitment, continued to try to check egregious and large-scale economic crime, they soon learned the limits of police power in attempting to cope with myriad other manifestations of corruption, and began to turn a blind eye. One could speculate that without official tolerance of the underground economy in the severe austerity of Romania today, daily life for the urban citizen would go from extremely difficult to impossible.[14]

Containment is the final, least tolerant, and most specialized response to the contra-system. This is usually the standard policy stance toward political and ethnic dissent and frequently religious protest as well. In adopting this position, the authorities are effectively declaring: we will not tolerate this contra-phenomenon, we are going to contain it. Containment, however, is a very complex policy which the various regimes use differentially, drawing on a wide range of policy tools from administrative through judicial political justice. Generally, religious dissidents are treated more leniently than political and ethnic dissenters. Within the pluralistic spectrum of political dissent, left-wing protest is usually not treated as harshly as center or right-wing dissidence. Other variables also affect containment policy: the tone of East-West relations or the cost-benefit ratio of repression; the stature of a defendant or target and his/her visibility in the West; the proximity to an important symbolic anniversary, official or otherwise (e.g., August 1988 will be the 20th anniversary of the WAPO invasion of Czechoslovakia); the status of East-East relations (e.g., periodically, Hungary has hardened its low-key containment policy to show its mettle to Moscow); whether or not, at a given time, a regime wishes to use a particular person or case to convey a "message" of warning or threat to one or another internal audience; and the domestic costs of repression if the intended victim is under the protection of a powerful constituency (e.g., the GDR regime backed off in late 1987 when establishment clergy came to the defense of environmental protestors).[15]

For East European regimes most in need of Western goodwill, the first variable or the cost-benefit ratio may impact most heavily on containment policy. Poland since the late seventies has developed what I would call a "revolving door" policy of repression, using grand amnesties when the need for Western credits or Vatican favor arises, followed by less conspicuous individual arrests to maintain a steady flow of dissidents through the door in both directions. If arrests are inexpedient, as they have been since the 1986 amnesty, then the less easily documentable "official hooliganism" is used against activists— a kind of Latin American-style extra-judicial justice which is not infrequently fatal for the victim.[16]

Romania is also in need of goodwill, American goodwill, annually in order to get its Most Favored Nation trading status renewed. Hence, a "seasonal cycle" of repression is practiced—

arrest and trial in the fall, imprisonment in the winter, and early release by spring as the summer of MFN renewal in the Congress approaches.[17] In the same spirit, the USSR since late 1986 has been using its human rights policy tactically, expediently, and instrumentally as part of its broader peace offensive in an effort to achieve overriding foreign policy objectives.[18]

DISSENT IN THE LATE 1980s

A map, so to speak, of the contra-systems of Eastern Europe in the late 1940s would have been a bleak and not very productive cartographic exercise. A few declining outposts of contra-action would have been engulfed in vast stretches of expanding state control over society. Even the Polish church was under unremitting pressure in those years. By contrast, four decades later, a map-sketch of just the contra ethnic, religious, and political landscapes of East Europe in the late 1980s reveals a rich, varied, multi-hued tapestry of dissent throughout the region. As state control has eroded in many areas and groups of contra-citizens have reprivatized large and small enclaves of public life, we are witnessing the re-emergence, albeit glacially, of civil society in the midst of communist systems.

On the ethnic map, the most visible terrain feature has been the rise of the ethnic Albanians of Yugoslavia. This is partly the result of a now familiar by-product of modernization. As literacy rises, social mobility spreads and large numbers of educated citizens are produced, ethnic nationalism tends to increase dramatically.[19] Other factors are at work in the Kosovo region of Yugoslavia as well, including a revolution of rising expectations and the proximity of the neighboring state of Albania, but Yugoslav modernization appears to be the precipitant. Although suppressed by force in 1981, the Yugoslav Albanians remain restive, venting their frustrated aspirations for greater autonomy within the Yugoslav federation on the Serbian minority which lives among them. The result has been a Serbian backlash at the national level, with angry petitions, marches, and anti-Albanian demonstrations in

Belgrade.[20] This is, of course, only the most vivid scene in the fabric of conflicting minority nationalisms within multi-ethnic contemporary Yugoslavia.

The plight of ethnic Hungarians in their East European *diaspora* constitutes another major landmark of contemporary ethnic nationalism in the region. The post-World War I breakup of the Austro-Hungarian empire left a sizeable number of Hungarians outside the new Hungarian republic's frontiers and within the boundaries of several post-Versailles successor states. Hungarian minorities today are located in Romania, Czechoslovakia, and Yugoslavia. In Romania, and to a lesser extent Czechoslovakia, the ethnic Hungarian communities are under cultural pressure from the majority (Romanian) or larger nationality group (the Slovaks).

The Hungarians resist the majority in peaceful ways by asserting and trying to maintain the viability and integrity of their ethnic identity within the respective nation-state. The problem is most acute in Romania, the second most multi-ethnic state in Eastern Europe after Yugoslavia, where the largest of the "overseas" Hungarian communities lives. For some time now, the Romanian regime has been persistently pressing a Romanianization program euphemistically called "national homogenization,"[21] in its Transylvanian province where the majority of the Hungarians are located. This has manifested itself gradually and bureaucratically through the closing of a Hungarian-language teachers college followed subsequently by the closing of Hungarian elementary schools for lack of Hungarian kindergarten teachers; limiting the number of minority students admitted to Romanian technical universities (Hungarians are the largest minority group); restricting the number of Hungarian clergymen (so that churches are understaffed); restricting the importation of books from Hungary; curtailing the number of Hungarian-language newspapers; reducing Hungarian-language programming on Romanian television; and shutting down the provincial Hungarian-language radio station.[22]

Admittedly, some of these policies (e.g., on radio broadcasting) have been applied to other nationalities as well, certain

policies (e.g., on training clergy) are standard communist practices, and other policies no doubt are influenced by the
Romanian austerity economy; but the net effect has impacted
most heavily on the ethnic Hungarians. The thrust of the
Romanian drive has been to promote assimilation by cutting
the Hungarians off from their ethnic past (e.g., through con-
fiscation of the archives of numerous parishes of the
Hungarian Reformed Church) and making extremely difficult
the intergenerational transmission of the ethnic culture (e.g.,
extensive educational restrictions) which is essential to sustain
a nation, especially in *diaspora*.

Ethnic Hungarian defense of the native culture has included establishing underground *samizdat* media to transmit
uncensored information within the community and to the
world outside Romania—the currently best known one being
the Hungarian Press of Transylvania. Certain individuals have
shouldered the burden of ethnic advocacy. Most notable has
been a former high party and state official Karoly Kiraly who
recently argued for continuing the struggle in the face of
Romanian repression: "The alternatives are to assimilate, for
the Transylvanian Hungarian to disappear as a national entity
in a matter of a few generations, or to fight for our national existence."[23] In recent years, neighboring Hungary has begun to
come to the rhetorical assistance of its brothers and sisters in
Transylvania. Initially, a few major Hungarian cultural figures
spoke out against Romanian nationality policy, then the
churches joined in the effort. Gradually, both the Hungarian
government, as represented by the provincial press, and the
dissident community added their voices in defense of the
Transylvanians.

Since the mid-1980s in a rare post-World War II expression of interstate ethnic conflict in East Europe, Hungary has
begun to take the case of the oppressed Transylvanians to international forums—first to the CSCE Cultural Forum held in
Budapest in 1985 and more recently, in the spring of 1987, to
the biennial Helsinki review conference in Vienna.[24] Clearly,
an "escalation" of this magnitude within the bloc would have
to have been sanctioned by the USSR.

By far the most tragic case of minority nationalism in Eastern Europe has taken place in Bulgaria since the mid-1980s. The largest minority are the ethnic Turks who constitute eight to nine percent of the population. The Turks have long been the target of Bulgarization by the ethnocentric majority. In quest of an "ethnically pure"[25] state, the Bulgarians have pursued four previous campaigns of forced assimilation against the Turkish minority in 1964, 1971, 1974, and 1981.[26] The latest and most violent campaign, launched in 1984, appears to have at least nominally effaced the Turks from the Bulgarian census register.

The most recent campaign has involved a well-planned, comprehensive, anti-minority program of cultural genocide. Turks have literally been coerced at gunpoint to take Bulgarian names in place of their Islamic names, newly-born Turkish babies are only being issued birth certificates with Slavic names, fines are imposed for speaking Turkish in public, letters in Turkish go undelivered, ethnic schools have been closed, Turkish-language newspapers are now printed only in Bulgarian, and Turkish-language radio broadcasts have been taken off the air.

Discrimination against the Turks is being applied in education. The practice of the Moslem religion by the Turks (it is also the religion of two smaller minorities) is being hampered: mosques have been closed, clergy arrested, tombstones inscribed in Turkish taken down, and circumcision of young males banned. The wearing of traditional Turkish clothes is being discouraged, administrative resettlement to primarily Bulgarian areas is being carried out in some cases, visits to families in Turkey restricted, and listening to radio broadcasts from Turkey prohibited.

The Bulgarian army and police used force on those Turks refusing to change their names. In many villages, the Turks mounted armed resistance to defend their ethnic heritage. As one Bulgarian party official put it, "some ethnic Turks had not yet matured sufficiently politically to accept new names."[27] The ensuing violence and counter-violence reportedly cost the lives of some 40 Bulgarian soldiers and police and possibly 500

Turks. The government of Turkey has vigorously protested these actions against its ethnic brethren, and there is even circumstantial evidence that the Soviet Union has privately tried to deflect the Bulgarian regime from its all-out assault on the Turks of Bulgaria.[28] In spite of the systematic effort to extirpate their traditions from the public domain, one can probably assume that many of the hundreds of thousands of Bulgarian Turks still surreptitiously strive to observe their religion and maintain the remnants of their culture deep within the contra-system.

Religious activity—both the part sanctioned by the state as well as subterranean religious dissent—also present a more peaceful but equally vivid tableau of spiritual yearning from the Baltic to the Adriatic in Eastern Europe. All of it represents another significant manifestation of the contra-system in the region. Religion in fact, in either its licensed or illicit forms, frequently tends to interface with related contra-phenomena in a given country.

In Yugoslavia, for instance, religious activity offensive to the regime is usually fused with and even considered as a surrogate for one or another of the ethnic nationalisms of the Yugoslav federation.[29] In the GDR, conversely, religious activism (most of which is legal) serves as a patron and protector of a curious mix of mass political dissent and the youth counterculture. Similarly, in Czechoslovakia, both state-sanctioned religion and the religious underground are loosely confederated with Charter 77, the cynosure of political dissent in the CSSR.

There are also more modest political linkages in Romania and Hungary. Some of the Romanian Protestant evangelical groups, after considerable hounding by the party-state, have made emigration their objective in order to practice the faith elsewhere in conditions of political freedom.[30] In turn, in Hungary, religious activism has led to a number of cases of young men declaring conscientious objection to serving in the military, a political obligation for all draft-age males in Eastern Europe. The cases have involved both Jehovah's Witnesses and members of the "Catholic basis communities" which have rejected the church hierarchy because of its compromises with the political realm.[31]

From what little is known about religious dissent in Bulgaria and Albania, it apparently includes elements of free-standing contra-religion as well as activism linked to an ethnic cause. In Bulgaria, there is circumstantial evidence of some evangelical Christian dissent and somewhat more indication of Turkish Muslim active resistance to the forced assimilation of the ethnic Turks.[32] In Albania, which prohibited all organized religious activity in 1967, all religious practice is purely of a contra-character. In the past two decades the regime has been equally harsh toward the clergy of the three major religious persuasions in the country, Albanian Orthodox, Albanian Moslems, and Albanian Catholics, the latter for instance have been severely persecuted for such contra-activity as conducting worship services in private and performing secret baptisms.[33] Similar to the Bulgarian treatment of its Turks, the Albanian party-state has been trying for a long time "to eradicate ethnic Greeks as a distinct minority" in the country, which has included persecution of the Greek Orthodox clergy who resisted the combined anti-ethnic and religious policies.[34] Although Albania has recently and finally embarked on a cautious course of de-Stalinization, there is no indication yet of relief for the indigenous religious communities.

Finally, there is the unique position of the Polish church which is virtually at the vortex of nearly all contra-action in Poland, and which is the subject, along with East German and Czechoslovak religious activism and dissent, of brief case studies below.

The contra-system in Poland is the most highly developed in the socialist commonwealth and, to a great extent, this is due to the immense temporal prestige and spiritual power of the Catholic church. The election of a Polish pope, the several papal visits to Poland beginning in 1979, and both the rise and the fall of Solidarity in 1980-81 have further strengthened the position of the church in society, and *vis-à-vis* the secular authorities.

The vitality of the church is testified to by the fact that there are more seminarians in Poland than in any country in the world, with 30 percent of all new priests ordained in Europe annually being Polish.[35] The church has over 22,000 priests and more than 27,000 nuns.[36] Given the church's leverage with the regime, a veritable religious construction boom has been underway since the mid-1970s with more than one thousand new churches erected since 1975, while hundreds of religious buildings are presently under construction.[37]

Recently, a Polish bishop declared that the church in Poland has attained *de facto* "freedom of worship."[38] In this sense, the church annually mounts huge pilgrimages, broadcasts the mass on Sundays, and teaches most children the catechism. The Polish episcopate also publishes over 30 newspapers and magazines with a combined circulation of several millions.[39]

The outreach of the church also extends throughout the alternate society of the contra-system as well. As the Polish political dissident Adam Michnik wrote in 1985:

> Nothing can change the fact that the Catholic church is a great asset for the Poles. And not only because churches serve as headquarters for various committees aiding victims of repression, or because chaplains speak up on behalf of the wronged and the persecuted; and not only because church buildings ring with the free words of Polish music, and their walls are adorned with the works of Polish painters; not only because the church has become an asylum for independent Polish culture. The church is the most important institution in Poland because it teaches all of us that we may bow only before God.[40]

Michnik is referring to the fact that since martial law in 1981, the church has provided sanctuary for and served as the patron of the Solidarity political underground, the parallel high culture, independent education, and even to some extent the youth counterculture. In the rural areas, some 10,000 "pastoral communities" under church auspices provide similar alternate opportunities to the peasant population.[41] In an important symbolic gesture of social and religious unity, the

Pauline order conferred on Lech Walesa, titular leader of the alternate society, the title of honorary monk.[42]

The Polish Church even provides ecclesiastical support to contra religious activity in neighboring countries by ordaining secretly trained priests from Czechoslovakia, and, on the occasion of the papal visits, receiving pilgrims from the CSSR, Hungary, Soviet Lithuania, and the Soviet Ukraine. The pilgrims, in turn, record the papal words and after returning home circulate the audiotapes within their own religious networks. The Polish regime, given its weaknesses, has little choice but to tolerate many of the church's activities in return for its role in helping maintain social peace, but there are limits to this tolerance of the church's official and contra-activities. The authorities regularly criticize the church for "abuse of the pulpit" or "political clericalism."[43] Pressure is put on the Cardinal-Primate to curb the more vigorous activist clergy. To reinforce the political pressure on the hierarchy, the police frequently, but covertly, resort to committing acts of "official hooliganism" against individual parish priests. The execution-murder of one such political priest, Father Jerzy Popieluszko, by secret police officers, served only to create a new martyr for the faithful.[44] In spite of harassment, repression, and episodic acts of violence, the spiritual and secular power of the Polish church grows and thrives.

The situation of religion in the GDR is quite different from Poland. The dissimilarities can be summarized as follows:

1. While the Polish church enjoys a near monopoly in Catholic Poland, the East German religious community is far more diverse and pluralistic. Catholics are outnumbered by Protestants who are subdivided among a number of different denominations of which the Lutherans are the largest. Aside from the various major evangelical churches and the Catholic church, there are 40 other independent denominations including Jehovah's Witnesses, Mormons, Christian Scientists, as well as Jews.[45]

2. While the *de facto* position of the Polish church is exceptionally strong, the *de jure* status of the East German churches is more secure.

3. While the Polish church receives more material benefits from the state, the Lutheran church in the GDR is the most autonomous church in Eastern Europe. The Lutheran minister is not dependent on the state for his salary, and the church is permitted to operate its own seminaries, hospitals, and even printing presses.[46]

However, the religious situations in Poland and the GDR do share at least one major similarity. In both cases, the regimes try to coopt organized religion for their respective political agendas. Of the two, the East German regime probably manages the church-state relationship more skillfully and certainly with greater consistency. The party-state accepts the point of view articulated by a Protestant pastor that the church will be neither for nor against socialism—it will be merely "a church in socialism."[47] In turn given its legal and financial dependence on the state, "the church can be utilized as an escape valve for social unrest, the opening and closing of which still permits a degree of party control."[48]

To this extent, then, one might say the regime legitimates to a degree the church's outreach to the contra-community, especially to the youth counterculture, independent education, and, to a lesser degree, a kind of mass para-political dissent. Unlike the Polish church though, the churches in the GDR do not play a major role in the parallel high culture. The near total exposure of the GDR to West German television makes this a less significant issue for the churches. The church in East Germany is also quite ambivalent about the burning, inchoate issue of socio-economic and political-dissent, the desire of thousands of citizens to emigrate to the FRG. The churches have noted that emigration has thinned their ranks, carrying to the West pastors, lay personnel, and parishioners.

The great issues for the official East German churches *qua* contra-religion are the intertwined political, social, and religious issues of peace, pacifism, conscientious objection to military service, and ecology. This cluster of concerns has drawn to the churches the youth of the country in increasing numbers, offsetting the inroads into church attendance arising from the secularization of society. While many young people are not believers or do not practice religion, they are attracted to the church by public discussion of such topics as sexuality, alcoholism, rock music, by "blues masses" and by such symbolic tokens as "Swords into Ploughshares" shoulder patches.[49] The churches in turn mobilize their, for the most part, unbaptized younger brethren for the larger issues which revolve in a loose constellation around the theme of anti-militarism. The result in the 1980s has been an impressive array of church-sponsored peace forums, petitions, vigils, hunger strikes, and the production of a "set of studies on the causes of the arms race and strategic issues...."[50]

How does the East German regime respond to the church's preemption of its erstwhile dominion over the public arena and political discourse? The authorities monitor the ecclesiastical political "front" constantly, trying to ensure that its social cathartic effect remains constructive without exceeding the parameters of permissible political-religious dissent. The policy response is a mix of coexistence and mild, very selective containment, the latter through short-term detentions (the C.O.'s), exemplary arrests (the pacifist activists), and periodic expatriations (of individual notables in the non-conformist ranks, thus depriving the followers of their leadership).[51]

Does this unusual church-state concordat work? The answer has to be yes for now—contra-religion provides a surrogate sphere for political dissent while the party-state deftly enforces boundary-maintenance. However, the issues capturing the attention of the young may change with the East-West disarmament process successfully underway. To hold its new constituency, the church, too, may have to shift its stance. One possible symbolic issue may be the removal of the Berlin Wall, a subject fraught with substantial potential for public disorder in East Berlin within the now more permissive atmosphere of *glasnost*' in the East.[52]

The situation of religion in Czechoslovakia, both permitted and contra-religion, stands in stark contrast to neighboring Poland and East Germany. Church-state relations are poor by comparison and the Czechoslovak regime overall policy response to religion is containment. Repression is the norm rather than the exception.

Of the 18 registered churches, the Catholic church is by far the largest. The next largest religious group encompasses a number of Protestant denominations, including the Czech Brethren, Baptists, Lutherans, Pentecostals, Seventh Day Adventists, and others. Jehovah's Witnesses and Mormons are officially banned because of their proselytizing activities; nonetheless, the secret police concedes that the underground Witnesses are the best organized religious group in the country.[53]

Representing 70 percent of the believers (who are officially estimated at 20 percent of the population),[54] the Roman Catholics are probably the most tightly controlled Catholic church in Eastern Europe outside of Albania. The hierarchy is weak and timid *vis-à-vis* the regime, which has resisted normalization with the Vatican for years. As a result, nine of 13 dioceses are without bishops, some for many years.[55] Of the four bishops (of whom only three are resident), the average age is 80. Only two seminaries are permitted, one in the Czech provinces and the other in Slovakia. Hundreds of parishes are without resident priests.

Key church offices are often in the hands of clergy who belong to the pro-regime priests' association, *Pacem in Terris*. For instance, the one official church publication is controlled by regime priests. Similarly, the Federal Chairman of *Pacem in Terris* heads the seminary in the Czech lands, and from that position leads the regime's continuing drive against monasticism which has been banned since 1950.[56] As a final indicator of church-state relations, "for many years, no new Catholic church buildings have been approved for construction."[57]

In response to official containment of the church, the existence of a subterranean church or "Church of the Catacombs"[58] became known to the West in the 1970s and is today a thriving contra-institution in spite of constant surveillance and stern repression. The clergy of the underground church include licensed priests working quietly on the side, retired priests, and, most of all, hundreds of priests deprived of their state licenses for their political beliefs or for their religious activism in the official church.[59] The parishioners include youth and children, precisely the demographic groups which regime policies are designed to discourage from religious practice. For many of the religious dissidents, clergy and laity alike, practicing "persecuted Christianity" may be more attractive than participating in an established church.[60]

The underground church meets irregularly in private residences in small secret groups of a half dozen to 20 people. In these settings, the clergy, mostly de-licensed priests, administer communion, hear confessions, and preach sermons. Catechism is taught to the young and Bible classes are held for adults, often using *samizdat* printed Bibles or Bibles smuggled into the country from Poland.[61] Given government restrictions on the publication of religious literature, underground religious publishing ventures have emerged to fill the vacuum. By the mid-1980s, three *samizdat* religious journals were in existence, with an estimated clandestine circulation of almost 10,000, and probably an even larger secondary readership.[62] Finally, the Church of the Catacombs has also kept alive the tradition of monasticism through its secret monastic orders. As with most of the de-licensed, underground priests, members of the orders lead a dual existence holding a regular job to earn a living while fulfilling the duties of their religious office in nonworking hours.

All of these activities constitute illegal religious dissidence and are punishable under various provisions of Czechoslovak law. During the 1980s, the regime has become especially assiduous in prosecuting clerical activists for practicing religion without a license or, in the case of licensed clergy, performing ecclesiastical functions outside of controlled religious premises without official permission.[63] Defending the party-state's restriction of religious activities to official church facilities, the government's chief administrator of religion offered the following invidious analogy that "a surgeon cannot perform operations except in a hospital."[64]

Clearly, the attention being given to the pursuit of religious dissidents reflects shifting priorities within the regime's general repression policy. Compared to the emphasis on prosecuting political nonconformity after the 1968 Soviet invasion in the late 1960s and early 1970s, and again in the late 1970s and early 1980s after the creation of Charter 77, the contemporary lists of Czechoslovak prisoners of conscience tends to include more religious than political dissenters, as well as a number of religious activists who are also engaged in political dissent.[65]

While the regime struggles with subterranean believers, a far more serious and open religious challenge had recently begun to emerge at the grassroots level in Slovakia and the Czech lands as well. A religious revival appears to be underway in Czechoslovakia as the post-1968 regime program of pacification through consumption has reached its natural limits. More and more people, especially in Slovakia and among the urban youth of the larger cities of Bohemia and Moravia, appear to be turning to religion in quest of moral and intellectual sustenance that lies beyond the regime policy of "bread alone," and is not provided for by the widely disregarded official ideology of Marxism-Leninism.[66] Manifestations of greater religiosity include petitions with thousands of names calling for a papal visit to Czechoslovakia as well as religious pilgrimages of tens of thousands of believers in 1985, on the 1,100th anniversary of the death of St. Methodius, the first Slavic archbishop and missionary. The celebration began in the spring with a gathering of 10,000 Czechs and Slovaks at Velehrad, in eastern Moravia and culminated on July 7 with simultaneous pilgrimages of an estimated 100 to 150,000 Catholic pilgrims each at Velehrad again, and at a site in Slovakia. The momentum of the summer events carried over into the autumn as an annual Slovakian pilgrimage, which normally draws only a few thousand, attracted some 40,000 faithful.[67]

In addition to the established church and the Church of the Catacombs, a new religious contra-phenomenon has arisen from the nominally still waters of society—in the words of an underground journal, "The silent church has spoken ...."[68] With the mass public experience of the first papal visit to

Poland just a year before the rise of the Solidarity labor movement in 1980 no doubt in mind, a prominent specialist on Poland has called attention to the potential socio-political impact of these great religious events within the Czechoslovak system:

> More important, the pilgrimages have furnished the public with an opportunity for self-organization. This is, of course, a natural consequence of the government's policy which, while not expressly forbidding such gatherings, forces their participants to take care of their own needs. Those could include such basics as food and housing, but they might also entail maintaining order among such crowds. Above all, the organization and conduct of pilgrimages tend to provide the pilgrims with an experience of authentic participation, true communal feeling, self-reliance, and self-determination. All those elements contribute to a possible evolution of greater self-assertiveness that, born from a religious experience, could eventually expand into other, more secular areas of public activity.[69]

The summer pilgrimage to Velehrad alone was the largest spontaneous gathering in Czechoslovakia since the days of the Prague Spring, the 20th anniversary of which occurs in 1988.

Undoubtedly emboldened by the successes of the "silent church," the Cardinal-Primate of the Czechoslovak church recently issued a broad 16-point "Charter of Believers in Czechoslovakia" in connection with his visit to Rome in the autumn of 1987.[70] Although none of the points would be remarkable by the standards of the Polish church, collectively they represent, in the Czechoslovak context, a dramatic and radical appeal for religious freedom. In effect, a majority of the points which cover, among other matters, catechism, monasticism, and the need for an independent religious press—seek secular approval, legitimation, and formal institutionalization of religious activities long underway in the contra-system in Czechoslovakia. In conclusion, the church "Charter" simultaneously provides a long-term composite agenda for the normalization of Vatican-regime relations, internal church-state relations, and relations within the church itself between the establishment and the catacombs.

The Eclipse of Political Dissent

As Eastern Europe approaches the 1990s, political dissent, long the leading edge of the contra-systems in the region during the 1970s, has been dulled by the vicissitudes of time and circumstance, and the relentless friction of repression.

Although political dissent, the "classic" mode of reformist dissent articulated by intellectuals, was frequently the catalyst for the rise of the contra-system, especially through its reprivatization of enclaves within political society and its creation of an alternate independent (internal and East-West) information system, it has generally experienced some slippage in status in the 1980s.

A kind of rotation is taking place in East Europe as political dissent is gradually being eclipsed by its contra offspring of ethnic and religious dissent. The latter are gradually becoming the new cutting edge of contra-behavior. A glance at East European police dockets confirms that political dissidents are no longer seen as quite as threatening to the status quo as their religious and ethnic counterparts. Generally, ethnic and religious activism along with the specter of blue-collar economic unrest now constitute the main challenge to the administered realm and the ultimate political authority of the communist regimes in Eastern Europe.

Of course, as always in dealing with a region as diverse as East Europe, the situation varies from country to country, so let me briefly survey the present status of political dissent in the eight countries.

Poland, the beacon of political dissent in the early 1980s; is relatively quiet. A cursory reading of the extensive underground press[71] suggests two reasons: (a) the leadership of underground Solidarity remains divided and unable to develop a durable consensus on how to cope with the Jaruzelski regime; and (b) the erstwhile followers appear to be suffering from political exhaustion, a form of combat fatigue from being so long in the fever zone of political conflict. As a result, the

Solidarity chieftains have been superseded by the church hierarchy, especially the cautious Primate-Cardinal Glemp, as the new contra-leadership of society. In turn, the average Pole has retreated from the political arena into the socio-economic and cultural dimensions of the contra-system. Privatism now appears to be the reigning social value and political ennui the dominant mood of the public. The problems of everyday life in a scarcity economy take their daily toll of the individual's social energy and, for the time being, seem to have foreshortened his/her political attention span. Of course, this quiescence is but a hiatus in the recurring cycle of Polish political dissent and popular unrest. The fact that neither pacification nor repressive tolerance are working effectively does not bode well for longer-term social peace.

In the GDR, political dissent is inchoate at best, finding diffuse expression in the mass emigration movement and the church-led peace and environmental campaigns. The regime has learned to coexist with emigration, even benefitting from it financially as hundreds of people serving sentences for illegally attempting emigration are "sold" to West Germany annually for substantial amounts of hard currency.[72] As of now, church-led dissent deals with relatively pacific and benign issues which do not appear to be a major irritant to the authorities. However, if the church loses effective control of its mixed constituency or, in order not to be left behind, decides to redeploy onto a more volatile issue, tensions could rise perceptibly. Classic intellectual political dissent, which has never figured as a major factor in the GDR, is presently at low ebb due to past expatriations (of Biermann and Bahro) and the attrition of time (the death of Havemann).

Charter 77, the umbrella association of political dissent in Czechoslovakia, having endured years of judicial and administrative political justice, in 1987 celebrated its 10th anniversary. Good to the word of its 1977 mandate, Charter 77 has never acted as a political opposition.[73] Instead, it has provided over the years a large number of intellectually oriented and well-reasoned alternatives to a wide array of regime policies. Charter 77's prodigious *samizdat* output has included several dozen major position papers, several hundred ancillary statements, and, through an affiliate VONS or the Committee for the Defense of the Unjustly Persecuted, another 500 case reports on specific human rights violations by the party-state. Although even this lower-keyed manifestation of political dissent has often riled the authorities who have responded with familiar containment techniques, Charter 77 has had a greater impact on Western public opinion than on Czechoslovak society.

The limited impact of Chartist dissent inside the country has been due to two factors: (a) Charter 77 has always been small in number, predominantly intellectuals, and effectively isolated from and denied access to society; and (b) it has been issue-directed rather than conflict-oriented, and the issues addressed have often tended to be broad-gauge and philosophically formulated, such as the papers on literature, historiography, the environment, and peace. Consequently, Charter 77, through its successive spokespersons, has never sought nor has it ever enjoyed any popular contra-mobilizational potential which might challenge the regime; certainly nothing ever even remotely akin to the great religious pilgrimages of 1985.

After initially over-reacting repressively to the small band of Chartists when they first began their work in the late 1970s, the party and police have settled into a pattern by which they primarily ensure that Charter 77 maintains a low profile at home. Conversely, in the past few years the regime has begun to display much greater concern with the potential challenge to its domination arising from the religious sector of the contra-system. This sector, in turn, has begun to receive substantial attention from the security police of Czechoslovakia.

Hungary, Albania, and Bulgaria can be discussed more succinctly. Hungary enjoys one of the relatively more relaxed political environments in Eastern Europe. Within a kind of zone of permitted dissent under the aegis of repressive tolerance, a domesticated para-opposition is allowed to engage in limited public discourse on selected policy issues. Outside of this "zone" by choice, there is a real political opposition, but it is tiny in size and largely marginalized through a set of subtle, low-visibility containment procedures designed to produce no attention-attracting political prisoners for the external image-oriented Hungarian leadership.[74]

Antithetically, Albania and Bulgaria rank among the least tolerant of any kind of nonconformist activity. Up until the recent death of the Albanian Stalinist Hoxha, any manifestation of deviance—political, ethnic, or religious—would have been extremely dangerous. It probably still is as de-Stalinization gets underway very guardedly. Since Hoxha's death, the main contra-activity which seems to be arousing concern, is the modest emergence of the first shoots of a youth counterculture in Albania.[75] Although a less coercive system on the whole, Bulgaria has been home to only the faintest suggestions of underlying political dissent in the past decade. In 1978, the appearance of Charter 77 in Czechoslovakia the previous year evoked a barely audible echo from Bulgaria in the form of a terse, anonymous supporting declaration. Nine years later in 1987, a bolder step was taken when several Bulgarian citizens affixed their names to a statement of human rights grievances addressed to the biennial Helsinki Review Conference meeting in Vienna. Predictably, the signatories have been subjected to political justice.[76] Possibly, something is stirring within Bulgaria, perhaps encouraged by Gorbachev's oft-repeated themes of *glasnost'* and democratization. Meanwhile, the Bulgarian authorities seem far more preoccupied with those they deem their ethnic and religious opponents.

Organized political dissent arose in Romania in the late 1970s, stimulated in part by the role model of Charter 77. It was, however, a shortlived phenomenon. By the early 1980s, the small group of intellectual dissidents centered around the writer Paul Goma had been contained through political trials, psychiatric internment and expatriation, and effectively silenced. Political activism has been reduced to small groups of urban professionals and evangelical Protestants from the provinces, seeking to emigrate to the West for different reasons—the urbanites to escape the domestic economic environment and the provincials to avoid the repression of their religious activity.[77]

Throughout the 1980s, the severity of Romanian economic austerity and the extremity of the Ceaucescu cult began bringing forth new expressions of protest. Although these protests tend to arise from common causes, they have been stratified and segregated from one another, making it easier for the regime to apply methods of social control. At the level of individual protest, a number of "cases" have reached the West, suggesting deep frustrations are being expressed in isolated acts of political desperation. One man set fire to volumes of Ceaucescu's speeches in public, another is serving a long sentence for trying to organize a demonstration against regime policies, while, most recently in 1986, three men "were arrested for displaying homemade anti-Ceaucescu placards on the eve of the regime's anniversary celebration."[78] At another level of protest, former leaders of pre-revolutionary political parties have petitioned, to no avail, for the rehabilitation of their banned institutions.[79]

Finally, in the late 1980s, in the most ominous development for the regime, working-class protest and violence, provoked by new austerity measures, has flared up again. Fragmentary information suggests that other population groups are supporting the protests this time.[80] The regime appears to be embarking on a familiar response pattern: isolate the blue-collar unrest from sympathetic groups by manipulating short-term measures of pacification through consumption, then identify and subject to political justice the "leaders," other major perpetrators, and principal supporters. But, will the containment machinery prevail this time?

Finally, there remains only the question of the status of political dissent in Yugoslavia. Given its deviation from the Soviet systemic model in the early 1950s and its multinational makeup, the Yugoslav system has always been different from its eastern neighbors. A case in point is the question of political dissent. Historically, it has never been in the vanguard of the contra-system for several reasons: (a) the decentralized Yugoslav system provides far more avenues for political expression than a standard Soviet-type system, so that what would constitute provocative dissent in Romania or Czechoslovakia is institutionalized and coopted in Yugoslavia; (b) where political dissent does appear beyond the bounds of repressive tolerance, it often reflects the prevailing fragmentation and diffusion of political authority in the Yugoslav communist system; hence the phenomenon tends to be regionalized, ethnically-oriented, or issue-specific. Not surprisingly then, official tolerance varies regionally from low in Bosnia to high in Slovenia; and (c) classic reformist dissent at the national level has generally been confined to small, informal groups of left and liberal Belgrade intellectuals whom the regime has traditionally vigorously contained through prosecutions for "hostile propaganda" under the Yugoslav criminal code.[81]

With only the few latter exceptions, then, ethnic advocacy in Yugoslavia tends to fuse with and color all expressions of political dissent with the result that diverse and corrosive "ethnic politics" have consistently been the main challenge to the fractured authority of the central leadership. Episodically, the system has been racked by ethnic politics. The late 1980s are witnessing again such an outbreak, but this time intensifying ethnic conflict is compounded by hyperinflation, working-class anxiety, and escalating strikes, all reflecting the country's deepening economic crisis.

In conclusion, the 1990s will most likely usher in a period of general crisis in Eastern Europe. Albania will be trying to manage the now familiar unintended consequences of decompression after decades of Stalinism. The Czechoslovak succession has just begun, while Bulgaria, the GDR, and Hungary will be facing or experiencing the instability of impending successions. Finally, the coming crisis is likely to impact most heavily in Poland, Romania, and Yugoslavia, all three of which have in common an acute economic situation, extensive evidence of blue-collar unrest,[82] and mass-based, inter-class movements of religious and/or ethnic activism contra to the communist leaderships of the respective countries. The Polish, Romanian, and Yugoslav regimes are all experiencing large-scale failure of social control (even Hungary experienced some sporadic, symbolic violence in 1987 in reaction to the implementation of its austerity program). Pacification through consumption has not been working for some time or is beginning to break down in Poland, Romania, and Yugoslavia, while the regimes' political justice machinery is increasingly inadequate to contain the sheer number of deeply disaffected contra-citizens, many of whose activities are beyond the effective reach of the state's police power.

One or more of these crisis regimes is likely to undergo a social explosion in the 1990s, perhaps sooner.[83] Whether such an event is followed by a full-blown legitimation crisis will remain to be seen,[84] but should one occur it will put to a severe test Gorbachev's "new thinking" on Soviet relations with Eastern Europe.

NOTES

The author expresses his thanks to Anne Mauboussin for her research assistance on parts of this chapter, and to the Union College Summer Research Fellowship Program which sponsored her.

1. See Robert Sharlet, "Dissent and the Contra-System in East Europe," *Current History*, Vol. 84 (November 1985), pp. 353-56 and 386.
2. Vladimir Kusin, "Gorbachev, Eastern Europe, and the Communist Movement," *Radio Free Europe Research* herearter cited as *RFER*, Vol. 12, No. 45, Part I of 2 (November 13, 1987), p. 2.
3. See Robert Sharlet, "Varieties of Dissent and Regularities of Repression in the European Communist States," In Jane L. Curry, ed., *Dissent in Eastern Europe* (New York: Praeger, 1983), esp. pp. 10-14.
4. The concept is Herbert Marcuse's.
5. See George Schopflin, "Opposition and Para-Opposition: Critical Currents in Hungary, 1968-78," In Rudolf L. Tokes, ed., *Opposition in Eastern Europe* (Baltimore: Johns Hopkins University Press, 1979), esp. pp. 142-45.
6. See Miklos Haraszti, *The Velvet Prison: Artists Under State Socialism* transl. by Katalin and Stephen Landesmann with the help of Steve Wasserman (New York: The New Republic/Basic Books, 1987).
7. See Robert Sharlet, "Dissent and Repression in the Soviet Union and Eastern Europe, " *International Journal*, Vol. 33, No. 4 (1978), esp. pp. 765-71.
8. See *Amnesty International Report 1982* (London: Amnesty International Publications, 1982), pp. 308-09.
9. This was the second military suppression in Romania, the first occurring in 1977. On the 1977 and 1981 events, see Anne Planche, "Workers' Revolts in Romania," In *World View 1983* (New York: Pantheon, 1982), pp. 124-25.

10. See George C. Malcher, *Poland's Politicized Army: Communists in Uniform* (New York: Praeger, 1984), Chs. 10-12.

11. See *Reinventing Civil Society: Poland's Quiet Revolution, 1981-1986* (New York: U.S. Helsinki Watch Committee, 1986), pp. 53-60.

12. In Prague, there is a place dubbed "Lennon Wall" where Czechoslovak youths scrawl irreverent graffiti which the authorities periodically whitewash away. In Moscow, attempts by Lennon fans to hold a silent vigil or otherwise mark the anniversary of John Lennon's death during the past few years have been discouraged by the police.

13. The new Soviet law took effect May 1, 1987.

14. Whereas unofficial "second currencies" are tolerated in Poland (the dollar) and the GDR (the West German mark), possession of foreign currency is a crime in Romania; hence unopened packages of Kent cigarettes serve as a surrogate currency in the Romanian second economy.

15. See "East Berlin Raids Staged on Church," *New York Times* (November 27, 1987), p. A24; and Henry Kamm, "In East Berlin, Dissenters Resist a Crackdown," *New York Times (November 30, 1987), p. A5.*

16. See *Repression Disguised As Law: Human Rights in Poland* (New York: Lawyers Committee for Human Rights, 1987), Ch. 3.

17. See Robert Sharlet's reply to a question by Congressman Tom Lantos in *Human Rights in Romania*—Hearing Before the ... Committee on Foreign Affairs, House of Representatives, May 14, 1985 (Washington, DC: U.S. Government Printing Office, 1985), pp. 91-92.

18. For instance, arrests for political offenses and political trials slowed to a trickle in Moscow, which is most visible to the Western press, while repression for ethnic and religious dissent has continued unabated in the provinces.

19. On the linkage between literacy and "re-nationalization" of ethnic consciousness, using the Soviet Georgians as a case study, see Ronald Grigor Suny, "Soviet Georgia in

the Seventies," Occasional Paper No. 64, Kennan Institute for Advanced Russian Studies (May 15, 1979), esp. pp. 1-2.

20. See Jackson Diehl, "New Serbian Leader Accused of Adding to Ethnic Tension," *Washington Post* (November 20, 1987), p. A21.

21. See *RFER*, Vol. 11, No. 17, Part III of 3 (April 25, 1986), pp. 4-5.

22. See *RFER*, Vol. 10, No. 42, Part IV of 4 (October 18, 1985), p. 36.

23. From a *samizdat* journal interview with Kiraly—see *RFER*, Vol. 12, No. 26, Part II of 3 (July 3, 1987), p. 29.

24. See "Hungarian Statements at the Vienna Conference," *New Hungarian Quarterly*, Vol. 28, No. 106 (Summer 1987), pp. 125-35.

25. David Binder, "Going Back: Bulgaria, 20 Years Later," *New York Times Magazine* (December 8, 1985), p. 159.

26. See Michele Lee, "The Persecution of the Turks," *Labour Focus on Eastern Europe*, Vol. 8, No. 1 (Summer 1985), p. 26.

27. Henry Kamm, "Aides in Ankara Say Bulgaria Has Slain 1,000 Ethnic Turks," *New York Times* (August 7, 1985), p. A10.

28. Generally, see *Destroying Ethnic Identity: the Turks of Bulgaria—An Update* (New York: A Helsinki Watch Report, 1987); *Bulgaria: Imprisonment of Ethnic Turks* (London: Amnesty International Publications, 1986); *Bulgaria: Continuing Human Rights Abuse Against Ethnic Turks* (New York: Amnesty International USA, 1987).

29. See, e.g., the case of Father Nedjo Janjic, a Serbian Orthodox priest charged in 1980 for inciting "chauvinist euphoria" during his son's christening at his house, in *Yugoslavia: Prisoners of Conscience* (London: Amnesty International Publications, 1982), p. 16-17.

30. On the persecution of Romanian neo-Protestants, see *Romania* (New York: Amnesty International USA, 1978), pp. 29-34; and *Romania: Human Rights in a 'Most*

Favored Nation' (New York: U.S. Helsinki Watch Committee, 1983), Ch. 7.

31. See *From Below: Independent Peace and Environmental Movements in Eastern Europe and the USSR* (New York: A Helsinki Watch Report, 1987), pp. 54-59.

32. See *Nineteenth Semiannual Report: Implementation of the Helsinki Final Act, April 1, 1985-October 1, 1985* (Washington, DC: U.S. Dept. of State, 1985), p. 14.

33. See *Albania: Political Imprisonment and the Law* (London: Amnesty International Publications, 1984), pp. 12-15.

34. See Nikolaos Stavrou, "Albania: The Little Country with the Big Gulag," *Washington Post*, Sun. ed. (December 9, 1984), p. C2.

35. Barry Newman, "Quiet Crusade: As Pope's Visit Nears, the Church in Poland Hews to Its Strategy," *Wall Street Journal* (June 1, 1987), p. 1.

36. *REER*, Vol. 12, No. 25, Part I of 3 (June 26, 1987), p. 9.

37. See Michael T. Kaufman, "1,000 Churches Rise in Poland ...," *New York Times* (May 26, 1986), p. 2.

38. Michael T. Kaufman, "Polish Church Awaits Pope, Bewildered by Its New Vigor," *New York Times*, Sun. ed., (June 7, 1987), Sec. 1.

39. Roman Stefanowski, "The Catholic Press in Poland," *RFER*, Vol. 10, No. 44, Part I of 1 (November 1, 1985), p. 1.

40. Adam Michnik, "Letter from the Gdansk Prison," *New York Review of Books* (July 18, 1985), p. 46.

41. See *RFER*, Vol. 10, No.11, Part I of 3 (March 15, 1985), pp. 17-20.

42. See *Help & Action Newsletter*, Vol. 7, No. 30 (1984), p. A5.

43. "Polish Leader Sees Long Conflict," *New York Times* (November 29, 1985), p. A10.

44. See *Help & Action Newsletter*, Vol. 8, No. 38 (1985), p. 63.

45. "For the First Time, Statistics from the GDR on Religious Affiliation," *Religion in Communist Dominated Areas*, Vol. 22, Nos. 7-8-9 (1983), p. 128.

46. See *Implementation of the Helsinki Accords*—Hearing Before the Commission on Security and Cooperation in Europe, May 22, 1984 (Washington, DC: U.S. Government Printing Office, 1984), pp. 55-56.
47. James M. Markham, "Luther Being Lionized in East Germany," *New York Times*, Sun. ed. (May 8, 1983), Sec. 1, p. 1.
48. Joyce Marie Mushaben, "Swords into Ploughshares: the Church, the State and the East German Peace Movement," *Studies in Comparative Communism*, Vol. 17, No. 2 (Summer 1984), p. 131.
49. See Pedro Ramet, "Church and Peace in the GDR," *Problems of Communism*, Vol. 33, No. 4 (July-August 1984), p. 49; and Adam Hochschild, "East Germany: Behind the Lines with Europe's Most Daring Peace Activists," *Mother Jones* (September-October 1982), p. 52.
50. Ronald D. Asmus, "The Peace Movement in Eastern Europe," in Vojtech Mastny, ed., *Soviet/East European Survey, 1983-1984* (Durham, NC: Duke University Press, 1985), p. 63.
51. For example, Wolf Biermann, a popular performing artist and intellectual dissident, was expatriated in 1976, while Rudolf Bahro, the critical left-Marxist social scientist followed in 1979.
52. See Elizabeth Pond, "Clashes in East Berlin Point Up Risks of *Glasnost'* in East Europe," *Christian Science Monitor* (June 10, 1987), p. 10.
53. See North Atlantic Assembly *Bulletin*, No. 38 (September 1 - December 31, 1985), p. 14.
54. See *RFER*, Vol. 12, No. 23, Part I of 2 (June 12, 1987), p. 11.
55. See *RFER*, Vol. 12, No. 47, Part III of 3 (November 27, 1987), pp. 22-23.
56. See *RFER*, Vol. 12, No. 23, Part I of 2 (12 Jun 87), p. 10.
57. U.S. Dept. of State, *Country Reports on Human Rights Practices for 1986* (Washington, DC: U.S. Government Printing Office, 1987), p. 895.

58. See David A. Andelman, "Czech Church Struggles With Itself and the State," *New York Times* (February 27 1978), p. A4.
59. By 1983, the number of priests de-licensed was estimated at 500. See *RFER*, Vol. 10, No. 3, Part I of 3 (January 17, 1986), pp. 27-28.
60. *East European Reporter*, Vol. 2, No. 3 (1987), p. 22. The statement is by Milan Simecka.
61. On Bible-smuggling, see, e.g., North Atlantic Assembly *Bulletin*, No. 37 (June 1-August 31, 1985), p. 6.
62. See William Erikson, "Religion Gains in Eastern Europe," *Christian Science Monitor* (January 5, 1987), p. 10.
63. See, e.g., the case of Father Adam Rucki, *Palach Press*, No. 26 (October 1985), pp. 79-80. This is from VONS Statement No. 430.
64. *RFER*, Vol. 12, No. 23, Part I of 2 (June 12, 1987), p. 11.
65. See *RFER*, Vol. 11, No. 7, Part IV of 4 (February 14, 1986), p. 13.
66. See George Schopflin, "Unity and Diversity in Eastern Europe: Poland, Czechoslovakia, Hungary in the Mid-1980's," *East European Reporter*, Vol. 1, No. 1 (Spring 1985), p. 4.
67. See *RFER*, Vol. 10, No. 48, Part III of 3 (November 29, 1985), pp. 13-15.
68. The quote is from the religious *samizdat* journal *Informace o Cirkvi*. See *RFER*, Vol. 10, No. 40, Part I of 3 (October 4, 1985), pp. 13-15.
69. J.B. de Weydenthal, "Religious Pilgrimages: A Step Toward Public Self-Assertion," *RFER*, Vol. 11, No. 29, Part II of 4 (July 18, 1986), p. 2.
70. See *RFER*, Vol. 12, No. 47, Part III of 3 (November 27, 1987), pp. 19-22.
71. See, for instance, *Uncensored Poland News Bulletin*, a periodical which surveys, and selectively translates and summarizes the Polish underground press.
72. This is called *"Freikauf"* or "buying out" and has been going on quietly between the FRG and GDR since the 1970s.

73. See Robert Sharlet, "Charter 77 Revisited," U.S. Information Agency, *Addendum*, No. 54 (1987), esp. pp. 5-7.
74. See George Schopflin, "Opposition in Hungary: 1956 and Beyond," in Jane L. Curry, ed., *Dissent in Eastern Europe* (New York: Praeger, 1983) esp. pp. 79-80.
75. See Louis Zanga, "Problems with Albanian Youth," *RFER*, Vol. 12, No. 20, Part II of 2 (May 22, 1987), esp. pp. 1-2.
76. See *Help & Action Newsletter*, Vol. 10, Nos. 47-48 (June-September 1987), p. 28.
77. On some recent emigration cases, see *Romania: Human Rights Violations in the Eighties* (London: Amnesty International Publications, 1987), pp. 17-18.
78. *Help & Action Newsletter*, Vol. 10, Nos. 47-48 (June-September 1987), p. a.
79. A former leader of the banned National Peasant Party was even preparing to petition Gorbachev during his visit to Romania in the spring of 1987 until the police intervened. See *RFER*, Vol. 12, No. 45, Part I of 3 (October 23, 1987), pp. 31-33.
80. For the most current information on the spreading social unrest in Romania, see *RFER*, Vol. 13, No. 3, Part I of 3 (June 15, 1988), pp. 21-28.
81. This is Art. 133 of the Federal Criminal Code of Yugoslavia. The law on "hostile propaganda" is similar to subversion laws found in all communist states such as Art. 70 of the RSFSR Criminal Code in the USSR.
82. Blue-collar protest could be considered a hybrid of *mass* political and economic dissent. See Ivan Volgyes, *Politics in Eastern Europe* (Chicago: Dorsey Press, 1986), pp. 197-202.
83. A Bulgarian philosopher recently warned of possible "spontaneous" social explosions even in Bulgaria. Quoted in Bennett Kovrig, "Fire and Water: Political Reform in Eastern Europe," in this volume.
84. See James O'Connor, *The Meaning of Crisis: A Theoretical Introduction* (Oxford, UK: Basil Blackwell, 1987), esp. Ch. 3 & pp. 110-11.

FIVE

THE SOVIET UNION AND EASTERN EUROPE

WILL THE REFORMS IN THE USSR MAKE A DIFFERENCE?

Otto Ulc

In 1953, three months after the death of Stalin and the week of Beria's announced arrest, I was taking final examinations at Charles University Law School in Prague.

The pivotal part of this ordeal involved a probe into the arcane matters of Marxism-Leninism, scientific communism and the like. "A hundred times nothing killed a donkey—provide a proper dialectical explanation!" demanded the examiner. The question was splendidly simple. The third law of dialectics, according to Stalin, the accumulating quantity becomes a new quality.

The professor nodded, the test proceeded without blemish until I stumbled over the following query concerning scientific communist affairs: "What is the most fundamental, distinguishing characteristic of a true, genuine communist?" After a few unsuccessful attempts to solve the enigma, the examiner terminated my embarrassing ineptitude: "The love for the Soviet Union, of course!" "Of course," I apologetically seconded. The granite-like verity of the decade of Stalinism was followed by decades of de-Stalinization, socialism with a human face, and post-invasion normalization. Soviet Union Our Model—the most loudly and frequently repeated slogan.

But not anymore. *Glasnost'* and *perestroika* are to be blamed for this unexpected turn of events and values.

Glasnost' is an old word, frequently used by the Russians in a political context even more than a century ago.[1] The contemporary usage of the term did not start with Mikhail S. Gorbachev, but with his mentor Yuri Andropov (November 1982 speech), former head of the K.G.B., the best informed force in the country. As the saying goes, in a police state only a policeman can afford to be a liberal.

But how liberal are these modernizers? Will the real Gorbachev please stand up? Western observers tend to reach contradictory conclusions from the same body of facts, though in at least one respect they are usually in agreement: always give a new leader in the Soviet Union the most generous praise for being the new, pragmatic, liberalizing force and hope for the country. Even Stalin used to be characterized as a "pragmatist" and a "moderate" by the experts of the day.[2]

According to Anatolyi Shcharansky, *glasnost'* is above all a public relations gimmick aimed at the incurably gullible West. Most of his fellow Soviet exiles do not share this pessimistic assessment. They point out that Soviet communism is running out of energy, that Gorbachev's reforms are not unprecedented, and that the drive for efficiency is always behind every Soviet political reform.

The Soviet society must be reformed but it cannot be too democratized, one is likely to surmise from Gorbachev's core belief that democracy, above all, is a "conscious discipline." For him (as well as for Bismarck and a host of distinguished non-democrats), an authority should be just, not liberal and permissive. *Demokratizatsia* means no democracy, as *glasnost'* means nothing more than a less restricted airing of ideas, information, and grievances, and whatever else *perestroika* may ultimately mean, it is not intended to introduce liberal ideas and practices into the Soviet society. On the opposite end of the political spectrum a rather extraordinary analysis is offered by Stephen A. Cohen who traces the birth of *perestroika* to as early as the 1950s, and who considers Gorbachev a leader who is finally able to implement this allegedly old, dormant "opposition program in the Communist Party."[3]

   "Gorbachev is a different manager, not a different communist," asserts[4] Milan Svec, a former Czech apparatchik of prime rank, and deputy ambassador to Washington until 1985. Unlike Khrushchev, an ebullient and not infrequently erratic reformer, Gorbachev has succeeded in projecting an image of the most intelligent, dynamic, self-assured leader since Lenin himself, a leader more cautious in actions than in his speeches.

   Words or deeds? Vladimir Morozov, a journalist who defected in October 1986, was asked by Westerners about the impact of *glasnost'*. An investigative reporter, he confessed it was the first time he had ever heard of this allegedly earth-shaking novelty. "Nothing has changed except for words," he maintains[5]. The only real change is the new anti-alcoholic laws. Vodka now costs over 10 roubles a bottle, more than the average pay for a day's work.

   The distinguished French publicist Alain Besancon offers a different view. In an interview with George Urban[6] he rated Gorbachev a more radical reformer than his activities have so far betrayed. Urban responded by labelling Gorbachev a "Leninist with a human face" who wants the world to see the human face but not the Leninism. Modernization at home will require substantial Western assistance, and *glasnost'* earmarked for export is to help in this effort.

   However, Gorbachev's very own words diminish the plausibility of such an assertion. If words were to be weighed gingerly in order not to alert the Western world (though it is almost always ready and eager to detect angelic impulses on the part of its sworn adversaries), why then characterize the Soviet military intervention in Afghanistan—one million dead, maimed, wounded, five million, i.e., a third of the nation, in exile—as a shining example of "the principle of strict non-interference into internal affairs"?[7] At the Party Congress in Warsaw, as well as during his subsequent visit to Czechoslovakia, Gorbachev did not disavow the legitimacy of the Brezhnev Doctrine—the responsibility of the socialist community to save socialism in whichever fraternal country by whatever means. Yet, verities like these are also subject to the laws of dialectics, the rule of perpetual change, as it has subsequently been the case, to the considerable displeasure of the officialdom in various quarters of the realm.

No democrat by Western standards, Gorbachev is striving to strengthen the system to prove that it can work; to avert the otherwise perhaps inevitable decline of the USSR to the status of a second-rate power. Even if he should succeed in this monumentally demanding venture, he would still have to cope with the crucial task of modernizing the economy, the state, and the society without endangering the power monopoly of the Communist Party, which is largely responsible for the cheerless state of affairs that necessitated all those risky remedial measures.

Without a fundamental change, the reform is impossible. With a fundamental change the reformed system will cease to be a socialist system of the Soviet type. Declining productivity and backwardness threaten the cause of socialism, yet modernization threatens the leading role of the party: to implement the reforms will inevitably diminish the power of its own apparatus. Vladimir Bukovsky put it this way:

> The emerging dilemma is truly paradoxical: if the party retains its control over the economy, socialism will be endangered and will finally collapse; if, however, the party loses its control over the economy (and, therefore, its control over the Soviet society), what Gorbachev calls "the position of socialism in the modern world" will collapse as surely. In short, the implacable logic of Marxist-Leninist analysis produces the inevitable demise of socialism.[8]

Furthermore, if the imperatives of modernization will require new criteria of recruitment, promotion, and demotion, without merits or political considerations in place, who would bother to join the party, to sacrifice for the "cause" in this thoroughly post-revolutionary, post-ideological age?

"Is 'glasnost' ' a Game of Mirrors?" is the title of an article prepared by a group of exiles, published in *The New York Times* on March 22, 1987, and reprinted in the Soviet weekly tabloid *Moscow News* (for this daring it was sternly reprimanded by *Pravda*). The authors stated:

> Even a fool can see by now that if 70 years of doctrine have brought to ruin one of the richest countries on earth, the doctrine must be faulty. Mr. Gorbachev admits that no one in all those years succeeded in putting the country right. Perhaps, then, the time has come to reject the system itself.

Meaningful, genuine change, the authors charge, would require the Soviet leaders to reject the basic fallacies of the Marxist-Leninist dogma—the indispensability of world class struggle, the inevitability of worldwide communist victory, the eternal monopoly of power of the Communist Party, the self-chosen vanguard, etc.—in sum, the dismantling of the very fundamentals on which the legitimacy of the system rests. This kind of suicide will surely not be undertaken by any ruling party, the Communist Party least of all.

Andrei I. Sakharov, expressing a great hope in Gorbachev's policies, and considering *perestroika* a historical necessity, nonetheless adds a cautionary note: "There is a clear distinction between what Gorbachev says and what the Central Committee approves, and still a greater gap between what they approve and what happened in real life."[9] After life-long experience with central planning, a command economy, and a command lifestyle where there is a missing link between performance and reward, how could the man in the street free himself from the habits of sloth, indolence, and inertia? To convert him to abstinence sounds as realistic as a party *ukaze* ordering a pork diet for devout Muslims in Uzbekistan.

With the exception of the parasitic bureaucratic strata whose existence is directly endangered by the reforms, the society is likely to welcome the changes but is sorely unprepared for the role of responsible decision making. As William Hyland, the editor-in-chief of *Foreign Affairs*, put it after his return from the Soviet Union: Everyone claims to be in favor of *perestroika*, but let the other guy start first—work hard, come to work and leave work sober, etc.

A great deal of energy, stamina, imagination, and sheer luck will be required to move this mountain of indifference, suspicion, even hostility in many cases, in the right direction. It is not the ambition of the architects of *perestroika* to play a solitary role against insurmountable odds, and neither is Gorbachev seeking the role of a Lone Ranger. *Glasnost'* is a campaign to gain the support of the intelligentsia and an appeal to the new middle class, the reformers' most natural ally and most receptive constituency.

The numerous strata of bureaucrats in the party, state, and economic structures, are *perestroika's* natural enemies. Their parasitic, nonproductive, redundant careers endangered, these instruments of oppression seek as their natural allies the people that they have thus far oppressed. This rather illogical, even bizarre united front ought not to be attributed to the officialdom's ability to manipulate the gullible masses, but rather to the latter's natural, conservative inclinations, and their distrust of unsettling changes.

Reforms initiated and orchestrated from above are bound to become diluted, whether intentionally sabotaged or merely weakened, through the chain of command. This dilution and weakening proceeds on both the vertical and horizontal planes. The civil rights movement in the United States went ahead faster in New York City than in the Mississippi delta. The same applies to the dismantling of apartheid—nowadays nonexistent in Cape Town or Durban but still alive in distant rural Transvaal. To an average citizen in the Soviet orbit, at the mercy of a provincial party despot, the thought of an enlightened distant Secretary General is of little comfort. As a rule, as the distance from the capital increases the responsiveness and adaptability to change decreases. Appropriately, the daring Czechoslovak reforms of 1968 were named after the capital city, it was the Prague Spring and not a spring named after some obscure provincial township. In the same vein, almost two decades thereafter, Marc Chagall's exhibition was hailed in Moscow but not in his native Vitebsk.

Marshall I. Goldman predicts that Gorbachev will not last four years. This view is shared by Peter Reddaway of the Kennan Institute. Others scoff at such doomsday scenarios. Jerry Hough compares Gorbachev's strength to that of Stalin in 1927-28 and considers Gorbachev's phenomenon broader than the man himself, he being the personification of a fundamental generational change. Such a view is seconded by Stephen A. Cohen.[10]

Seen from the East European capitals, Gorbachev's reforms mean destabilizing, politically risky cures—cures that are even more risky for governments with a precarious legitimacy.

The old Stalinist serf-landlord relationship, an example of unimaginative simplicity devoid of regional integrative ambitions, is no longer required. When Stalin died, the Czechoslovak mini-Stalin, Klement Gottwald, followed suit immediately upon returning from the master's funeral. Khrushchev's pledge of polycentrism—of legitimate different roads to socialism—did, however, have its rather narrow limits, as proven by subsequent events. While Tito was absolved from the mortal sin of having deviated from the approved path, the rest of the East European leaders continued to perform their mirror image roles with regard to Soviet matters and values. Accordingly, the changing political fortunes of Nagy and Rakosi reliably reflected the contest between Malenkov and Khrushchev in Moscow.

In January 1968 the utterly faithful Antonin Novotny faced a precipitous fall. Brezhnev, responding to an urgent request to intervene in Czechoslovak matters, arrived in Prague for a prolonged visit. After a few hours stay he departed, startling his host with three very memorable words: "Eto vashe dyelo" (It's your own business).

It was not Moscow's business to bail out losers and inept managers, no matter how loyal. The Russian word *dyelo* soon became the politico-semantic symbol for sovereignty in those self-constrained Czechoslovakian circumstances. *Dyelo* (*delo* in Czech) also means a cannon. During the May 1 parade, enthusiastic students were pulling small papier-mâché artillery pieces in front of Dubcek and company.

Three months later, the Soviets arrived with five thousand big tanks to end the inadmissible interpretation of polycentrism. With *"eto vashe dyelo"* put aside, Brezhnev fairly convincingly documented his doctrine of limited sovereignty.

Svec asserts that "Moscow has never been good in appreciating who is who."[11] This view is seconded by Rudolf Tokes: "USSR has had a singularly poor track record in picking the winning ponies in various leadership races."[12]

The record confirms Moscow's flexibility in overlooking past blemishes of individuals who showed promise of further political utility. Such an imprimatur was extended to former political felons and long-term inmates Kadar and Husak, as it was *pro tempore* to the nationalist proletarian deviationist Gomulka, and subsequently to the nationalist aristocrat Jaruzelski (son of a minor nobleman deported to the USSR– the father died in Siberian exile, the son joined the Soviet-led Polish troops).

Khrushchev unmasked Stalin and within a year revolutionary upheavals swept the realm. Since Gorbachev's ascent to power in 1985 no such turbulence took place, no East European leader has been toppled, and no regime has changed or even been challenged.

Willingness to follow Gorbachev's modernization program depends on several considerations: confidence in the stability of the respective East European system, the perceived potential to survive should the implemented reform get out of hand, and the opportunity of the office holders to disassociate themselves from the past policies.

With regard to the involvement in and responsibility for the current deficient state of affairs, the East European leaders are at a distinct disadvantage. Unlike the newcomer

Gorbachev (1985), they all predate him, appointees in the Brezhnev or even the preceding era: Zhivkov (1954), Kadar (1956), Ceausescu (1965), Husak (1969), Honecker (1971), Jaruzelski (1981).

All septuagenarians, members of the fading generation—except for Jaruzelski, with whom Gorbachev has apparently established a rather close rapport. In 1986, at the Party Congress in Moscow as well as in Warsaw, Gorbachev strongly endorsed Jaruzelski, thus rendering true international assistance in the elimination of the hardliners Olsowski, Milewski, and Grabski. After Gorbachev's significant address at the 70th anniversary of the October Revolution in November 1987, Jaruzelski was the first non-Soviet leader to address the Kremlin gathering, and the first East European leader to meet the Secretary General in private. Jaruzelski's speech was printed in full, and, *The New York Times* observed, "There was perhaps unintended irony in his characterization of Mr. Gorbachev's blueprint for change as a 'Soviet Springtime'...,"[13] the phrase bound to evoke memories of the Czechoslovak heresy of 1968.

Unlike the rather subdued response in East Germany, the Polish press exulted over the address. This euphoria notwithstanding, the Polish nation seems the only one in Europe to be convinced that their system cannot possibly work no matter how resourceful and imaginative the communist leadership.

General Jaruzelski's policy has remained unchanged since Brezhnev's days: nonconfrontational relations with the Catholic Church, no dialogue with Solidarity, and the attempted revival of the party and the economy.[14] Alternating toughness and accommodation with the opposition, the regime has at times responded in a way thoroughly unacceptable and, indeed, unimaginable in the immediate—the East German and the Czechoslovak—neighborhood: Jaruzelski touching a super-taboo such as the Stalin-Hitler Pact, and condemning Molotov's notorious characterization of the independent Polish state as a "monstrous bastard of the peace of Versailles." Only Katyn has yet to wait. Minister of

Culture Alexander Krawczuk, a classics professor from Jagellonian University, and a nonmember of the Communist Party, ventured an opinion hitherto unheard of from official quarters, namely, that Poland's prolific underground and illegal press was a "good thing."[15]

Yet, the nation at large remains rather unresponsive to this wooing. Participation in a "parallel society" has given the nation a feeling of freedom, unattained in any other part of the socialist orbit.

The response and receptiveness to Gorbachev's program of modernization covers the entire scale, ranging from enthusiastic embrace and warm reception to frosty reaction and hostile rejection.

Next in line to the cooperative Polish Party are the Hungarians, the pioneers of *glasnost'*—like novelties implemented several years ago. Though imitation still remains the most gratifying expression of flattery, the leadership in Budapest has not rushed forward to claim credit for this parentage. Instead, a considerable silence prevails in Hungary. "Kadar reportedly sought to pose as the bloc's elder statesman paternally accepting Gorbachev into the family, but the General Secretary remained aloof," asserts V. V. Kusin.[16]

Georgi A. Arbatov, Director of the Institute for the Study of the USA and Canada, and Gorbachev's public relations man, commented on the Hungarian experience: "Nobody can automatically take a model from another country and implement it."[17]

Whereas in Budapest a picture of Andrei Sakharov appears in newspapers and he is treated as a "positive hero," in Prague he remains a dangerous, treacherous nonperson. It would require Gorbachev to leap forward greatly, well ahead of the Russian political experience and temperament, in order to match Hungary in modernization—visa-free arrangement with Austria, free travel to the West, and open political debates in the media with impunity (e.g., one in which a former cabinet member who allegedly invited the Red Army to intervene, characterized the matter as a colossal error). Imre Pozsgay, former Minister of Culture and a current member of the party's Central Committee, is expressing doubts as to the preservation of the one-party system: "Sooner or later the position of the opposition, as such, should also be settled"; furthermore, "The country has no need for underground literature. Let's have it completely publicly printed and distributed according to the norms of the Constitution."[18] Revisionist heresies such as these represent a new version of the notorious "salami tactics," this time chopping off the smelly totalitarian product in pieces of substantial size. The relatively free Hungarians are currently burdened with absolutely the highest per capita foreign debt among the CMEA members. Except for Poland, a country with similar economic troubles, the rest of the socialist community is not prepared to engage in such daring pluralistic flirtations. Instead, a search for modernization of the economy without tinkering with the political structure and processes characterizes the East European climate.

Bulgaria, her international reputation tarnished (the KGB connection with international terrorism and drugs, the drive to eliminate the Turkish ethnic minority), implemented a thorough reorganization of the governmental and economic structure, with ministries merged and leading cadres reshuffled: "We started in 1980 to try to give more power to lower levels. It didn't work. We have to change totally," admitted Ognyan Panov, the director of the Institute of Social Management.[19]

In response to the widening technological gap that separates East from West, and also to the critical prodding on the part of Gorbachev himself, the reforms announced are such that if fully carried out, "this country is likely to emerge as the most thoroughly revamped of the Communist nations."[20] At the July 1987 meeting of the party's Central Committee, the program of self-management throughout the economy was introduced, as were tariff-free zones and vigorous initiatives aimed at Western markets.

Unlike the Bulgarians—"the Prussians of the Balkans" as they are sometimes characterized—the real, genuine Prussians in the GDR ignore similar steps with forceful justification:

their centralized, competently managed economy works. Over the past two decades, East Germany's economic performance has outstripped that of the Soviet Union and the rest of Eastern Europe. "We can say with complete justification that we have built a society that can stand any comparison,"[22] boasts the successful nonreformer Erich Honecker.

Disciplined, efficient, without Hungary's debt-ridden market economy, without Czechoslovakia's overall malaise, and without Poland's substantial breakdowns—considerable self-confidence characterizes the GDR's leadership. Indeed, "The tone of this congress (SED, April 1986) is one of incredible arrogance. In Honecker's speech there is a tone of self-satisfaction that approaches eulogy."[23]

Laudatory marks for economic performance provide sufficient justification for the failing effort in other spheres of modernization. No such compensatory consideration applies to the resolutely antireformist Romania, a country with malfunctioning political and economic systems with extreme suppression and the lowest living standard (monthly meat ration one pound). The food lines are getting longer and the officials dismiss this trend with a reference to optimistic statistics of alleged production and consumption. At the same time, no energy is spared on the grandiose project of construction of a vast avenue in the center of Bucharest to mark "the Ceausescu Epoch, the Age of Gold"—an exceedingly high price to pay for symbols of national independence.

Romania does in fact emulate the traditional Soviet practice of equating the cause of socialism with the interest of its own nation. The Moscow leadership may not like it but it surely understands it (unlike the thoroughly misunderstood intentions of the Prague reformers in 1968).

A scenario of undernourished Romanians, genuinely welcoming Soviet fraternal invaders, once a scenario suitable only for the stage—perhaps written by the great Romanian master of the theater of the absurd, Eugene Ionesco—has increasingly become a matter of realistic plausibility.

Where does Czechoslovakia fit on this scale of responsiveness to Gorbachev's initiatives with *perestroika* and *glasnost*?

A case study on this subject follows:

Next to the 1979 invasion of Afghanistan, the 1968 invasion of Czechoslovakia ranks as the weightiest legacy of the Brezhnev Doctrine. Vassily Aksyonov, the Soviet Union's leading prose writer, now in exile, characterized the reaction to the Soviet invasion in 1968 as one of insult, felt by those circles most closely committed to the current drive of *perestroika*. Aksyonov put it in these words: "They are Dubceks, actually. They are fascinated with the idea of socialism with a human face. The great difference is that now it has sprung up in the center of the Empire."[24]

In Czechoslovakia genuine implementation of Gorbachev's reforms is simply incompatible with the country's current political course, and, more importantly, with the current political leadership.

Unlike Poland, where Jaruzelski has held power for a relatively short time, and unlike Hungary, where Kadar still enjoys a degree of popularity, Husak's team is neither popular nor new and thus in no position to disassociate itself from the past record of governing. Whereas Gorbachev can and does put the blame for the sorry state of "real socialism" on his predecessors, the ruling *nomenklatura* in Czechoslovakia can only blame themselves—"eto nashe dyelo." They were put into office by Brezhnev, whose appointees in the Soviet Union have been swept away by Gorbachev within one year.

The current Soviet media provide the normalizers with a cheerless experience. Various hitherto sacrosanct facets of the system are being touched upon. The party's being mocked for its pretensions of infallibility and collectivization of agriculture is being characterized as a colossal mistake. "If three years ago I had ever said one tenth of what he (Gorbachev) is saying now I would have been hanged by the Central Committee of the CPCS in Prague,"[25] commented the former top apparatchik Svec.

Gorbachev seems to advocate the kind of innovations that in 1968 triggered the invasion and led to the removal of the reformers and their replacement with normalizers who were responsible for the following twenty years of sorry state affairs.

Was Dubcek wrong in substance or merely in timing? How big and reprehensible a sin is being prematurely correct?

The nation at large started to view *glasnost'* and *perestroika* as a vindication of the 1968 Prague reforms. In the opinion of the hardliners like Vasil Bilak, the slogan "Soviet Union Our Model" has allegedly been usurped by the enemies of the regime with the implicit message "With the Soviet Union Against the Communist Party of Czechoslovakia."

The exemplary docility of the normalizers toward all things Soviet has been aptly encapsulated in the dictum: "Czechoslovakia is the most peace-loving country on earth. She does not even interfere into her own affairs." Husak's personal association with Brezhnev used to be stressed with monotonous regularity. Husak never attempted to initiate a tolerant, conciliatory course like that pursued by Kadar in Hungary. Instead, harsh punitive measures became the order of the day. Over half a million, i.e., one third of the total party members, were purged, dismissed, or reassigned to menial labor (such as Professor Bedrich Placak, a member of the International College of Surgeons and the first Czechoslovak to perform open heart surgery: because of his politically immature views he was made a member of a subway construction crew). Some 150,000 went into exile, thousands of scientists were dismissed. "I would not hesitate to fire Albert Einstein!" has become a notorious vow, characteristic of its time, expressed by a cadre chief, prompting the comment that whereas in the Soviet Union sane people are being put in lunatic asylums, in Czechoslovakia lunatics are being put in charge of once sane institutions. Heretics purged and existentially destroyed, dissidents imprisoned, cultural life and scholarship emasculated with Stalinist vigor, total ideological rigidity and eager voluntary vassalage to the USSR were all reintroduced.

Along with the strident condemnation of foes domestic and foreign, real and imagined, one encountered an extravagantly sycophantic adulation of all things Soviet. Thus, *Tvorba*, a cultural weekly, published by the Central Committee of the party, in ascribing to Brezhnev's words "a special hypnotic power" and "an overabundance of logic"—expressed just a touch of amorous infatuation.[26]

The Czechoslovaks were also frequently reminded of the "matchless character of the Soviet people."[27] "We owe everything to the Soviet Union and to the Communist Party. Without them we would have absolutely nothing."[28] It is difficult to imagine the Kremlin demanding tributes of such humiliating servility.

When Brezhnev died, *Rude Pravo*, the main party daily, reported that the sun refused to shine, "covering itself in a mourning shroud of clouds." On Andropov's and Chernenko's demise, the elements once again paid their respect.

Hand in hand with the glorification of all things Soviet came vitriolic, chauvinistic, oddly antiquated attacks on the capitalist, imperialist West, the United States in particular: stories about American soldiers piling up ears cut from the Vietnamese communists;[29] the CIA running the terrorist networks, such as the Red Brigades, in Western Europe;[30] West Germany promoting fascist literature such as *The Guns of August* by Barbara Tuchman;[31] Ronald Reagan the madman who tramples all things democratic and progressive (in the view of Jan Fojtik, secretary of the party's Central Committee),[32] this vulgar and cynical president,[33] a megalomaniac who dreams of world domination,[34] equal to Hitler;[35] the United States violating international rights, expressing contempt for all humanity, engaging in the most vulgar acts of aggression, cynical acts of banditism, "the insane craving of American imperialism to conquer the world."[36]

Recent history is not exempt from this ideological overkill. Accordingly, it was the Soviet Army that defeated the Japanese Empire in World War II, it was South Korea that attacked North Korea, and it is socialist North Korea whose sterling accomplishments both in economic and political advancement earn the respect and admiration of the world.[37]

The advent of Gorbachev's *glasnost'* notwithstanding, the Prague propagandists continued to beat the same drum; the West is charged by the authoritative *Rude Pravo* with engaging in "antihuman propagandistic campaigns" and "ideological diversions" in preparation for direct political and psychological warfare, and with trying to undermine the insufficiently vigilant masses.[38] In an article entitled "Monument of State Terrorism" *(Pomnik statniho terorismu)*[39] President Reagan is unmasked as a de facto murderer of Grenada's Premier Bishop (who had been disposed of by his Marxist-Leninist comrades). In 1987 *Rude Pravo* reported on the colonial status of Puerto Rico, the exploited, suffering masses, their yearning for independence callously denied.[40]

Milan Matous, a principal ideologist and the deputy director of the party's Marxism-Leninism Institute, when asked what he admired in the Soviet program of *perestroika*, replied, "What we appreciate highly is everything in Mr. Gorbachev's views."[41]

Yet, some facets of *perestroika* are less difficult to live with than others. The least difficult ones are the exhortations toward disciplined hard work, honesty, and a drive against corruption that has been waged with no success whatsoever for a generation. Greater use of market mechanism has also met with approval, albeit a grudging and conditional one, whenever the matter of private initiative has been mentioned. In the opinion of Ota Sik, a prominent economist on Dubcek's team and in Swiss exile since 1968, the new (1987) law on state enterprises "does not substantially differ from the reform proposals in 1968."[42]

The confines of *glasnost'* have been delineated: all that strengthens the party and adds safe efficiency is fit to print. "Thus far we have not lived up to the basic principles of socialism.... We have only two choices, either to march to high Leninist norms or to further fall behind," is the party line.[43] "Criticism is to be aimed publicly, without fear, in no way would such initiative signalize a return to the perilous year 1968."[44]

Why should party meetings proceed to a prearranged calendar with comments from the floor carefully rehearsed? Why are we so timid? The editorial board of *Rude Pravo* turned to the readers for suggestions on how to improve their work. The advice received ranged from demands for promptness and accuracy of reporting to the admonishment, "Write in such a way so that after some time you will not have to feel ashamed!"[45]

Worries were also expressed over the critical reprints from the Soviet press (dangerous to the foundations of socialism): "Until recently all the reporting with regard to the Soviet Union was the so-called positive one, but now, since the 27th Congress and further meetings of the Central Committee we have been reading one negative news after another," protest the members of the local No. 55 party organization in Hradec Kralove.[46]

Prague normalizers, however, resolutely reject the kind of *glasnost'* that would legitimize loosening of censorship and toleration of pluralistic views– a Trojan horse, a dagger stuck in the back of the post-invasion order. Out of step with the experimentation in some of the fraternal countries, Czechoslovakia still relishes the archaic electoral charade, the totalitarian results proudly reported. In the May 1986 general elections a total of 10,884,947—i.e., 99.39 percent of eligible voters—participated; of these 99.94 percent voted for the candidates of the National Front with the result that every single one of the 197,404 candidates was elected—the one citizen who attempted to run as an independent candidate was swiftly arrested and sentenced for subversive provocation. In sum, the election did take place in a "festive, dignified atmosphere, characterized by its profound democratic nature *(demokraticnost)*."[47]

Alain Besancon in his interview with George Urban [48] quotes the late Boris Souvarine with having said that the lie was the very core of the Soviet system, that the whole unreality of Soviet ideology was as if socialism had really happened, and that the rulers have a need to pretend that things exist that do not. The electorate participates in non-elections so that parliamentarians can be non-chosen into a non-parliament. A tyranny of words, an unreal language casting a spell of bewitchment. And suddenly, *glasnost'* is posing a threat to the spell.

Much was expected from Gorbachev's speech inaugurating the celebrations of the 70th anniversary of the Bolshevik Revolution. Gorbachev satisfied neither the reformers, by not going far enough, nor the hardliners, for going much too far. "You cannot be completely frank without undermining the existing system," commented Adam B. Ulam.[49] However, on the trampoline of *glasnost'* a considerable leap forward was executed in the right direction, away from the ever-present, entrenched lie.

- "Many thousands"—hence, not millions—of people suffered because of Stalin, whose crimes were "enormous and unforgivable."

- A kind word was uttered on behalf of Bukharin but not for Trotsky.

- The policy of fighting kulaks was "basically correct" but the entire collectivization program was not.

- The Nazi-Soviet Non-Aggression Pact was "not the best" and the appended secret protocol dividing the spoils of aggression was not mentioned at all.

- The Soviet invasion of Czechoslovakia in August 1968 was not among the subjects mentioned in this significant revisionist speech. This omission offered no great comfort to the normalizers, the beneficiaries of the invasion, in view of the likelihood that the subject will be brought up in the future.

The weekly *Tvorba* devoted three full pages[50] to the cogitation of eleven experts as to the meaning of the terms *perestroika* and *glasnost'*:

Éva Fojtikova of the School of Philosophy, Charles University, opined that "In the USSR this all has its own specific features as it is also quite unique in our country, due inter alia to the lesson we have drawn from our crisis in the late Sixties (for example, by having abolished censorship)."

Evzen Paloncy, director of the publishing house Svoboda: "In translation it (i.e., *glasnost'* and *perestroika*) concerns only the Soviet Union; should it affect also other countries, *prosim*" (*please* in the sense of a reluctant gesture: "All right, let it be so, if you insist").

Ivan Mann, editor-in-chief of Czechoslovakia's state television: "In the Western media the term '*perestroika*' has frequently been used untranslated, in the original. Is it perhaps due to the fact that the bourgeois society, a capitalist socioeconomic formation, is incapable of such restructuring?"

Moderator Josef Vesely: "An interesting view, indeed."

Semantic difficulty is dwarfed by political worries over the destabilizing potential of this vexatious novelty. The nation, however, remains skeptical, thus far translating *glasnost'* as *hlasitost* (i.e., plenty of noise about nothing) and *perestroika* as *prestrojeni* (i.e., the change of one's overcoat).

Milan Syrucek, a hardliner publicist, summarized the matter thus: "The truth is, and no-one is hiding it, that *perestroika* is complex and for numerous comrades a painful process."[51]

Given their different political culture, the Czechoslovak people who embraced with enthusiasm the liberalization program in 1968 (a generation ago) are more likely to welcome *perestroika* than are their Soviet counterparts. It is estimated that not more than 10 percent of the Czechoslovak public, the direct beneficiaries of the post-invasion regime, are in favor of preserving the status quo. Yet, skeptical hesitancy and, indeed, pessimism characterize the mood of the public, disappointed in the past and distrustful of the present opportunities, given the precarious quality of leadership at hand. The very same people are still in charge, those who voted for and against Novotny, for and against Dubcek, and those who condemned Sik's economic reforms in order to endorse them thereafter.

The opportunistic, wait-and-see tactics are based on a firm precedent, established by Husak's foe and predecessor, Novotny, who managed to delay Khrushchev's de-Stalinization course from 1956 to 1963. The impatient Khrushchev stepped on many toes, as Gorbachev has been doing with his challenges to too many ingrained Russian habits. Both innovators, more popular abroad than at home, have incurred resolute opposition on the part of the entrenched bureaucratic interests. Even if not removed from office, Gorbachev's reforms may run out of steam, wither away, one musician after the other leaving the stage as they do in one of Haydn's symphonies, as was the fate of promised innovations in Gomulka's era—such are the consolations of the opponents of *perestroika*.

The Polish historian and veteran dissident Leszek Moczulski asserts that Gorbachev wants to eliminate Husak and to liberalize the situation there, that "Czechoslovakia is the first country where it is very likely that the leadership of the Communist Party will be changed."[52]

Evidence in support of such a trend has yet to surface. By June 1987, when the Plenum of the Central Committee of the Soviet Communist Party met, 67 percent of the ministers and 55 percent of the provincial apparatchiks were replaced;[53] only 3 full members of the Politburo predate Gorbachev's rule. In Czechoslovakia, only one individual, the aged Josef Korcak, is known to have resigned.[54] At the 17th Congress of the Czechoslovak Communist Party, held in March 1986, immediately after the 27th Congress of the Soviet Communist Party (the USSR was not represented in Prague by Gorbachev but by Mikhail Solomentsev, an apparatchik of second rank), plenty of lipservice was paid to *perestroika* but no changes were made in the leading cadres to implement it.

Unlike the apprehensive officialdom and the distrustful public, the deposed authors and implementors of the Prague spring view Gorbachev's initiative with a great deal of optimism.[55] For them, the true nature of *perestroika* boils down to a single question: rehabilitation of their own political course, thwarted a generation ago.

Thus far their expectations have not been met: Gorbachev, during his spring 1987 visit to the country, characterized the invasion as a matter of the past, painful but necessary; he did not respond to the reformers' public endorsement of *perestroika* and neither did he call on pensioner Dubcek, as was widely expected.[56]

It seems certain that the entire generation of leaders, whether proponents or opponents of the 1968 reforms, are unacceptable to the nation, on grounds of both their age and political accomplishments. Nor is hope placed in middle-aged cadres, those in their fifties who entered public life after the invasion, largely perceived as beneficiaries of "negative selection."

The party is currently undergoing a fundamental generational change; the majority (52 percent) of members joined the party after 1970—in the period in which one's membership was motivated not by dedication to the "cause" but to one's self-interest. The conflict between the neo-Stalinist "healthy core" and the "revisionists" that characterized the period shortly after the invasion was replaced by the conflict between the nostalgic, conservative old-timers and the new breed of pragmatic opportunists, immune to any ideology. It is the latter who are becoming represented in the party, state, and economic apparatus in increasing numbers.[57]

In the entire Czechoslovak leadership only Prime Minister Lubomir Strougal–a durable pragmatist whose career stretches back to the days of Novotny–has publicly and promptly (in his Kosice speech, April 4, 1985) expressed his support for Gorbachev's reform program.

The opposite end of the political spectrum is represented by the hardliner ideologue Vasil Bilak, by far the most hated person in the country[58] with a penchant for rather flamboyant utterances. In one of his typical hyperbolic invectives he likened the leaders of the United States to criminals of the Hitlerian fascist variety. According to Bilak:

> For the sake of American glory and global domination, the world is to be destroyed and the United States is to become a kind of new Noah's ark in which only the chosen few will have the right to be saved. We know from history that many times an adventurer or madman has had the power to decide the fate of whole nations and continents.[59]

Vice President George Bush has also been a recipient of Bilak's severe verbal lashing:

> ...a sick, mad, ferocious anticommunist. It is undignified and uncultured. Only a person ignorant of the history and culture of the European nations can behave this way. When and

how did Czechoslovakia harm the United States and make Vice President Bush hate us so much? Is it because we have chosen our own and not the American way? We do not blame the American government or its people for not marching on the path of socialism. They have not yet matured enough.... Does Mr. Bush know the meaning of the word civilization?[60] etc., etc., etc.

Bilak, an embarrassing anachronism, hides (not altogether successfully) his distaste for *perestroika*, and most resolutely rejects any commonality between the Prague deviations of 1968 and Moscow reforms of today.[61]

Husak performed his role as a merciless normalizer. Exceptionally ambitious, unscrupulous, and the most experienced among the normalizers, he decided to sit on the fence and watch the race. This procrastination lasted two years. Only then, with Gorbachev still in charge and his reforms still in force, Husak, sensing danger from further delay ("Whoever wanted to restructure himself has already done so and has gotten down to work. And those who have not ... are in actual fact sabotaging *perestroika*," Gorbachev told the June 1987 Plenum[62]) jumped on the bandwagon with youthful vigor. After all, before the Soviet invasion he belonged to the most radical pro-Dubcek reformers. "The enemy propaganda accuses us of being afraid to use the term *reforma*. Why should we be afraid?" declared the born-again reformer Husak in August 1987, though conceding that "the term *reforma* was, in the course of 1968, discredited."[63]

No shiny prospects for democratization were unveiled, however. "As to the leading role of the party there are no, and can be no, doubts about it. Therefore it is necessary to remind us of this leading role in every paragraph,"[64] Husak the modernizer opined.

Yet, on December 17, 1987, less than a week after Husak's return from East Berlin (where he had attended a briefing delivered by Gorbachev en route from Washington to Moscow), he was deposed as the head of the party, and replaced by Milos Jakes, a colorless apparatchik of Czech nationality, a veteran chief of the party Control Commission, some half a million comrades in the early 1970s. His reputed ties to the secret police and his credentials as a die-hard conservative notwithstanding, the elevation of Jakes is likely to be welcome to the nation-at-large as it does represent the first crack in the frozen political realm in almost two decades. Husak, the symbol of hated normalization, was removed in a way less reminiscent of the fall of Khrushchev (an abrupt dismissal, humiliation, and relegation to history's black hole) than of the fall of Husak's countryman and personal foe, Novotny (first the loss of party leadership, and a few months thereafter the loss of the presidency). Whether Husak will be able to keep his ceremonial office as the head of state is yet to be seen.

In Czechoslovakia the artists and the writers in particular have been placed in the roles which in other societies are performed by political elites: this was the case in the revolution of 1848 as well as during the challenge of 1968.

As a result of normalization, their ranks have been substantially depleted. Some were forced into exile or silence, others intimidated into sterile collaboration. And yet, in March 1987 at the Writers' Fourth Congress, presided over by the notorious Stalinist poet Ivan Skala, various refreshing voices were heard, like that of Slovak publicist Lubomir Feldek:

"Soviet literature is being rationed to us much too cautiously."

"If we try to write a political poem we are reconciled in advance to the fact that the result will be an inferior one."[65]

By far the most daring statement was delivered in May 1987 at the Fourth Congress of the Dramatic Artists by Milos Kopecky, a "national artist," whose public reputation was tarnished by his role in a vituperative campaign against the exile community. Kopecky, in his address to the Congress, demolished several taboos and called for the resignation of the entire state and party leadership in these words:

> Your time has run out, leave in time, or otherwise you will have to leave later, with far less dignity, as mere comical figures. ...If the fate of socialism is so dear to your heart, as you are constantly assuring us, you have now got a splendid

opportunity to do something useful for socialism, to render
it a distinct service: to resign.

This sensational challenge, published in a heavily censored
version,[66] was not left unanswered. The hardliner Alois Indra,
in his address to yet another Congress (of the Creative Artists),
resolutely rejected Kopecky's arguments, without, however,
naming the culprit, as "pure-blooded, petty bourgeois
radicalism" that demands heads of merited comrades roll.

As some observers have been pointing out, Gorbachev the
innovator may and indeed does have to lead, but the led masses must not lose sight of their leader. He in turn must watch
his steps and measure his speed while also remaining aware
that excessive caution may dilute the reforms and, with the assistance of many willing saboteurs, drown them in inertia. For
a successful leader skillful timing is of crucial importance. He
must expose society to novelties in an incremental way, to ration them with an increasing amount of spice. A revolutionary,
shocking novum of yesterday may well become a perfectly acceptable norm of today, a foundation on which to build and
augment one's programmatic designs—hence, not an over-
night ambitious cure but a protracted transformation, administered in prudent doses.

In February 1986 a new Program of the Communist Party
of the USSR replaced the blueprint adopted during the
Khrushchev tenure in 1961. The embarrassing boasts were
omitted, the bellicose cliches of the standard dogmatic bent
were kept. In Part I, Section 2, this superpower's permanently
ruling party condemns the non-communist part of the world
for "innumerable crimes that remain forever the most sordid
chapters in the history of imperialism."[67] The general crisis of
capitalism is deepening, its historical doom is increasingly obvious, the forces of imperialism, unwilling to accept the inevitability of their own destruction, pose the main danger to
world peace. No quarter is given to the adversary for whom the
only course of action is total surrender.

Whether a mere tactical public relations adjustment or a
substantive ideological shift, in less than two years after the

adoption of this binding Party Constitution, Gorbachev in his festive November 1987 address neither disavowed nor did he mention the credo of capitalism's inevitable doom. Instead, Gorbachev declared:

> the inevitability of conflict between Communism and capitalism was giving way to a new era of guarded cooperation in an interrelated, interdependent world. ... Since an alliance between a socialist country and capitalist states proved possible in the past, when the threat of fascism arose, does it not suggest a lesson for the present, for today's world which faces the threat of nuclear catastrophe?....[68]

Tactics or strategy? A verbose oratory with a faulty logic, paralleling inanimate permanent nuclear weapons that cannot be disinvented with the impermanency of the Hitlerian foe, or a daring ideological pirouette with fundamental implications? If the foundation stone of implacable hostility, conflict, and predestined victory of the superior social order were removed from the edifice of Marxist-Leninist ideology, and were replaced by a state of normalcy, of live-and-let-live, would the edifice not fall apart along with the ruling party whose legitimacy is based precisely on these militant principles of global class confrontation? What kind of life expectancy could be expected of the Communist Party of Czechoslovakia?

"Our Party does not suspect any leader of wishing to change the view of 1968," asserted Zdenek Horeni, editor of *Rude Pravo*.[69] The normalizers stress the allegedly fundamental difference between the reforms of 1968 and of today: whereas the aim of *perestroika* is the perfection of socialism, the aim of the Prague Spring was the abandonment of socialism and restoration of capitalism.

These severe charges notwithstanding, in a few months' time Moscow altered its assessment of the "painful event." In the spring of 1987 Gorbachev soothed the normalizers and upset the reformers with assurances as to the correctness of the international assistance rendered, yet in the autumn of the same year the principles of the Brezhnev Doctrine appear to be questioned. Georgi L. Smirnov, head of the party's Institute of

Marxism-Leninism, and a former aide to Gorbachev, announced at a news conference the need "to think over the events of 1968, the intervention." This was seconded by Georgi A. Arbatov, also not known for expressing views without approval from the highest places.[70]

The irony of history sneers at the socialist orbit, as it has done several times before. The Soviet Union, after having crushed the reforms in Czechoslovakia, is introducing them on its own turf. The loyalists, ready to fulfill all Soviet wishes, are put in charge of punitive normalization of the wayward country. Their mandate is derived solely from the act of foreign military intervention and the imposed status of limited sovereignty. The moment that the rationale for the invasion is invalidated will be the moment their own rule is invalidated.

However, the cause of their predicament may inadvertently become their rescuer, namely, Gorbachev. He also has reinterpreted the norms of proper behavior and relations within the socialist community from one of unconditional docility ("always and in everything to remain loyal to Marxism-Leninism and proletarian internationalism," i.e., to the interests of the USSR—so decreed in *Pravda*, June 15, 1985) to a looser community of more sovereign components. "Unity does not mean identity and uniformity anymore," "arrogance of omniscience" officially ceased to be an acceptable basis for Moscow's relations with its allies.[71]

Thus a helping hand was extended to the opponents of modernization, individuals with a record of sycophantic admiration and emulation of all things Soviet. Attempting to circumvent Gorbachev's reforms is by no means considered an act of disloyalty to the Soviet Union. The dangerous novelties of the new Secretary General are viewed as essentially anti-Soviet, harmful to the interest of the international socialist movement in general (and in particular to maintain their power).

In the name of *glasnost'* and redefined responsibilities within the socialist community, their invoking national specific conditions sounds hollow, transparent, fraudulent, and even less popular than the nationalistic maneuvering and pretensions of Ceausescu in Romania. Bilak, an ethnic Ruthenian—hence, neither a Czech nor a Slovak—is least suited to masquerade as a paragon of national integrity, sovereignty, or honor.

> Never must we forget the experience we gained in the strug-gle against the enemies of socialism, especially in the late 1960s. There are people among us all too eager to endorse the new policies. We know what they are after. They want to exploit the ongoing changes in the USSR for their own nefarious goals.[72]

This is the message of the hardliners of Bilak's ilk who bristle and consider provocative, even subversive, the slogan "USSR Our Model"—for decades the most durable expres-sion of verbal vassalage.

As the ultimate twist of irony, these unreconstructed Stalinists attempt to justify their hardline course with reference to past errors caused by a too faithful following of the Soviet model. Ergo, in order to avoid repeating the same mistake we shall keep prudent distance between our tested ways of "real socialism" and what Gorbachev is experimenting with in his distant, substantially different realm. Such transparent, self-serving rationalization presented by politicians already so thoroughly discredited found very few converts. "Prostitutes preaching virginity—same thing," remarked the man in the street. Publicist Feldek aptly summed up the national mood at the Writers' Congress in March 1987:

> The Soviet Union our model ... but not in all its aspects. We are proceeding on our own road. Not a bad idea except for the fact that this claim for one's own road is also being ad-vocated by those individuals who until recently had labelled such a road a crime. And that they happen to demand it just now when fifteen million Czechoslovaks see absolutely no reason to search for one's own path.

> What special road is needed by an individual who trusts Gorbachev's principle that more democracy means more socialism?[73]

The changed attitude of the Czechoslovaks public toward the Soviet Union is reminiscent of the image transformation of Kadar, the despised traitor, into a bona fide accepted, even popular leader of punished post-invasion Hungary (no such credit was given and neither was it sought by Husak in his land). In Czechoslovakia the impossible, indeed unimaginable, change of heart has been achieved with regard to Gorbachev; the head of a hated land, considered the cause of the nation's misfortunes, attains genuine popularity among the people who reserve for their own leaders contempt and indifference, at best.

When the Gorbachevian reforms started, the Czechoslovaks whimsically recommended that the Brezhnev Doctrine be applied in reverse and that the tanks of the satellites be dispatched to fraternally flatten the heresies in Moscow.

However, as *glasnost'* and *perestroika* proceeded in a surprisingly pleasant, welcome direction, the jokes about the Brezhnev Doctrine in reverse gave way to a sincere wish for the application of a would-be Gorbachev Doctrine to erase, with military force, the hated policies that the same Soviet military force a generation ago had imposed upon the country to the subsequent damage of both parties. Wounded nationalism of yesterday offers no prospect for betterment and, as far as the hardliners' ostensibly defiant patriotism of the Romanian and even Albanian variety is concerned, its appeal does not reach beyond the circle threatened by the reforms.

That the Soviets are looked upon as the only force to unmake the damage is a somber testament to a country dispirited, lacking self-confidence and willingness to take risks to accomplish goals which in other parts of the socialist community, in Poland in particular, are considered ones own primary responsibility. Frequent references to the Munich legacy and subsequent traumas provide an alibi to withdraw into the cocoon of inaction and self-pity. "If Gorbachev succeeds in the Soviet Union, it's the only hope for us,"[74] a Charter 77 activist said, reflecting the mood of the nation.

Vaclav Havel, the internationally recognized playwright who is banned in his own country, commented that the

Czechoslovak reaction to Gorbachev's visit indicated a nation that will never learn and that is eager to applaud a man whom it expects to be the deliverer of freedom: "They perhaps truly believe that Gorbachev came here to liberate them from Husak."[75]

This nation, with its fingers crossed, is waiting for the advent of a truly welcome fraternal invasion. The first one in 1968 was allegedly triggered by a plea of 40 concerned citizens (whose letter of invitation has yet to be released). The second invitation is likely to be signed by millions of patriots, once again delegating the fate of their country into the hands of powerful outsiders.

It was announced in Moscow that after a pause of almost half a century (since 1941), the All-Union Party Conference will be convened in June 1988—a perfectly timed opportunity to reevaluate the 1968 invasion, to disavow its correctness and blame it on the fallen and, by now, semi-disgraced Brezhnev. (A step less difficult to undertake than the amendment of the Party Program concerning abandoning the doctrine of the inevitability of the destruction of the capitalist foe, a doctrine that cannot be credited to Brezhnev but to Lenin himself—a step his Leninist disciple, Gorbachev, will surely be hesitant to undertake.)

Gorbachev defined the rationale of his program with lucidity. Unless we change radically, the position of world socialism will be in jeopardy.

But how can the Soviet system reform itself into something different without ceasing to be Soviet? In the words of Rudolf Tokes, *"glasnost"* may be used for tactics, may be a bait, may be a 100-flowers scenario, but it cannot remain a built-in permanent part of any so-called reform oriented party strategy because that would be signing its own death warrant."[76]

Two possibilities for further development of the USSR are suggested:

1. The country would change in such a substantial degree that it would become a status quo partner in the international community, free of expansionist designs wrapped in ideological, messianistic pretensions.

2. As it is the nature of an empire to expand or else decline, and since its growth becomes increasingly expensive, the Soviet Union may well be on its way to losing its superpower status and becoming no longer vitally relevant to global developments — a reduction in role experienced by the Ottoman and later by the British Empire.

Regarding the impact of Gorbachev's reforms on Eastern Europe, it should be emphasized that *perestroika* and *glasnost'* are remedies intended primarily, if not exclusively, for the Soviet Union rather than for its extended, peripheral realm.

From Moscow's vantage point "Love for the Soviet Union as a distinguishing characteristic of an honest, genuine Communist" may, even today, still be considered the valid principle that it was at the Prague university examinations on Marxism-Leninism the year Stalin died. This love, however, is to be interpreted in strictly utilitarian and pragmatic terms as a willingness and a capacity to perform the role of a reliable, dependable ally and economic partner who will always look out for the interests of the USSR.

Accordingly, the leaders of the GDR will be permitted to adhere to their unreconstructed ways, as long as they continue to meet the above criteria of desirable partnership. Should the quality of their goods deteriorate to the level of Bulgarian shoddiness, East Berlin will be castigated and urged to reform, just as Sofia had been. If too much *perestroika* and *glasnost'* should lead to destabilization rather than reconstruction, causing any country to become beset by a crisis of Polish proportions, the restoration of the pre-Gorbachevian state of affairs will be demanded by the very same Gorbachev.

The provinces tend to prosper and are given more breathing space whenever the center is preoccupied with vital worries like the issue of succession—a power struggle in a power vacuum—or a crisis over a vital policy course. The provinces may further gain as the various factions in the center begin to lobby for allies in support of their respective causes.

Similar leverage may eventually apply to the East European countries, with their mandate toward socialist polycentrism, if not pluralism, further enhanced by Gorbachev's November

1987 renunciation of the validity of any binding Soviet model.

Yet, despite this pledge of enhanced sovereign rights, the room to maneuver remains fairly limited for at least two fundamental reasons: 1) The fairly anemic legitimacy of the East European regimes in the eyes of their populace; 2) the economic dependency on the Soviet Union—the supplier of raw material and energy, and the market for goods which cannot find customers in the West. Facts of life like these should suffice to dissuade temptations to disloyalty.

As reconstruction has been declared the prime programmatic task of revolutionary proportions, the possibility of eventually reversing to Brezhnevian business-as-usual inertia seems unlikely. Whereas the political survival of Gorbachev and his program remains in doubt, in the absence of any creative, imaginative alternative to *perestroika*, time is on the side of the modernizers and not with the obstructionist bureaucrats. Further duration of the reforms adds to their ultimate durability.

"Are the reforms in the best interests of Western democracies?" is a frequently asked question. "Do you suggest that the West should support Gorbachev by making concessions?" asked the Polish-born publicist Jan Nowak at the symposium on *glasnost'*.

"No. The best policy for the West is doing nothing," responded the Czech-born diplomat Milan Svec.[77]

It is frequently pointed out that history knows not a single case of a successful reform of communism. No ruling class will voluntarily give up its power and privileges, and no other force in a totalitarian state can arise to challenge the powerful monopolists.

This black and white dichotomy fails to distinguish between very substantial shades of gray that may mean the difference between life and death for a great many people: Kadar's Hungary and Pol Pot's Cambodia offer exemplary comparisons. Even disregarding the likelihood of extreme terror, it remains a matter of paramount concern to the people whether they live under benign and intelligent or intolerant and inept despots, whether they are allowed to travel to the West as the Hungarians are or whether they are subjected to Orwellian police supervision (e.g., periodic registration of typewriters, as is the current predicament of the Romanians). Surely a substantial difference in quality of life has been recognized by most of the Chinese who had experienced both Mao's and Deng's rule. If such changes are considered a mere "difference in degree," then so be it: a stone and a nuclear bomb are also weapons that merely differ in degree.

NOTES

1. The Soviet exiled historian Alexander Nekrich noted that one of the writers of that time, Kurochkin, wrote a satire on the subject of *glasnost'*. *Glasnost': How Open?* (New York: Freedom House, 1987), p. 5.
2. Gorbachev is not being compared to Khrushchev by all the analysts. Alain Besancon, in his interview with George Urban (*Encounter*, May and June, 1987), compares Gorbachev to Stalin in the early 1930s: "He is conscious, as Stalin was, that the system needs to undergo radical change if the Soviet Union is not to be fatally handicapped in its bid for world domination." June 1987, p. 20.
3. David K. Shipler, *The New York Times*, November 1, 1987, p. E1.
4. *Glasnost', op. cit.*, p. 78.
5. *Ibid.*, p. 11.
6. *Encounter*, June 1987, p. 21.
7. *Rude Pravo*, December 13, 1986.
8. "Will Gorbachev Reform the Soviet Union?," *Commentary*, September 1986, p. 20.
9. *The New York Times*, November 1, 1987, p. A22.
10. Shipler, *The New York Times, op. cit.*
11. *Glasnost', op. cit.*, p. 71.
12. *Ibid.*, p. 77.
13. *The New York Times*, November 4, 1987, p. A12.
14. Cf. V.V. Kusin, *Problems of Communism*, January-February, 1986.
15. *The New York Times*, February 5, 1987, p. A4.
16. *Problems of Communism, op. cit.*, p. 39.
17. *The Los Angeles Times*, September 27, 1985.
18. Henry Kamm, *The New York Times*, October 25, 1987, p. A11.
19. *Op. cit.*, October 8, 1987, p. A10.
20. *Ibid.*
21. *Eastern Europe Newsletter*, October 28, 1987, p. 7.

22. John M. Starrels, *The New York Times*, September 6, 1987, Sect. 3, p. 3.
23. James M. Markham, *The New York Times*, April 22, 1986.
24. *Glasnost'*, *op. cit.*, p. 2.
25. *Ibid.*, p. 71.
26. Jan Janu in an article entitled "Slovo jako pohlazeni" ("A Word as a Caress"), *Tvorba*, June 7, 1978.
27. Miluse Hajkova, *Tribuna*, November 29, 1976.
28. Karel Mach, *Tribuna*, July 26, 1978.
29. Jiri Bagar, *Tvorba*, December 15, 1984, p. 4.
30. Tomas Rezac, *Tvorba*, February 18, 1982, pp. 6-7.
31. *Halo Sobota*, March 5, 1983, p. 3.
32. *Rude Pravo*, April 21, 1982, p. 3.
33. *Rude Pravo*, editorial, May 19, 1984, p. 1.
34. The distinguished party veteran Vilem Novy, *Praha Moskva* No. 2, 1984.
35. *Rude Pravo*, May 19, 1984, p. 6
36. *Rude Pravo*, editorial, April 16, 1986, p. 1.
37. *Tvorba*, June 6, 1984, p. 1.
38. *Rude Pravo*, June 6, 1986, p. 4.
39. *Rude Pravo*, February 22, 1986, p. 7.
40. *Rude Pravo*, April 1, 1987, p. 7.
41. Interview with Henry Kamm, *The New York Times*, November 17, 1984, p. A14.
42. BBC interview quoted by *Panorama* (Melbourne, Australia), November 1987, p. 7. Cf. detailed account in *Listy*, October 1987.
43. *Rude Pravo*, April 25, 1987, p. 5.
44. *Rude Pravo*, February 7, 1987, p. 1.
45. *Rude Pravo*, June 27, 1987, p. 3.
46. *Rude Pravo*, May 16, 1987, p. 3. (Thanks to the liberating rays of *glasnost'*, some taboos were broken with frankness exceeding the permissible standards of 1968. For example, the weekly *Tvorba*, October 7, 1987, p. 10, printed a devastating review of several Soviet movies as asinine, ideologically counterproductive, with laughable, puerile plots in which a handful of pathologically heroic comrades are knocking out hordes of American aggressors. Yet, the

reviewer, not to risk much of his own heroism, did shield himself with an equally critical quote from a Soviet source, pointing out that movies just as stupid with roles reversed are produced in the United States. "Yet there is none who could prohibit it–unlike in our case."

47. *Rude Pravo*, May 26, 1986, p. 1.
48. *Encounter*, May 1987, p. 3.
49. *The New York Times*, November 4, 1987, p. A12.
50. *Tvorba*, February 25, 1987.
51. *Tvorba*, April 2, 1987, p. 5.
52. *Glasnost'*, *op. cit.*, p. 77.
53. Thane Gustafson and Dawn Mann, "Gorbachev's Next Gamble," *Problems of Communism*, July-August 1987, p. 5.
54. Korcak's resignation "for reasons of health" was front page news. Dalibor Hanes, a speaker of the Parliament, resigned quietly. This political dinosaur did, for example, claim—in Bratislava's *Pravda*, January 7, 1986, p. 4—that not a single prisoner existed in Czechoslovakia, in contrast to the plight of the multitude of political prisoners in Western democracies.
55. E.g., Cestmir Cisar, Dubcek's Minister of Education, *Listy* (Rome), August 1987, pp.16-21.
56. Nor is it known whether Gorbachev contacted in nearby Vienna his old friend and classmate from Bratislava, the exile Zdenek Mlynar, former Secretary of the Central Committee in the days of socialism with a human face. It is certain, however, that Jiri Hajek, Dubcek's foreign minister and thereafter an active dissident, was allowed to travel to Vienna to establish contacts with his banned comrades.
57. *Listy*, October 1986, p. 1 ff.
58. In 1984-1985 I conducted a survey among recent refugees as a part of a major project delving into matters of dissent and non-dissent in Eastern Europe. Question #65:"The most hated person(s) in your circles in Czechoslovakia." Bilak was a clear winner.
59. *Rude Pravo*, June 18, 1984, p. 2.

60. *Rude Pravo*, October 8, 1983, p. 7.
61. *Rude Pravo*, February 1987, p. 1.
62. *Pravda*, June 26, 1987, cited by Gustafson and Mann, *op. cit.*, p. 6.
63. *Rude Pravo*, August 29, 1987, p. 1.
64. *Rude Pravo*, October 17, 1987, p. 1.
65. *Tvorba Kmen*, June 3, 1987, p. 3.
66. *Rude Pravo*, May 7, 1987. Full text in *Listy*, August 1987, pp. 5-8.
67. Full text in *Rude Pravo*, March 8, 1986.
68. *New York Times*, November 3, 1987 pp. 1, 10. Alexander N. Yakovlev, a member of the Politburo and one of Gorbachev's closest advisers, confided: "The forecasts of the capitalist system, of the boundaries of its viability and the reserves of its survival were found to be largely oversimplified. It all has to be abandoned, which is not at all easy." (*The New York Times*, November 1, 1987, p. A22)
69. *The New York Times*, November 10, 1987, p. A7.
70. *The New York Times*, November 5, 1987, pp. 1, 7, and November 10, 1987.
71. *The New York Times*, November 5, 1987, p. A 1.
72. *Glasnost'*, *op. cit.*, p. 89.
73. *Tvorba*, June 3, 1987, p. 3.
74. *The New York Times*, November 23, 1987, p. A23.
75. *Listy*, October 1987, pp. 47-48.
76. *Glasnost'*, *op. cit.*, p. 92.
77. *Glasnost'*, *op. cit.*, p. 75.

SIX

EASTERN EUROPE, THE WARSAW PACT AND NATO

THE IMPACT OF CHANGES ON THE MILITARY BALANCE

Aurel Braun

T here is a sense of movement in Eastern Europe as Gorbachev seeks to put his ideas into practice and yet there is also apprehension that form may well differ from substance. The Soviet leader's approach is a broad one covering the realms of politics, ideology, economics, and the military. The Warsaw Pact represents only part of the picture and it cannot be equated with the whole although this military/political organization is, to an extent, symptomatic of the state of the Soviet/East European relationship as the latter itself operates within the international system. There is, therefore, at least the potential for dramatic change in Eastern Europe, in the Warsaw Pact and, consequently, in the military balance between East and West itself.

It is not inconceivable that political and military developments in the bloc may be at variance. Soviet, political, ideological, and economic concerns in Eastern Europe need to be balanced with their interest in the correlation of forces between East and West within which the strategic security factor plays a seminal role. Though ultimately military developments and relationships need to mesh with the others, it may be possible that movement takes place at a different pace. Indeed, the Soviet Union may find certain advantages in employing a variable rate of change in its relations with Eastern Europe where political flexibility may not be matched by a diminution of military dominance. Unfortunately, though, it is not inconceivable that rigidity in the latter may slow or ultimately even stifle progress in the former. The Soviet Union pays keen attention to the East-West military balance in shaping the military relationship with the bloc which, in turn, determines the evolution of the Warsaw Pact itself. Changes in East-West military relations including arms control and reduction agreements, therefore, have a profound effect on the development of the Warsaw Pact even though they may play a secondary role to intra-socialist, political, and perhaps even economic relations.

Thus the December 1987 Washington summit between Soviet and American leaders where they initialed an agreement on the elimination of intermediate-range nuclear (INF) missiles in Europe, has produced openings that could ultimately lead to significant change. There have also been a variety of claims and hints from the Soviet Union regarding changes in doctrine, force postures, and reductions of forces and military assets. Among the more intriguing ones, for example, both in terms of Soviet policies and motives and of West German domestic politics is a purported Soviet offer of tank reductions. According to a December 1987 statement by West Germany's Foreign Minister, Hans-Dietrich Genscher, the Soviet arms negotiator, Viktor Karpov, told him that the Warsaw Pact was ready to bargain away its two-to-one advantage in tanks. It may be particularly intriguing that Genscher then publicly declared that he found this "very interesting."[1] This illustrates, in some measure at least, how the Gorbachev regime is attempting to fit its military policy and that of the Warsaw Pact within the context of East-West relations and the type of Western reactions which, in turn, may affect future socialist/military policies.

Despite these elements the political factors are still prime in relations among the socialist states and in military developments. The latter then operate within the larger political context. And as such, the Warsaw Pact needs to be understood within the totality of that context even though we may focus on specific military developments. For, if not exclusively, then at least in large measure the Warsaw Pact remains an instrument of Soviet foreign policy. The attitudes of the Gorbachev regime toward the region as well as specific policies are bound to have a major impact on the Warsaw Pact.

What then is Gorbachev's vision as far as relations with Eastern Europe are concerned? First, he sees Eastern Europe and the Warsaw Pact through a domestic prism. There he has emphasized *glasnost'* (giving voice or openness or making things public), *perestroika* (restructuring or even reconstruction), *uskornie* (acceleration), and democratization which (unlike the last two terms which apply to political and social development) should be seen mainly as a means to better economic performance. These are not only the pillars for his policies but also the yardsticks by which Gorbachev measures domestic change. And it is this yardstick that he brings to the Warsaw Pact.

Secondly, from the beginning of his tenure, Gorbachev has presented himself not only as the leader of the Soviet Union but also of Eastern Europe. Thus, he has continued the tradition established by his predecessors of what Hélène Carrere d'Encausse aptly called the "big brother and little brothers relationship."[2] Shortly after he came to power Gorbachev declared that close ties with Eastern Europe would be his first commandment. For such a supremely confident leader heading the socialist superpower, close ties would allow ideas to circulate better from the Soviet Union to Eastern Europe. Though Gorbachev may on occasion praise development in Eastern Europe, he is unlikely to emulate East European models of reform, ideals in politics and, least of all, seek input in military affairs. If Gorbachev feels admiration towards any East European state, it would appear to be the German Democratic Republic (GDR), not for its reforms but for its Teutonic efficiency. To an extent he views Eastern Europe as part of the domestic system and the flow of power would still emanate from Moscow. Thus, despite proposals for change, there is important continuity in Soviet East European relations. Such continuity, or even rigidity, may be especially important in the future if it turns out, for instance, that *glasnost'* is no more than a control mechanism designed to enable the Soviet state to identify problems.

Still, Gorbachev's attitude towards Eastern Europe is not entirely clear not only because we in the West have received vague and at times contradictory signals, but also perhaps because Gorbachev has yet to define firmly, in his own mind, goals and precise processes in domestic and foreign affairs. He is pushing, though, for change in the status quo and he has continually stressed that further changes will occur. What has emerged, in terms of relevance to Eastern Europe and to the Warsaw Pact, is a pattern or at least a tendency in his policies. He has been firm on key principles but has been, or at least has conveyed the impression that he is, flexible on certain applications of policy. It should not be surprising, therefore, that we see Gorbachev trying to balance continuity and change. As far as the Soviet bloc is concerned, though, it is worth reiterating that Gorbachev, within this context, desires to improve the management of the Soviet bloc and not preside over its dissolution.

Ultimately, though, what is important in the nature of the changes taking place and their impact on the Warsaw Pact and the military balance? Especially in the case of the Warsaw Pact, how does one test the validity or the magnitude of changes? From a conceptual perspective, therefore, it may be useful to approach developments in the Warsaw Pact in subareas. The four most relevant are decision-making, military doctrine, arms control, and modernization. To an extent, all four are interrelated but their separation for analytic purposes may be useful.

SOVIET CIVIL-MILITARY RELATIONS AND DECISION-MAKING

When he came to power in 1985, Gorbachev stressed the urgency of implementing social and economic reforms. He also sent signals to the military that there would be a greater need for efficiency both in restraining spending and in improving military preparedness. The military thus was being asked to do more with fewer resources.[3] Its initially low-key and slow moving response displeased Gorbachev and, within a few months, the General-Secretary began to take a very tough line.[4] And it appears that Gorbachev has continued to press home the need to economize. In contrast to Brezhnev, who in 1982 promised the military everything that they needed,[5] the party at the 27th CPSU Conference, led by the new General-Secretary, was willing to promise no more than that it "will make every effort to ensure that the USSR armed forces are at a level that excludes strategic superiority on the part of imperialism forces...."[6]

Gorbachev, then, has been consistent to the extent that in his application of *perestroika* all elements of society are affected, including the military. Moreover, he has maintained continuity in Soviet civil-military relations in that he has emphasized the primacy of politics and of the party as had every other General-Secretary. He has exercised the party's control over military appointments to promote those who support *perestroika* and to remove those who have not shared his vision or who have not lived up to his standards of efficiency. In his first two and a half years in power he made ten changes at the level of deputy and first-deputy minister of defense[7] as well as dismissing or rotating lower-ranking military officials.[8]

On May 28, 1987 a West German youth, Mathias Rust, flew a Cessna 172 through Soviet air defenses and managed to land unhindered in the center of Moscow. This instance of gross negligence on the part of the Soviet military gave

Gorbachev an added opportunity to bring major changes, including the retirement of the minister of defense.[9] But the outcome of this event bears careful analysis because it reflects Gorbachev's views on civil-military relations in the Soviet Union and ultimately on policy towards the Warsaw Pact. The Soviet leader disciplined the military but he did not choose to humiliate it. He promoted a general, Dmitri Yazov, to the post of defense minister when he could have appointed a civilian. In a sense, therefore, it was a proportional response to military inefficiency whereby Gorbachev tried to maintain a fine balance between continuity and change. He was going to push the military along the road of *perestroika* but he was not going to bludgeon it.

Gorbachev's approach, at least so far, is to employ a division of labor while maintaining political and party primacy. In this respect it is a policy favoring continuity. He appears to be satisfied, at least for the time being, that under the present system party authority can be maintained and military efficiency enhanced. Consequently, he has not yet chosen to restructure a mode of decision-making that organization theorists such as W. Richard Scott call a "loosely coupled" system.[10] In this type of system there is a division of labor with the leadership concentrating on defining broad policy outlines whereas the professional core is involved in option formation and implementation.[11] The Soviet Union does not have a parallel civilian/political apparatus for analysis and option formation. The Soviet military makes the crucial decisions in the purely military areas of strategy, on force posture, and in matters of organization.[12]

Even though this appears to be an extensive, and clearly important, area of responsibility for the military, with its monopoly on expertise, information, and the generation of options, it plays a very much subordinate role in terms of domestic and foreign policy formulation. For what Gorbachev has inherited and is continuing with is a system where the Politburo and the Defense Council provide guidance in formulating defense policy and render major defense decisions.[13] This model in turn acts as a filter for the

Soviet Union's and Gorbachev's vision of the role of the East European forces in the Warsaw Pact. Given the political relationship with Eastern Europe it would then be logical that Gorbachev should assume that the same Soviet bodies should exert power, on Warsaw Pact defense policy and major defense decisions.

An extensive network of political officers in the Soviet (and East European) forces helps ensure control but this is different from the creation of a civilian management network that parallels the General Staff. In many ways it is a more streamlined approach but it still does not fully explain the effectiveness of civilian control. Perhaps the most important element in civilian control is that through a variety of means, including *nomenklatura* (the Communist Party approves the list of candidates), they hold the military responsible and accountable for the execution of their duties rather than delegating authority.[14] Thus far Gorbachev has reinforced this approach instead of substantively altering it.

In its application towards Eastern Europe through the framework of the Warsaw Pact, there is one other crucial factor at work. For several decades the Soviet leadership, at both the political and military level, have recognized the need for a combined-arms control, and this has led to the pursuit of a single strategic view. That, in turn, both assumes and necessitates coordination and, ultimately, centralization of a variety of functions and encourages efforts to integrate. In extending the precepts of civil-military relations from the Soviet Union to Eastern Europe, Moscow consequently tends to follow a pattern where the Soviet military is held responsible and accountable for strategy covering the entire Warsaw Pact and for the execution of military policy within the entire region. As such it is only to be expected that the Soviet military would insist on control over military policy in its application in Eastern Europe (with the exception of Romania, which is a special case).[15] And, in such circumstances, the Soviet Union has tried to ensure that it alone conducts operational planning in the Warsaw Pact.[16] Nor would such an approach be affected by Soviet concerns or reappraisals of the doctrine of coalition warfare which envisions the East European states' armed forces operating together with those of the Warsaw Pact.[17] If anything, it may reinforce Moscow's assumption that the leading role in all joint military operations would be played by Soviet forces in the event of East European unreliability.[18] This would not, however, exclude the Soviet Union from employing East European military assets within the Warsaw Pact in other productive but less risky ways. As noted, then, the Soviet approach to civil-military relations and strategy is transferred to the Warsaw Pact and in turn affects the decision-making process itself within the organization.

DECISION-MAKING IN THE WARSAW PACT

In cases of crisis in Eastern Europe the Soviet Union has been able to resolve military problems within the Warsaw Pact with relative ease. In 1968 the official Warsaw Pact operation in Czechoslovakia was really a Soviet one since the "allied socialist" troops were commanded by the commander of the Soviet Ground Forces.[19] The invasion was a substantive action. The Warsaw Pact commander was merely involved in maneuvers in and around Czechoslovakia during the crisis which preceded the invasion. There were difficulties within the Warsaw Pact to the extent that some Soviet officers such as the Chief of Staff, M.I. Kazakov (who was replaced on August 5, 1968), were less enthusiastic than others[20] but ultimately the military leadership of the Pact (with the exception of Romania), which is totally dominated by Soviet officers, came down firmly on the interventionist side.[21] At the very least, therefore, one may conclude that while the invasion of Czechoslovakia was Warsaw Pact in form, it was clearly Soviet in content.

It is true that in 1969 there was a structural reorganization of the Warsaw Pact. But the creation of such units as the Council of Defense Ministers did not alter the decision-making process. Further, rumored changes in 1979, which provided for greater integration of the best-trained and equipped East European forces (the Category 1 troops) directly into Soviet formations, if anything, reinforced Soviet control. As Ross Johnson and his co-authors have suggested, then, the 1969 changes have been cosmetic and the Pact's "multilateral military institutions have failed to grant the East European military establishments a meaningful role as junior partners. Moreover, the Pact institutions evidently still lack wartime functions."[22] The Warsaw Pact, therefore, has continued as an instrument of Soviet hegemony and in its implicit intra-bloc mission to ensure the survival of socialism in the Soviet bloc states. This, in turn, brings us full circle to Soviet civil-military relations in the Gorbachev period because Soviet military decision-making needs to change before there can be significant changes in the decision-making process within the Pact.

RELIABILITY

In maintaining the pattern of civil-military relations and preserving a single strategic view that is determined by Moscow, together with a method of holding the military responsible and accountable for the execution of their duties, Gorbachev has not altered the parameters within which the question of reliability of the East European military forces operates. There is a considerable body of Western scholarly literature on this question of reliability and there is a consensus among Western observers that the Soviet Union cannot think of the East European forces in the same fashion as their own. There have been particular problems with Hungarian forces since 1956, Czechoslovakian ones in 1968, and Polish ones since 1980.[23] And Romania's development of a doctrine of "peoples' war" and its refusal to allow Warsaw Pact maneuvers on its territory have created doubts about the participation of that country in Warsaw Pact military actions. There have been attempts to deal with the conceptual problems of reliability. Ivan Volgyes has provided a valuable framework for analysis in terms of behavioral expectations and values.[24] Others have assessed the mobilization potential of the East European forces[25] or approached the issue of reliability in terms of Soviet perceptions about the military utility of their East European allies.[26]

As important as the reliability of these military forces may be, it is possible however that Western analysts have overemphasized its centrality. As Malcolm Mackintosh has suggested, in Eastern Europe and in the Warsaw Pact nothing succeeds like success.[27] Furthermore, it may be entirely possible that given the decision-making structure in the Warsaw Pact and Soviet civil-military relations, we may be looking in the wrong places to ascertain the significance of reliability. We should keep reminding ourselves, as John Erickson suggests, that operational planning is an exclusively Soviet matter.[28] The Soviet goal has been to try to ensure that the East European states and their military forces are not given an opportunity to become disloyal. In the first place this involves stressing the inevitability of Soviet success in a military operation and, given the pattern of civil-military relations in the Soviet Union, this will mean that the East European military specifically will be held responsible for any acts of disloyalty. Secondly, for some time now, the Soviet Union has instituted a system whereby East European forces are "corsetted" by Soviet ones and therefore they do not have the ability to act independently in operational units of any significant size. Thirdly, and this ties in with the previous point, the Soviet Union has made certain that they control logistics in terms of the most crucial supplies and especially that they retain control over communications. Fourthly, we have seen a compartmentalization of the Warsaw Pact with a far greater emphasis on the utility of the northern tier forces, which comprise those of the GDR, Poland, and Czechoslovakia, rather than those of the southern tier. And lastly, the latter ties in with an additional element, a newer Soviet approach which places greater emphasis on the integration of Category I East European divisions with Soviet forces.

It has been suggested that the Soviet Union will have to expect less of the East European forces in the 1980s and beyond[29] partly because of the question of reliability. Unfortunately, such a conclusion may be missing the point that even in the 1960s and the 1970s the Soviet Union envisioned a role for the East European forces that was very limited in significant respects. It is unlikely that the Soviet Union has ever held great illusions about the reliability of the East European forces and therefore the role that it assigned to them would have taken this into account. That is, the Soviet Union could and can work *around* the problem of reliability by placing most of the East European forces in roles where they can make significant contributions without endangering the military operations of what has been called "coalition warfare."[30] The assumption that in offensive operations, for example, East European forces would fight shoulder-to-shoulder in a massive, rapid operation that quickly moves onto enemy territory may well have come from a misunderstanding in the West. Whereas this scenario may apply to a few select East European units, the basic role of the East European forces might well be played in the areas of logistics, including the securing and defense of airports, behind the front lines, and of safeguarding depots and lines of communication essential for the rapid movement of the well-equipped and highly motivated Soviet forces.

This may be viewed as a relegation of the East European forces to the rather unflattering function of "hewers of wood" and "drawers of water." For this reason it is conceivable that the Soviet Union, in order to help East European morale, would have stressed full East European participation in "coalition warfare," but in actual terms these forces are far more important in creating and maintaining the infrastructure which allows Soviet forces to fully exercise their tremendous mobility and fire power. It is not entirely surprising, therefore, that the less "glamorous" role of the East European forces has been apparent to elements of the East European military. Though a Hungarian publication deplored this "secondary" mentality within the Hungarian army, the latter view may be far more in line with actual Soviet intentions in terms of the role of the East European military forces. The publication derided the view that "the Soviet army should fight the battle instead of us..., that we cannot be engaged in the main front-line operations, but will only secure the communications and base areas of the Soviet army, or that the Soviets will in any case deal with problems...."[31]

There is one other important implication of the "secondary role" of the East European military forces. If the East Europeans are to concentrate on infrastructure, then military expenditures in general, and not just those on the armed forces themselves, become particularly important. That is, the Soviet Union would wish to make sure that the East Europeans carry a commensurate portion of the total defense burden of the socialist commonwealth.

BURDEN SHARING

Warsaw Pact defense expenditures affect not only Soviet and East European economic concerns but may also have a significant impact on decision-making itself within the organization. Gorbachev has made it very clear since he came to power that he wants the East European states to increase their contribution to the socialist commonwealth in all areas. This includes not only better economic performance and contribution to economic integration but also shouldering more of the military burden. In this Gorbachev does not differ from his predecessors who had also applied pressure to the East European governments to increase military spending.[32] Romania's Nicolae Ceausescu, for instance, complained openly of Soviet pressure after the November 1978 meeting of the Warsaw Pact Political Consultative Committee at which the Soviet Union pushed the other members to increase expenditures.[33]

But now there is even greater need than in the past for the East European states to assume a greater portion of the military burden. The Soviet economy is performing especially poorly and there has been increasing frustration, at least in Soviet eyes, that the East Europeans have not been pulling their own weight. Consequently, Moscow cannot afford to, and will not likely, be "as generous" as it has been in the past. This is already reflected across a whole range of economic relations with Eastern Europe.

Since Gorbachev came to power, there have been increases in military spending among the Soviet bloc states (with the exception of Romania),[34] however reluctant they may have been to assign additional funds to the military. The East European states, themselves, have encountered economic difficulties and military expenditures appear to be closely tied to increases in utilized national incomes.[35] Consequently, poor economic prospects in several of the East European states will limit increases in expenditures, but so far this does not appear to have diminished Soviet pressures.

There is something puzzling, though, about Soviet pressures on Eastern Europe to increase military expenditures. First, increases in spending have not brought East European forces up to the standards of the Soviet ones. Moscow has not yet entrusted the East European states with such advanced weapons as T-80 tanks or MiG-29 or MiG-31 aircraft.[36] Third World allies of the Soviet Union, such as Syria or India, have been able to purchase more advanced Soviet equipment than the East Europeans in the past.[37] There is no indication that Gorbachev intends to alter this purchasing pattern. Secondly, there is the assumption of linkage between input in decision making and burden-sharing in an alliance. It has been assumed at times that the relatively low defense spending by the East European states correlates with a lack of input in Warsaw Pact decision-making.

Defense budgetary allocations, in themselves, may not be an adequate indicator of a defense burden share in an alliance even if one has an accurate reading of what is spent on the military forces. As Daniel Nelson has written, there is a difference between the extractive burden and the performance burden (that is when resources are *taken* or when duties are *performed*).[38] Nelson's approach may also be inadequate because analysis in this area should be dynamic and should be related to the role of East European states in Soviet strategy itself. Consequently, there may be considerably more logic to Soviet pressure for increased burden-sharing in Eastern Europe despite the two points above. Increases in East European expenditures do not necessarily need to go to improving the fighting capabilities of their forces but rather they may be directed towards building the infrastructure of the Warsaw Pact. If that is the primary goal of the Soviet Union, then it is quite understandable why it would have been so insistent even though the economic performance of the East European states has been and remains relatively poor.

It is true that the East European states have resisted and if one examines real increases in military expenditures in Eastern Europe, one may conclude, as Keith Crane has, that the Soviet Union does not appear to have been very successful in inducing the East Europeans to spend more on the military.[39] Of course this does not take much of the performance burden into account, but perhaps even more importantly, it fails to appreciate adequately the fact that given the dire economic circumstances of the East European states, Soviet ability to prevent decreases in spending itself is an indication of the effective power that Moscow wields in the Pact. But the Soviet Union has actually (with the exception of Romania) managed to induce the East European states to increase their expenditures at least modestly, if not always in a linear fashion. The GDR, in fact, has substantially increased expenditures.[40] Only Romania has managed to decrease unilaterally military spending. In 1986 it decided to reduce force size and military spending by five percent.[41] But then Bucharest has pursued a different policy from the other East European states for some time now and the Soviet Union has managed successfully to compartmentalize the Romanian challenge.

In the case of the second issue relating to linkage between burden sharing and decision-making input, it is important not to equate correlation and causation. Even if one can establish a correlation, there is no evidence that a causal relationship exists in the Warsaw Pact and one cannot assume that the corollary is correct. There is no indication that an increase in burden-sharing on the part of the East European states would give them a larger voice in the decision-making process, especially in view of the fact that Soviet strategy directs their investments towards infrastructure rather than towards operational planning. East European states, consequently, may have increased expenditures in the past in order to diminish Soviet pressure, knowing full well that the potency of their own military force would not be increased.[42]

This could change if Moscow would revise Soviet and Warsaw Pact doctrine. If it would change military doctrine and strategy and thereby allowed more East European input, quite likely there would be greater willingness on the part of the East Europeans to share the defense burdens. For changes, under Gorbachev, in doctrine, in modernization, and in the areas of arms control could profoundly alter how the Warsaw Pact functions.[43]

DOCTRINE

Though there has been no substantive change in the decision-making process of the Warsaw Pact to date, there is nevertheless a sense of some movement in terms of doctrine, modernization, and arms control. The agreements signed by Ronald Reagan and Mikhail Gorbachev in December 1987 at least present new openings and possible opportunities. There have been strong signals and perhaps even some circumstantial evidence that changes in Soviet Warsaw Pact doctrine may be taking place. This may be no more than public relations, part of the effort to create an impression that new ideas are at work in the Soviet Union under Gorbachev. Nevertheless, it is worth assessing current developments in terms both of separating that which is new from that which is not, and examining those policies or developments which, either by design or as a result of unintended consequences, are likely to bring about significant change.

This is not the first time that the Soviet Union has proposed or attempted to alter its military doctrine. The vigor with which Gorbachev is pursuing, or at least appears to be pushing, reforms in all areas of Soviet domestic and foreign policy, however, creates the impression that something new and profoundly different is taking shape in Soviet Warsaw Pact military doctrine. At the 27th Congress of the CPSU in February-March 1986, Gorbachev emphasized what appears to be changes in the military doctrine.[44] The destructiveness of nuclear weapons, he contended, necessitated the creation of new forms in the relations among states with different social systems. He also spoke about the impossibility of winning a nuclear war. Significantly, he concluded, that there was a need to hold military forces to "a reasonable sufficiency." This seems to have become a guiding principle of Soviet military doctrine under Gorbachev.

Sufficiency also logically implies a defensive approach and this the Soviet Union has continually emphasized. Furthermore, the concept, as expected, has been transferred to the Warsaw Pact itself. At the May 1987 meeting of the Warsaw Pact in East Berlin, the organization issued not only a communique but also a statement, "On the military doctrine of the Warsaw Treaty Member States."[45] The doctrine emphasized the "defensive nature" of the Pact. It stated that the Warsaw Pact would never be the first to use nuclear weapons or begin military action against any state or alliance if it was not subject to an armed attack itself. The document also declared that the doctrine was based on the necessity of maintaining the balance of military power at the lowest possible level and on the expediency of reducing military potential to the level "sufficient to defense and for repelling any possible aggression."[46] Furthermore, the doctrine outlined as one of the fundamental Pact objectives the reduction of the armed forces and conventional armaments to "a level where neither side, maintaining its defense capacity, would have the means to stage a surprise attack against the other side or (engage in) offensive operations in general."[47]

Does this represent a radical departure from past Soviet Warsaw Pact policy? And, even if it is just a modest change, what are the implications? There is one element that has clearly been constant. The nuclear doctrine of the Pact is still Soviet nuclear doctrine. In the 1980s the Soviet Union demonstrated this when it unilaterally decided to deploy additional missiles in Czechoslovakia and the GDR in order to counter the deployment of American intermediate-range missiles in Europe. And, thus the Soviet Union continues to decide the balance between conventional and nuclear forces as part of its own and the Pact's doctrine. For this reason the evolution of Soviet doctrine is important. Gorbachev seems to be emphasizing is the relative decline of the role of nuclear weapons in Soviet strategy.

Especially vigorous efforts were made to change the balance between nuclear and conventional forces under the leadership of Nikita Khrushchev, a Soviet leader who much like Gorbachev sought to introduce major changes in the Soviet system. Khrushchev attempted to modify Soviet doctrine and military organization by stressing the nuclear missile forces beginning in 1960. He sought to de-emphasize the Soviet conventional forces and reduce them in size. In order to change the balance between the nuclear and conventional forces, Khrushchev understood that he had to alter doctrine and the role of the East European armed forces in the Warsaw Pact. Consequently, he emphasized Soviet conventional capacity for surprise, rapid movement, and massive firepower over mobilization capabilities. He also attempted to assign a more substantial role for the East European forces in order to compensate for proposed reductions. In the early 1960s, therefore, under Khrushchev the Soviet military developed a concept closer to *coalition warfare*[48] by assigning a greater role to East European forces.

But it should be instructive in terms of assessing changes under Gorbachev to note that Khrushchev at best was only partially successful. However, this was due not only to internal opposition but also to a variety of international developments. Although the strategic rocket forces were organized in 1960 and great emphasis was placed on building nuclear forces which would at the very least achieve parity with those of the United States, there were only minimal reductions in the level of Soviet ground forces in Eastern Europe.

Furthermore, the concept of coalition warfare was only partially implemented. The Warsaw Pact, in fact, continues to lack an operational command structure. The Soviet Union has employed a selective approach whereby it can incorporate specific Warsaw Pact elements in certain "battle group" configurations and it can involve certain non-Soviet commanders in operational tasks. But this is done on a bilateral rather than on a militarily multilateral basis. Though this facilitates the organization of "battle groups" led by Soviet officers, it precludes the creation of an independent Warsaw Pact doctrine and denies or greatly minimizes the role of any national doctrine (including that of Romania). Thus, in the end, despite Khrushchev's efforts, the balance between conventional and nuclear forces in Soviet doctrine was only partially altered rather than radically changed and Soviet doctrine continued to be superimposed on the Warsaw Pact.

Nevertheless, the evolution of Soviet military doctrine beginning in the 1960s tended toward greater emphasis on the nuclear component. Gorbachev is not the first leader to try to reverse this trend nor is he particularly original in putting forth the notion of sufficiency. One can go back at least to January 1977 when Leonid Brezhnev laid down what became known as the "Tula line" in a speech that he made in the city of that name, south of Moscow.[49] Brezhnev disputed the utility of nuclear superiority and contended that the Soviet Union needed only nuclear forces that were "sufficient" to deter those of the United States. Nuclear forces were, it seemed, to deter other nuclear forces rather than to incorporate the dual function of deterring both conventional and nuclear forces.

This represented a shift in emphasis to conventional weapons which, though perceptible earlier, was now made explicit. Moreover, in the same month Brezhnev appointed as chief of the Soviet general staff Marshal Nikolai Ogarkov, a controversial officer who had wanted to shift spending from nuclear weapons to advanced conventional ones. Furthermore, he had been the top military representative to the Strategic Arms Limitation Talks (SALT) where he saw arms control agreements on nuclear weapons as a means of enhancing Soviet conventional forces. Though Ogarkov lost his job as chief of the general staff in 1984, he retained an influential position as the commander of the group of Soviet Western forces, a position which is so vital in Soviet strategy that the change may indeed have been a lateral move rather than a demotion. But even if he was demoted, this was due more to his reputed arrogance than to a conclusion by top Soviet leadership that he was wrong.

In de-emphasizing nuclear weapons, Moscow also wanted to achieve the denuclearization of the American military presence in Europe. In particular, the Soviet Union wanted to ensure that the United States would not be able to deploy land-based missiles on the periphery of the USSR that could directly threaten Soviet territory. Arms control agreements would need to take this into account. Gorbachev has gone further and has called for massive reductions in strategic elements and, eventually, complete denuclearization of both superpowers.

But how would Gorbachev move Soviet doctrine into what Edward Luttwak has called "the post-nuclear era?"[50] He would need to convince the West that its security was not endangered through the transformation of Soviet doctrine. Western doctrine as enunciated in NATO has as its cornerstone the use of nuclear weapons in order to compensate for a perceived conventional inferiority.

There are debates in the West about to the magnitude of this conventional inferiority and the Soviet Union has argued in various fora that either there is no Soviet conventional superiority or that it is insignificant. Western analysts have devised a variety of analytic tools for comparing Warsaw Pact and NATO conventional forces. These range from counting numbers of men and equipment to enhanced static comparisons which look at firepower capabilities, to dynamic measures which assess concentration of firepower, attrition models, and relative combat potential, among others.[51] Whereas these various assessments lead to significant differences among analysts as to the degree of superiority that Soviet conventional forces and its allies enjoy in Europe, there seems to be a consensus that they are superior to those of the West.

A not insignificant part of this superiority, in Western eyes, derives from the Soviet doctrine which emphasizes the need to carry the fight onto the territory of the enemy through the employment of surprise, mobility, and massive firepower and thereby retain the initiative. Consequently, if the Soviet Union is to succeed in downgrading nuclear weapons (on more than a unilateral basis, which would be dangerous to its own security), it has to reassure the West by changing its military doctrine and by negotiating arms control agreements. In fact, if the intermediate-range nuclear forces agreement that it has reached with the United States in December 1987 is to be followed by other agreements on nuclear weapons, there is a good likelihood that changes in doctrine that relate to conventional weapons will become a *sine qua non* for maintaining the momentum. At the very least, Soviet conventional forces need to appear to be more defensive.

It is, therefore, quite logical that Gorbachev should signal that Soviet doctrine is becoming defensive. It is also in his interest to suggest that this is new. Consequently, the Soviets have proclaimed that they have a new military doctrine and that they are even ready to discuss problems of surprise attack in Europe. As noted, the Warsaw Pact declaration in May 1987 tried to reinforce this. Unfortunately the mere proclamation that a doctrine is defensive does not necessarily make it so. And so far, in operational terms, the Soviet Union and the Warsaw Pact have not done anything that has brought about substantive changes in the actual deployment of conventional forces in the Warsaw Pact. This does not exclude the possibility of future changes and it is not inconceivable that Gorbachev could move the Warsaw Pact towards a more defensive posture.

First, however, there is the conceptual problem of what constitutes a defensive rather than an offensive policy. Not only the Soviet military but, interestingly, also civilian specialists have been writing on the development of a defensive doctrine. L. Semeiko, a prominent researcher at the USSR Academy of Science's Institute of the USA in Canada, has written a series of works on military and political problems. He has devoted particular attention to the concept of "reasonable sufficiency" and the dimensions of a defensive doctrine.[52] He emphasizes the linkages between "reasonable sufficiency" and a defensive doctrine. He notes that the former is among the most important political tenets of the new thinking in the Soviet Union and that it, in turn, relies on the "purely defensive" purpose of the armed forces of the Soviet Union and the Warsaw Pact. He contends that specific levels of military potential must confirm the defensive nature of the military doctrine. He adds that the military power of a state or coalition of states must be such that no grounds arise for other states to fear for their security. There must not be an "unreasonable excess of military potential" and the orientation of a defensive doctrine "must be borne out by the scale and deployment of one's armed forces, their structure and the nature of their weapons, the military operations they carry out and, of course, by constructive actions to lower the level of the military-strategic balance."[53] He points out, as well, that mere declarations about the defensive nature of one's military doctrine do not suffice. There must be, he contends, accuracy in assessing the Soviet Union's capabilities as well as restraint and great responsibility in its decision-making.

In order to further this defensive doctrine of the Soviet Union and the Warsaw Pact, which Semeiko claims is already in use,[54] the armed forces and conventional weapons in Europe should be reduced to a level at which neither side would have the means to launch a surprise attack on the other or to undertake offensive operations in general. He claims that this tenet is truly revolutionary, for it would involve a mutual renunciation by both the Warsaw Pact and NATO of military action considered offensive. Moreover, policies would be implemented which would require mutual withdrawal of the most dangerous offensive weapons from the zone of direct contiguity between the two military alliances and, according to Semeiko, the concentration of armed forces in that zone could be reduced to a minimum agreed-upon level.[55]

As innovative as the measures suggested by Semeiko (and other Soviet officials) may be and as reassuring as the doctrine of "reasonable sufficiency" may seem, there are major problems with this analysis and the implementation of these suggested policies. It is not just a matter of its being perhaps too early to take Soviet proclamations of a new military doctrine at face value. Semeiko's detailed exposition shows that much of the old thinking is still present and his analysis contains too many contradictions in addition to being conceptually muddled. He argues that in order for "reasonable sufficiency" to work, the Soviet Union must be able to deliver "a crushing rebuff to the aggressor."[56] Furthermore, he contends that sufficiency for conventional forces means that they must be able to ensure the *collective* defense of the socialist commonwealth countries. Consequently, there is to be no separation between Soviet and Warsaw Pact doctrine because ultimately Moscow assumes responsibility for the defense of the Soviet bloc.

There are also problems with the terms "reasonable sufficiency," "sufficiency," and "defensive." Semeiko uses "reasonable sufficiency" and "sufficiency" synonymously even though one would think conceptually there would be significant differences. (This is in addition to a linguistic contradiction.) It is one thing to try to define "reasonable" in Soviet terms, it is something else to try to define it in general terms. In law, the "reasonable man" is a mythical creature but the term is nevertheless a vital tool in deciding guilt or liability. Consequently "reasonable sufficiency" should operate at a more abstract level than a particular national perception. Yet it is at that national level that Semeiko and other Soviet analysts operate. He does not hesitate to claim not only that the armed forces of the USSR and the Warsaw Pact are already based on the concept of "reasonable sufficiency" but also that this is in sharp contrast to NATO's military doctrine.[57] Moreover, he stresses that the development of the U.S. armed forces "is presently based not on the concept of reasonable sufficiency but on the concept of military superiority."[58]

Though one may find differing assessments among independent observers of the nuclear dimension of the American doctrine, there is little doubt that NATO doctrine as a whole is defensive if for no other reason than that the Western alliance does not currently have the military resources to pursue an offensive one. It may be, of course, that Semeiko and others feel that NATO- and US-bashing are required in order to establish the credentials that would allow them to put forth new ideas. This then, of course, raises the question whether there is an environment in the Soviet Union where truly new ideas can flourish. On the other hand, these assessments of what is defensive may also indicate that the Soviet purpose is to reassure the West that denuclearization would not lead to an increased Soviet conventional threat. Statements by some Soviet leaders tend to reinforce this impression. The new Soviet defense minister, D.T. Yazov, asserted in June 1987 that the Warsaw Pact doctrine is already defensive.[59] Given that operational planning in the Soviet Union and the Warsaw Pact still stresses the rapid offensive, contentions that a defensive doctrine is already in force should cause considerable skepticism.

Nevertheless, even if one assumes that Soviet analysts such as Semeiko are somewhat premature in their characterization of Soviet Warsaw Pact doctrine, there are further questions. Semeiko, for instance, contends that sufficiency not only does not rule out strategic parity but in fact presupposes it. The terminology, therefore, may have been drawn from Western literature but the concepts have not, or if they have, they have been utterly muddled. Traditionally, in the West, strategic sufficiency has been considered different from parity. Sufficiency could be achieved at a significantly lower level as long as it fulfilled the criteria for effective deterrence. In large part the concept of sufficiency was developed as an alternative parity. At the very least, then, there is a need for Soviet conceptual clarification of the terms "reasonable sufficiency," "sufficiency," and "defensive doctrine."

What is relatively clear, however, is that the Soviet Union does wish to de-emphasize nuclear weapons, that it hopes to eliminate American nuclear weapons in Europe, that it would like to see a de-coupling of the United States from its European allies, and that it would like to reduce its own military spending. If Moscow wishes to achieve a genuine accommodation, then, proclamations of a defensive military doctrine do have utility, but substantive steps must be taken if Western skepticism is to be overcome. The best way it would seem for Moscow both to convey the message and to implement such steps would be to reach mutually beneficial arms control agreements with the Western states.

ARMS CONTROL

Gorbachev has pushed hard for the reduction of nuclear armaments and has hinted that this could be followed by reductions in conventional forces. If the Soviet Union is able to maintain the momentum of arms reduction agreements in the area of nuclear weapons, this would have a profound impact on its conventional doctrine and on its relations with the East European states in the Warsaw Pact. On the other hand, the Soviet Union is faced with a dilemma—unless it first convinces the West that there are genuine changes in its conventional doctrine, it may not be able to sustain the momentum in the reduction of nuclear weapons in Europe. For NATO it has always been important to maintain coupling with the United States and the most important aspect of the military linkage in the alliance has been through the nuclear element. Consequently, NATO has viewed nuclear weapons as the kernel of its deterrence (both as a means of maintaining coupling and of compensating for conventional inferiority).

The West thus has perceived denuclearization as a potentially dangerous development. As Henry Kissinger has warned following the December 1987 Washington summit, NATO "must not in the name of arms control make the world safe for conventional war."[60] Consequently, the Soviet Union has to offer the kind of changes in conventional doctrine and deployment that would be sufficiently reassuring to the West that they would be willing to denuclearize Europe. The Soviet Union may indeed then have to implement a truly defensive doctrine and might be required to withdraw troops from Eastern Europe as NATO forces also withdraw from Central Europe.

Thus, if arms control and reductions were successful in the denuclearization in Europe, the Soviet Union's military relationship with the Warsaw Pact itself could change radically. First of all, in a post-nuclear world or even one where denuclearization is limited to the continent of Europe itself, territory becomes more important. Though the danger of conflict would diminish and a variety of confidence-building measures would undoubtedly be implemented, Eastern Europe would play a more significant role as a territorial buffer zone when the threat was an overwhelmingly or exclusively conventional one. Under no foreseeable circumstances would the Soviet Union wish to allow fighting on its own territory and, consequently, it would need to make certain that Western forces would not be able to to use Eastern Europe as a launching pad for a future conventional war against it.

Now the East European states, devoid of Soviet forces, would have to reassure the Soviet Union that their territory could not be employed for such purposes by the Western states. Entirely new questions of reliability would arise and the Soviet Union would have to devise new means to ensure the loyalty of the East European states. Furthermore, the role of the Warsaw Pact in suppressing revolutions in Eastern Europe would be more difficult since the Soviet Union would need to bring forces from the outside. Therefore it is not inconceivable that conventionalization of the Soviet/Warsaw Pact doctrine may result in increased coercion, directed at the Warsaw Pact states, to ensure their reliability as well as in the imposition of greater defense burdens in order for them to develop (and demonstrate) an ability to counter Western threats.

It may be that at this point, politically, the Soviet Union might find it expedient to be more flexible and accept greater political divergence in Eastern Europe. But ironically it may turn out that greater strategic concerns brought about as the value of territory becomes more important would limit the flexibility of Soviet foreign policy in Eastern Europe. As the Soviet Union would need to move away from the doctrine of rapid offensive, it would likely need to increase its mobilization capabilities in order to ensure its security. In the case of Eastern Europe, even if the Warsaw Pact would be dissolved, bilateral relations in the military realm would need to be maintained. In order to maintain or increase mobilization potential, the Soviet Union would need to pre-position huge quantities of weapons in Eastern Europe and to ensure the safety of its lines of communication along potential axes of offensive and defensive operations. Deprived of the surprise factor which, as John Erickson has written,[61] is a primary element of Soviet military doctrine, in practice, Moscow would need to ensure that it in turn would not have to face surprises. And it would not be just the West that would have to provide this assurance, but Eastern Europe would have to reassure the Soviet Union that it would remain a reliable buffer zone.

If one employed a best-case scenario and the Soviet Union and the Warsaw Pact accordingly transcended to a post-nuclear Europe and implemented defensive doctrines with reduced forces, would they achieve the goals of reduced military spending and thus the transfer of funds to the civilian economy? Reduction of military spending is a key goal of Gorbachev and this is one area where he has the enthusiastic support of the East European leaders and peoples. Smaller armed forces should lead logically to reduced spending on armaments. There is, however, another factor at play: Western nations have learned that in military matters, smaller does not always mean less expensive. High technology is costly. Gorbachev has strenuously pressed for the modernization of the military as part of the general restructuring of Soviet and Socialist society. The potential impact of modernization, therefore, deserves to be dealt with in detail.

MODERNIZATION

Military organizations have an often well-deserved reputation for wasteful spending. Niether featherbedding nor cost overruns are uncommon. Hammers and toilet seats costing several hundred dollars in the military have enjoyed widespread publicity in the West. Waste in the Soviet military and throughout the Warsaw Pact has been of great concern to the political leadership. Gorbachev rightfully believes that things can be done more efficiently. It is not illogical to assume that modernization can increase efficiency and cut costs in certain areas. Furthermore, if accompanied by a reduction in the size of the armed forces, then savings could be substantial. Since nuclear weapons and forces consume but a small fraction of the total budget in the Soviet Union, the bulk of savings would come from economizing on the conventional forces.

Modernization, though, is a complex phenomenon. Linear logic does not always bring about the desired results. The consequences of modernization may differ significantly from what was intended. The impact of modernization can affect not only defense costs but also the nature of civil-military relations in the Soviet Union and ultimately the military decision-making process in the Soviet Union and the Warsaw Pact.

Modernization of the military under Gorbachev involves changes in the management and training of military personnel as well as the introduction of more modern technology. The old methods of military leadership which too often according to Soviet reports, involved a dressing down by superior officers and insults to the dignity of subordinates,[62] was counterproductive according to the new regime. Under Gorbachev there has been widespread condemnation of military bureaucratism and sham efficiency. There have also been complaints that the military spent too much time doing various kinds of housekeeping and construction work rather than combat training.[63]

Since personnel matters in the military (and elsewhere) have been a high priority for Gorbachev, it is not surprising that Dimitri Yazov was chosen to replace Sergei Sokolov as the USSR defense minister on May 30, 1987. Though more junior than some other officers in the Soviet military, Yazov had a distinguished military career, including commander of the Far East Military District. What is particularly important about his career is that he had stressed personnel matters for several years. In 1978, for instance, he argued in an article that the most important characteristics of a commanding officer included initiative, creativity, a spirit of motivation, competence, selflessness, good relations with troops, and a high standard of discipline balanced by a willingness "to assume responsibility for decisions."[64] He advocated innovative approaches to training[65] and adapting military affairs to the rapid scientific technological changes.[66]

The first goal of improved personnel management is to increase the effectiveness of Soviet armed forces. This is a reasonable goal although, as we shall discuss later on, it can create problems. The second goal, of saving on military costs, however, may be even more difficult to attain. In the short run there may be savings as waste is discouraged, and a reduction in the size of the armed forces would, of course, reduce the military bureaucracy. On the other hand, the measures that have been advocated by Yazov and others who support the Gorbachev line are much more likely to increase defense costs. In order to foster initiative and to create confidence, flexibility must be applied to all levels of command, from the smallest military unit up. Living conditions must be improved and material rewards must be shared by all ranks rather than only the privileged elites who are now being condemned for their ostentatious lifestyles. Revised training methods are likely to increase costs sharply. Better pilots and tank crews will need far more extensive training. More flying time, more training with sophisticated equipment, as NATO forces have found out, is extremely costly.

In terms of equipment, modernization creates further problems if Gorbachev wishes to reallocate resources from the military to the civilian sector. Procurement of military equipment for the upgrading of conventional forces has not slowed down in the Soviet Union. The INF agreement has not, and for some time will not, lead to a cut in conventional forces so the momentum of conventional modernization will continue. There have been significant increases in the delivery of the T-80 tanks (which can carry reactive armor), armored personnel carriers, reconnaissance vehicles, TU-26 *Backfire* medium-range bombers, MiG-29 *Fulcrum, Mi-31 Foxhound* A fighters, Su-24 *Fencer*, Su-25 *Frogfoot* ground support aircraft, and Mi-8 *Hip* E combat helicopters.[67] These sophisticated and expensive pieces of equipment cost far more than the weapons that they replace.

In the short run the Soviet Union also suffers from not being able to convert defense production to civilian use. A study by the United States Joint Economic Committee has concluded that "in view of the immense costs for plant and installed equipment in the defense production facilities and the fact that these cannot be readily converted to civilian use, the industrial modernization goals are unlikely to significantly impede the completion of the major strategic weapons that the Soviets have programmed through the 1980s."[68] It is little wonder, therefore, that the military in general has supported modernization for they know that more sophisticated equipment is likely to force a commitment to large-scale funding by the civilian authorities.

Modernization of the Soviet forces poses particular problems for the East European states. There has always been a generation gap between the weapons that the Soviet Union and the East Europeans deploy. In order to prevent this gap from growing wider the East Europeans will have to keep pace with the Soviet modernization program. Although none of the East European states have the MiG-29 and MiG-31 fighters or the T-80 tanks, they have pursued a continuous, if slow, process of modernization.[69] For instance, the Polish army has received a significant number of T-72 tanks, Czechoslovakia has doubled its inventory of Su-25 *Frogfoot* close support aircraft, and Bulgaria has acquired the MiG-25 aircraft for reconnaissance.[70] It is highly unlikely that the Soviet Union would tolerate East European policies (with the exception of Romania) that would allow the "generation gap" in weapons to grow wider. Furthermore, if the Soviet Union truly adopts a more defensive doctrine, new demands on East European territory as a buffer zone may mean additional pressure on the East European states to purchase better weapons and to institute training programs commensurate with the new Soviet doctrine.

Modernization, however, presents an additional danger for the Soviet Union and the Warsaw Pact allies that may not be fully appreciated by the Gorbachev regime. Soviet military interest in the technical sciences and military economics developed strongly in the early 1960s and grew sharply under the influence of new methods of planning, especially those being developed under the American Secretary of Defense, Robert McNamara. In fact, this fascination with the scientific approach produced officers trained in the "scientific" methods of planning and analysis by the late 1960s.[71] In 1977 this trend was further reinforced by the appointment of Nikolai Ogarkov, a "commander engineer," as Chief of the General Staff.

The Soviet armed forces have sought to improve the management of the military-technological side of defense planning. The fact that Ogarkov has retained an influential position in the Soviet military, in charge of the most potent element of the Soviet forces facing the West, indicates that this approach has not been rejected. On the contrary, with Gorbachev's stress on both modernization and the scientific approach, the Soviet "McNamarites" may truly come into their own. However the Soviet Union and the Warsaw Pact may encounter major problems in the future because they may draw the wrong lessons from the McNamara "revolution."

First, in terms of effectiveness and cost, it may be wise for the Soviet Union to view the scientific approach and modernization with skepticism. McNamara and his "whiz kids" helped introduce systems analysis on a wide scale. They employed cost-effectiveness analysis and "prioritized" choices. It undoubtedly produced benefits and it seemed to cut waste. Unfortunately, as Edward Luttwak has persuasively argued, linear logic was applied to strategy, whereas strategy should be looked at in its horizontal dimension and is paradoxical.[72] McNamara and his aides, using this linear logic, identified the optimum anti-aircraft missile and fighter bomber. It seemed an efficient way of doing business in the military, but this created false efficiencies and ultimately tremendous waste. For instance, the F-111 aircraft, that was supposed to serve both the army and the navy, in the end satisfied neither. It resulted in wasteful expenditure of money and demoralization in both services.

Furthermore, the McNamarite approach set the stage for building extravagantly expensive weapons systems where the unit cost became so great that the American armed forces were forced to purchase progressively fewer numbers. Thus, a seemingly sophisticated approach failed to incorporate the true complexity of strategy and ultimately decreased efficiency while greatly increasing costs. This occurred in the United States, a country which has a vastly superior technological base to that of the Soviet Union.

Among the great advantages that the Soviet Union has enjoyed have been its "inefficiency" and lower technological level. Though Soviet weapons have not been as sophisticated as those of the United States, they have been reliable and their relatively lower cost has allowed Moscow to take advantage of the savings produced by long production runs. The simpler weapons produced in large numbers have also greatly facilitated the training of recruits who do not have a strong technological background. Furthermore, the relatively low cost of Soviet weapon systems has allowed the creation of necessary redundancies—a layered approach which has afforded the Soviet Union and its Warsaw Pact allies more military options. But as the influence of the Soviet McNamarites grows rapidly under Gorbachev, the Soviet Union is likely to suffer from problems similar to those of the United States: producing fewer weapons with vast cost overruns. As noted, the training of military personnel will become far more expensive. In a sense the Soviet approach to modernization may mean that it will have to compete with the West on a qualitative/technological basis where most of the advantages lie with the latter. The impact on the East European members of the Warsaw Pact may be delayed but not indefinitely for, as noted, they cannot allow the technological gap with the Soviet Union to widen further.

Perhaps the most significant impact of modernization may occur on the personnel side. Some of the most deleterious effects of the McNamara approach were felt in the area of military leadership. Leadership was replaced by "management" which emphasizes the organizational and political skills of military commanders rather than their ability to lead men. Soviet emphasis on military management under Gorbachev should recognize dangers of moving from one extreme of a brutalized and rigid hierarchical approach to the other extreme of detached bureaucratic-managerial style. As far as the Warsaw Pact states are concerned, they should also be wary of the centralizing tendencies of technological modernization. The centralizing trend in communications, intelligence, and air defense in the Warsaw Pact could be further reinforced with the new approach under Gorbachev.

Another significant aspect of modernization in the Soviet Union is the new role of civilians in at least the analysis area of strategy. There are similarities here to the McNamara approach. It is, of course, important not to over emphasize the similarities between what is happening in the Soviet Union under Gorbachev and what occurred in the United States in the 1960s. The Soviet General Staff is still in charge of formulating military strategy, but greater civilian involvement may set the stage for jurisdictional battles. Though Gorbachev may find natural allies within the Soviet military, such as Marshal Yazov, his approach to modernization necessitates a broader involvement and a greater range of expertise. Civilians are thus likely to play a larger role.

The Soviet leader has signaled to the military, as noted, that they will have to do more with less, but in order to have the economics of restructuring explained to the average serviceman, Gorbachev has had civilian specialists write articles on the subject in the military journals.[73] Even more importantly, many of the articles on the "new" military doctrine, as we have seen, have been written by civilians.[74] It is one thing for Gorbachev to use civilian experts who understand the economics of defense. It is something else entirely for civilian experts to formulate options for Soviet military strategy or for force posture. In allowing or encouraging members of the Academy of Sciences and other institutions (perhaps even the International Department of the Central Committee) to become more active in the study of national security issues, he might be setting the stage for future debates on such issues with the General Staff. This would alter the nature of civil-military relations. The system of loose coupling, of division of labor between the political elite and the military, would be altered. This would cause not only disruptions in the decision-making process in the Soviet Union itself but also within the Warsaw Pact. Greater civilian involvement in the Soviet Union at the level of operational planning could be replicated in Eastern Europe only with grave risks. And yet in the future the Soviet Union may find itself confronting a situation in which security concerns in Eastern Europe become greatly magnified just as its military decision-making process is in turmoil.

THE MILITARY BALANCE

Much of Soviet/Warsaw Pact strategy cannot be adequately understood unless one examines it within the context of NATO policies and military doctrine. Whatever changes Gorbachev makes, he is not likely to acquiesce to a shift in the correlation of forces between East and West and, as noted, the military component plays a vital role. Given the Soviet Union's economic performance and the decline in the attractiveness of its ideology during the past two decades, the military factor has played a growing role in the correlation of forces. It is difficult to gauge the East-West balance of military power in Eastern Europe because the problems of measurement are intrinsic. It is not merely a matter of counting tanks and aircraft, although these provide some useful indications of strength and trends. As noted, the various methods employed, such as enhanced static comparisons or a variety of dynamic measures, have helped though they cannot entirely compensate for data problems and uncertainty.

Nevertheless, there is a consensus that Soviet/Warsaw Pact forces do enjoy superiority over those of NATO in the conventional area though the degree or magnitude of that superiority is subject to debate. It would seem, however, that it is a significant one the Soviet Union has tried hard to preserve. At the same time the Soviet Union has sought to ensure that it achieved or maintained a balance in nuclear forces in Europe that would cast doubt upon the credibility of NATO's "first-use" doctrine of nuclear weapons. Lastly, it has been Moscow's ultimate goal, pursued with various degrees of vigor depending on the available opportunities, to decouple the United States from its Western European allies.

In trying to achieve these goals, the Soviet Union has attempted to exploit inherent weaknesses within NATO. Gorbachev's "charm" offensive in Western Europe shows he is persuing the policies of his predecessors, though with considerably more sophistication. For, despite its remarkable longevity and great successes in maintaining alliance cohesion in the face of divisive issues, NATO is vulnerable.

In certain ways NATO has functioned as an enabling factor for Soviet/Warsaw Pact military doctrine and deployment. Key aspects of Soviet/Warsaw Pact doctrine relating to offensive operations in particular would be illogical and risky were it not for a NATO doctrine that for a variety of reasons, both political and economic, rightly stresses defense. (There have been some changes on the margins such as the possibility of using follow-on force attacks.) NATO's vulnerability stems not merely, and perhaps not even primarily, from the numerical inferiority of its forces. The fact that in the NATO Guidelines area Warsaw Pact ground forces outnumber the NATO ones 995,000 to 796,000[75] should not pose an insurmountable problem for NATO since defense does enjoy certain intrinsic advantages. NATO has suffered from a variety of "self-inflicted wounds" which Gorbachev has exploited and is likely to continue to do.

There are, of course, limits on what NATO can do given the size of its conventional forces and the defense allocations. Standardization of equipment or even greater inter-operability would significantly enhance NATO's military potential. Some progress on inter-operability has been made but standardization of equipment is a planner's pipedream, given political and economic realities within the alliance. There are too many national interests in the alliance that need to be satisfied and, ultimately, perhaps the lack of standardization may be a price worth paying in order to maintain the political cohesion of the alliance. After all, one of the great strengths of NATO is that it is a voluntary association of states where each has a genuine input in policy formulation.

But, as the former Supreme Allied Commander in Europe (SCACUER) General Bernard Rogers has stated, the political decision to mobilize is the key to any successful defense.[76] Though NATO agreed twenty years ago to put its air forces and air defenses on the central front under a native command even in peace time, this has not happened in the case of the ground forces. Progress in this area might be made but democratic nations wish to retain as much control over their military as possible and this limitation on the integration of national forces as well as the method of decision-making is likely to continue for the foreseeable future. There are also problems with burden-sharing in NATO, with the Americans becoming increasingly dissatisfied with the West European defense efforts. Given the economic problems in Europe, however, it is unlikely that political leaders there will decide to increase spending substantially on conventional forces. This has probably entered into Gorbachev's calculations in pushing for the denuclearization of Europe. However there have been modest improvements in the West European conventional forces. West Germany, for instance, has increased its inventory of the excellent Leopard 2 tanks to 1800, and Britain has been progressively introducing the new MCV-80 *Warrior* MICV.[77]

Perhaps the biggest problem for NATO in organizing an effective defense against the Warsaw Pact is the alliance's official policy of "forward defense." This is not only an issue of military doctrine; it reflects one of the greatest dilemmas in the alliance: the role of West Germany which has the most powerful conventional forces in Western Europe. "Forward defense" makes little, if any, military sense and is, possibly, the greatest "enabling" factor for the Warsaw Pact's offensive doctrine. It is an alliance concession to West Germany, its political logic being that decisive battles should be fought on the borders with the East rather than deep within the country itself. It is an understandable desire in a country that suffered great losses in World War II. Unfortunately, "forward defense" both deprives the allied forces of maneuvering room and provides an incentive for the Warsaw Pact forces to search for a breakthrough point to reach an ill-defended West German and West European heartland.

Political primacy is essential, of course, and military strategy should be subservient to political goals. And "forward defense" seems to be good politics in West Germany because of both the noted desire of the population to avoid conflict on its soil and the continued commitment of the country to reunification with the GDR. West Germany is a special case. The greatest economic power in Western Europe, it continues to be hobbled by the legacy of World War II. It cannot become a nuclear power nor would the states of the East or the West tolerate a vastly increased West German conventional force. Most importantly, though, West Germany has not given up its dream of reunification with the GDR. The Soviet Union holds the key to that goal. Reunification may be unrealistic for the foreseeable future; nevertheless, Bonn has maintained close ties with East Berlin through special economic concessions and has gained a steady flow of immigration from the East. As long as there is hope for reunification, even if this is to take place in the form of a neutralized Germany, Bonn remains highly vulnerable to Soviet pressures and blandishments. And the Gorbachev regime has been particularly skillful at exploiting West German vulnerabilities and susceptibilities.

Politically it is important that NATO should try to accommodate West German wishes. A country which makes the kind of conventional force contributions that West Germany does should have a significant input in alliance decision-

making. On the other hand, the vulnerability and/or suscep-
tibility of West Germany to Soviet pressures poses particular
problems. Though one may understand or even sympathize
with West Germany's position, it seems both illogical and unfortunate that the alliance member that is most vulnerable or
at least susceptible to external pressure would play the central
role in deciding alliance strategy in Central Europe.

Yet this is precisely what has happened and the problem
goes beyond "forward defense." Though there are no technological "quick fixes" to compensate for the weakness of this
policy, West Germany, for a variety of domestic and political
reasons, has further limited alliance options. Even "forward
deployment" could be made more effective, according to
many analysts, by creating a series of relatively inexpensive
defensive barriers along the inter-German border.[78] But barriers, whether they would consist of anti-tank ditches or 40-
degree gradients, that would stop tanks, are unpopular in
West Germany because they symbolize the permanent
division of the country.

Given East-West divisions, German reunification as a
member of NATO is clearly not possible. Withdrawal from
NATO and reunification as a neutral or neutralized state may
also be extraordinarily difficult to achieve. And West
Germans will be wary about losing the security that they enjoy
under NATO. This is a dilemma not only for West Germany
but for the Western alliance as well. As long as there is a dream
of reunification, the Soviet Union can manipulate West
German policy by holding out hope. Thus it becomes particularly important for the Germans not to agree to the
Soviets' "provocative" military measures.

The Soviet Union could further tilt the balance of conventional forces in its favor. The elimination of certain categories
of nuclear weapons magnifies the potential role of West
Germany in Western defenses. The removal of INF missiles
means that the remaining short-range missiles (those under
500 km) would be targeted on the two Germanies. West
Germany, consequently, would have a strong incentive to
press for the elimination of this category of weapons. That, in

turn, would further magnify the role of conventional forces. In that area the Soviet Union enjoys a significant advantage and, historically, military superiority eventually turns into political advantage. British and French nuclear forces are not large enough nor could they be built up sufficiently in order to provide credible compensation for Western conventional inferiority. West Germany cannot go nuclear and a massive conventional build-up would be unacceptable, for both political and economic reasons.

On the other hand, it would make sense for the Soviet Union to reduce its conventional forces because this is where Gorbachev could, in the longer term, achieve significant savings which he could transfer to the civilian economy. But, he is not willing to allow an unfavorable shift in the "correlation of forces"and there is no reason he should not improve the Soviet Union's military position. Again West Germany can play a key role in Soviet calculations. Given its reluctance to "provoke" the Soviet Union into political retaliatory action via the GDR, Bonn's options are limited. In order to diminish the Soviet/Warsaw Pact military threat and to maintain its ties to and hopes for the GDR, Bonn may find offers of reducing and/or pulling back conventional forces particularly attractive.

Yet even asymmetrical cuts could leave the Soviet Union with the kind of military strength that would stretch NATO defensive forces to an extent that a Warsaw Pact breakthrough would become easier than it is now. Gorbachev has hinted that he may be willing to entertain asymmetrical reductions with the West. (Yet without dramatic changes in Soviet/Warsaw Pact doctrine, these cuts would need to be so heavily weighted in favor of the West[79] that the Soviet leader may have difficulty in getting domestic acceptance even if he himself were inclined to accept them.) The second advantage that the Soviet Union enjoys is that it has much shorter lines of communication than the West. Therefore, Soviet forces that could be withdrawn even several hundred miles could be kept at a high level of preparedness and they could return far more quickly than forces brought in from the United States.

Currently, the United States can deliver only seven brigades to Europe in ten days. It might take a month to deliver the other seven brigades which would be needed to boost total American forces to the ten armored divisions that it is committed to put in the field.[80] Lastly, the Soviet Union and the Warsaw Pact states have a mobilization capacity that is superior to NATO's because they maintain a significantly higher percentage of ready reserve forces than NATO does in Central Europe.[81] The Soviet Union alone has total reserves of 6,207,000 men with military service within the last five years.[82]

It is hardly the case that these risks are not apparent to West German policymakers. Rather, a combination of increased threat, both in the military and the political realm (via the GDR), combined with a feeling of military impotence in coping with this danger could potentially induce West Germany to seek accommodation with the Soviet Union. Therefore, West Germany could be the means for Gorbachev to achieve an arms reduction agreement with NATO which would further tilt the military balance against the West.

In a worst case scenario the Soviet Union could follow a success in the first scenario by decoupling both West Germany and the United States from the NATO alliance. Success in decoupling the United States would likely result in both the destruction of NATO and the significant political transformation of Europe. Decoupling the United States, of course, has been a long-term goal of Moscow's, but despite American problems in Greece and Spain, the Soviet Union has not been successful. In the future it might try to achieve decoupling through a German route. Reduction and withdrawal of Soviet/Warsaw Pact and NATO forces would diminish (or at least seem to) the threat of armed conflict in Central Europe. Soviet writers are touting the possibilities of both reducing conventional forces and reducing or eliminating the ability of either side to launch a surprise attack.[83] But these developments, would also give rise to new hopes for German reunification.

A neutral or neutralized West Germany could achieve the desired Soviet goal of destroying NATO but it would not be without risks. A reunified, though neutral, Germany would exert a tremendous economic pull in Eastern Europe where now the two German states individually enjoy significant success. From an ideological point of view, the integration of the GDR with a democratic state would mean that for the first time the Soviet Union allowed the "wheels of history" to move backwards. This would be a terrible blow to the legitimacy of the socialist regimes elsewhere in Eastern Europe. A neutralized or neutral unified Germany could also pose a future hypothetical military threat to the Soviet Union although this (and other risks) should not be overstated. A unified Germany with a population of only 77 million (demographic trends point to a decline of people of military age) means that the Soviet Union should be able to cope with any German military threat in the foreseeable future. On balance, the dissolution of NATO likely to accompany a West German withdrawal, may be sufficiently attractive to induce Moscow to assume the risks.

But, even if the Soviet Union would not wish to allow reunification, it could create a condition just short of it and count on Western opposition to German reunification. This would stem not only from Western worries about the dissolution of the NATO alliance. A neutral or neutralized Germany outside of NATO might leave the European Community. That, in turn, could fatally weaken an organization already beset by enormous difficulties in its attempts at integration. On the other hand, if Germany could manage to stay within the European Community, its economic primacy would become so overwhelming that it could lead to political preponderance. Historical memories and animosities aside, this would be unacceptable to France and perhaps to most other members. Western European concerns would then appear to the German public that the West rather than the Soviet Union was preventing reunification. In that case, the Soviet Union would be releasing a German fox among the

West European hens. The ensuing weakening of the Western alliance would greatly strengthen the Soviet position.

Yet, even if the Soviet Union is able to push towards the above scenarios, any success would not necessarily benefit the East European states. On the contrary, Soviet hints of allowing German reunification require strong Soviet signals and measures to ensure that the Eastern Eurpean states have no illusions about escaping Soviet dominance. In military terms the reduction of conventional forces and their withdrawal from the central front would require the Soviet Union to ensure its ability to rapidly re-establish itself within the defensive *glacis* that Eastern Europe represents. Thus the East European states would not escape control but may be faced, as noted, with additional expenses for supplies and pre-positioning that would ensure a rapid redeployment of Soviet forces.

CONCLUSION

Current measures undertaken by the Gorbachev regime in Eastern Europe have the potential to achieve significant change but so far little has altered in the Warsaw Pact and in Soviet/East European relations. Decision-making in the Warsaw Pact adheres to the established pattern though it eventually may reflect greater flexibility in Soviet/East European relations. We are dealing with continuity rather than change, and military change in the Warsaw Pact will be more difficult to achieve than in the political realm because its security is the last area where the Soviet Union will be willing to make concessions to the East Europeans. Thus strategic considerations may limit greater Soviet political flexibility in the region.

It appears that the process of denuclearization that began with the elimination of intermediate-range missiles may shift the military balance further in favor of the Warsaw Pact. Unfortunately for the East Europeans, increasing Soviet demands to carry a greater defense burden will not diminish even if there is a significant shift in the balance of military power in favor of the Soviet Union. Moreover, even if the East Europeans undertake increased defense burdens, they would not have a greater input in decision-making, especially in the military dimension of the Warsaw Pact.

There are, however, some crisis scenarios which could bring about dramatic changes in the nature of the Warsaw Pact or even lead to its dissolution. Changes in the civil-military relationship in the Soviet Union could lead the government to accept a sphere of influence in Eastern Europe. There could also be multiple political upheavals in Eastern Europe which could conceivably lead to Soviet compromise and/or retrenchment. It is also possible that Gorbachev could fall from power in the near future and be replaced by a leader who is far less adept at dealing with both Eastern Europe and the West.

Gorbachev, though, despite his rhetoric, seems to be a rather cautious individual. In the Warsaw Pact, as elsewhere, he seeks a balance between continuity and change and, throughout Eastern Europe, between cohesion and viability. In his relations with the West he has been particularly adept at exploiting Western hopes and susceptibilities. So far, NATO has been slow in responding to his challenge and he may shift the military balance further in the Soviet Union's favor. In sum, for Eastern Europe and the Warsaw Pact, the prospects for a diminution of Soviet control are dim. A variation on an old publisher's line may be applicable to the current process in the Warsaw Pact. In the case of the East European members of the Pact, under Gorbachev, much of what is good is not new and much of what is new is not good.

NOTES

1. *Toronto Star*, December 16, 1987.
2. Hélène Carrere d'Encausse, *Big Brother: The Soviet Union and Soviet Europe*, (New York: Holmes and Meier), p. 240.
3. See the excellent article by Dale R. Herspring, "On Perestroyka, Gorbachev, Yazov and the Military," *Problems of Communism*, July-August, 1987, pp. 99-107 and *Newsweek*, November 18, 1985.
4. *Ibid.*, pp. 100-101, the Minsk speech of July 1985.
5. *Krasnaya Zvezda*. October 28, 1982.
6. *Pravda*, March 7, 1986.
7. Herspring, *loc. cit.*, p. 106.
8. *Krasnaya Zvezda*, June 17, 1987. Marshal Anatoli Konstantinov, commander of the Moscow district troops, was replaced before the "Rust affair" for not being able "to translate the Party Congress' political directives into the language of specific, practical actions."
9. *Pravda*, May 31, 1987; *The Economist* (London) June 6, 1987, p. 47; and *The New York Times*, May 31, 1987.
10. W. Richard Scott, *Organizations: Rational, Natural and Open Systems* (Englewood Cliffs, N.J.: Prentice-Hall, 1981), pp. 256-57.
11. Condoleeza Rice, "The Party, the Military and Decision Authority in the Soviet Union," *World Politics*, Vol. XL No. 1, October 1987, pp. 55-56.
12. T.J. Colton, *Commissars, Commanders, and Civilian Authority* (Cambridge, Mass: Harvard U.P., 1979), p. 234 fn. 6.
13. Rice, *loc. cit.*, p. 66 and H.F. Scott and W.F. Scott, *The Armed Forces of the USSR*, (Boulder Co: Westview Press), 1979.
14. Rice, *loc. cit.*, p. 76.
15. Braun, *Romanian Foreign Policy ...*, *op. cit.*, pp. 98-138.
16. John Erickson, "The Warsaw Pact—the Shape of Things to Come?" in K. Dawisha and Philip Hanson, *Soviet-East*

European Dilemmas (New York: Holmes and Meier Publishers, 1981), p. 166.

17. T. Rakowska Harmstone, et al., *Warsaw Pact: The Question of Cohesion*, Vol. 1, (Ottawa: ORAE, 1984), pp. 65-165.
18. A. Ross Johnson, R. W. Dean, and A. Alexiev, *East European Military Establishments:The Warsaw Pact Northern Tier,* (New York: Crane Russak, 1982).
19. Johnson, et al *op. cit.*
20. Karen Dawisha, *The Kremlin and the Prague Spring* (Berkeley: University of California Press, 1984).
21. Jiri Valenta, *Soviet Intervention in Czechoslovakia, 1968: Anatomy of a Decision*, (Baltimore: Johns Hopkins University Press, 1979).
22. Johnson, et al., *op. cit.,* p. 146.
23. A. Ross Johnson, "The Warsaw Pact: Soviet Military Policy in Eastern Europe," (Santa Monica, Rand Report, July 1981), p.65-83.
24. Ivan Volgyes, ed., *The Political Reliability of the Warsaw Pact Armies: The Southern Tier* (Durham, NC: Duke University Press, 1982).
25. Daniel N. Nelson, *Alliance Behavior in the Warsaw Pact* (Boulder, CO: Westview Press1986). pp. 27-62.
26. Malcolm Mackintosh, "Military Considerations in Soviet-East European Relations," in Dawisha and Hanson *op. cit.*, pp. 134-48.
27. *Ibid.*
28. Erickson, *op. cit.*, p. 166.
29. Johnson, *The Warsaw Pact ...*, *op. cit.,* pp. 44-45.
30. *Ibid.,* p. 28.
31. As quoted in R. Rubin, "The Hungarian People's Army," *RUSI* (London), September 1976, pp. 59-66, Note 36.
32. Michael Checinski, "The Costs of Armaments Production and the Profitability of Armament Exports in COMECON Countries," Research Paper No. 10, The Soviet East-European Research Center, The Hebrew University of Jerusalem, November 1974: p. 24 and Jeffrey Simon,

Warsaw Pact Forces: Problems of Command and Control (Boulder, CO: Westiew, 1985), p. 126.

33. A. Braun, *Ceausescu: The Problems of Power* (Toronto: Canadian Institute of International Affairs, 1979/80).

34. *The Military Balance* 1987/8, (London: International Institute for Strategic Studies, 1987), pp. 46-53, herein after referred to as *The Military Balance*.

35. Keith Crane, *Military Spending in Eastern Europe* (Santa Monica, Rand, R-3444-USOP, 1987), p. vi.

36. *The Military Balance, 1987/8 op. cit.* pp. 32-52.

37. *The Military Balance, 1987/8, 1986/7, 1985/6.*

38. Nelson, *op. cit.*, pp. 71-107.

39. Crane, *op. cit.*, p. 49.

40. Crane, *ibid.*, p. 80, Table 12. The GDR has increased military spending at the rate of 6.8 percent between 1979-85 see Crane, p. 66.

41. *Izvestia,* May 28, 1987.

42. Crane, *op. cit.*, p. 51.

43. Herspring, *loc. cit.*, p. 102.

44. *Ibid.*

45. *Pravda* May 30, 1987.

46. *Ibid.*

47. *Ibid.*

48. Johnson, "The Warsaw Pact: Soviet Military Policy in Eastern Europe," *op. cit.*, p. 261.

49. Strobe Talbott, "The Road to Zero," *Time* pp. 2-3.

50. Edward N. Luttwak, *The Paradoxical Logic of Strategy* (Berkeley: Institute of International Studies, 1987), p. 46.

51. *The Military Balance 1987/8.* London I.I.S.S. 1987, pp. 226-29.

52. *Izvestia*, August 13, 1987.

53. *Ibid.*

54. *Ibid.*

55. *Ibid.*

56. *Ibid.*

57. *Ibid.*

58. *Ibid.*

59. *Pravda* June 27, 1987.

60. Henry A. Kissinger, "The Dangers Ahead," *Newsweek*, December 21, 1987, p. 36.
61. Erickson, *op. cit.*, p. 152.
62. *Krasnaya Zvezda,* June 17, 1987.
63. *Ibid.*
64. *Krasnaya Zvezda*, April 2, 1978.
65. *Krasnaya Zvezda*, November 24, 1981.
66. *Kazakhstanskaya Pravda* (Alma Ata), 6 February 1981, translated in *Joint Publications Research Service*, (Washington, D.C.), No. 77681, March 26, 1981.
67. *The Military Balance 1987-8*, pp. 27-9.
68. As quoted in *The Military Balance 1987-8*, p. 32.
69. *Ibid.*, pp. 47-52.
70. *Ibid.*, pp. 47-52.
71. See John Erickson, "Soviet Cybermen: Men and Machines in the Soviet System," *Signal*, December 1984.
72. Luttwak, *op. cit*, pp. 10 and 48-49.
73. See, e.g., V. Kulikov, "The Main Jumping-off Point," *Krasnaya Zvezda*, May 22, 1986.
74. See L. Semeiko, "Instead of Mountains of Weapons," *Izvestia*, August 13, 1987.
75. *The Military Balance 1987-8*, p. 231.
76. *Newsweek*, December 7, 1987, p. 33.
77. *The Military Balance, 1987-8*, pp. 54-81.
78. William Kaufman has estimated that effective barriers could be built for $800 million which would decrease the effectiveness of a given offensive force by as much as 40 percent, *Newsweek*, December 7, 1987, p. 37 and "Non-Nuclear Deterrence" in John D.Steinbrunner and Leon V. Sigal (eds.) *Alliance Security and the No-First-Use Question*.
79. Rand Corporation studies indicate that reductions must be 5 to 1 in the West's favor to prevent the Soviet Union from gaining a position from where a breakthrough would be made easier, *Newsweek*, December 21, 1987.
80. *Newsweek*, December 7, 1987.
81. *The Military Balance, 1987-8*, pp. 28-83., p. 3.
82. *Ibid.*, p. 33.

83. See, e.g., L. Semeiko "Instead of Mountains of Weapons," *Izvestia*, August 13, 1987.

SEVEN

U.S. POLICY TOWARDS EASTERN EUROPE

PAST, PRESENT, AND FUTURE

John Lukacs

Allow me, as a historian, to engage in a long-range view of that complex region of the world called Eastern Europe, with all of the inevitable shortcomings that such a general perspective entails.

Forty years ago it seemed as if the existence of states and nations in Eastern Europe had become devoid of meaning; that the dominant reality was their incorporation into a Soviet imperial and communist dictatorial system. The only exceptions were two states at the extremities of Eastern Europe: Greece (which may be regarded as a Southern, rather than an Eastern European state); and, perhaps, in 1947-48, Finland (a Scandinavian rather than an Eastern European state).

Less than ten years later—this means, more than thirty years ago—this ominous picture began to change. Since that time it has become increasingly obvious that the *existence* of the states and nations of Eastern Europe is, again, the *primary* reality in that portion of the Old World. Their relative independence and their social, economic, and cultural conditions remain, of course, influenced and compromised by the fact of Russian presence and power; but these conditions are, in reality, *secondary* to the principal reality of the continued existence of these states and nations, while the allied condition of a communist ideology is merely *tertiary* and, in some places and cases, increasingly devoid of meaning.

Now allow me to remind you that this prevalence of the factor of states over political ideologies is not new; that it goes back, indeed, to the centuries when what happened in Eastern Europe became, for the first time, a principal factor in the history of the world.

Consider the contrast between the Western and the Eastern portions of Europe during the eighteenth century, which was the peak of the Modern Age. The so-called Enlightenment, the Age of Reason, and the French Revolution were great events, with great consequences in the Atlantic world, with only faint echoes in Eastern Europe (that, too, was a long-standing reason for the general disinterest and ignorance about Eastern Europe in the English-speaking world).

Yet at the same time possibly the most drastic and revolutionary changes on the map of Europe occurred in the eastern, not the western, part of the continent. In 1700 the three principal powers and states in Eastern Europe were Sweden, Poland, and Turkey. By 1815 they were replaced by Russia, Prussia, and Austria. Sweden had retreated into a middle-size Northern European kingdom; the Polish state had entirely disappeared (though the Polish nation had not); and the Ottoman Empire had lost all of its domains north and west of the Balkans in Europe.

Because of the long-range consequences of the rise of Russia and Prussia it may be argued that these geographic changes may have been more important, in the long run, than the great French Revolution itself—especially if we consider that no comparable change occurred in Western Europe during that time; and that both the frontiers and the general foreign policy of France did not essentially change consequent to her different governments, which had radically different political philosophies.

In a similar way, it may be argued that in the history of Europe during the nineteenth century, the revolutions of 1820, 1830, and 1848 were not as important (by which I mean consequential) as the changes on the political map of Europe—that is, on the state level—as the unification of Germany (and of Italy).

The relative, but very considerable, prosperity and peace during the so-called Hundred Years of Peace, from the fall of Napoleon to 1914, was due to the fact, among others, that Prussian Germany, Austria-Hungary, and the Russian Empire continued to exist, with their Eastern European frontiers largely unchanged, for one hundred years or more. Now it is true that during the nineteenth century—more precisely, during the 55 years before 1914—a number of new Eastern European states came into existence. But keep in mind, first, that all of them—that is, Serbia, Romania, Bulgaria, Greece, and Albania—broke off not from the three great Eastern European empires but from the decaying Ottoman empire. More important, not one of these (with the possible exception of the tiny mountain bandit state of Montenegro) could become independent *by its own efforts*. For that they needed foreign (Russian or British or Austrian or joint) help.

The next group of independent states in Eastern Europe came into existence consequent to World War I. They were: Finland, Estonia, Latvia, Lithuania, Poland, Czechoslovakia, Yugoslavia, and Hungary (the latter passing from partial to full independence in 1919, but at the cost of territorial mutilation). Keep in mind, again, that the creation of these states was possible only because of the break-up of the Russian and Austrian (and, to a much lesser extent, of the diminution of the German) empires. In this respect we should at least consider that the Bolshevik Revolution in Russia proved to be a benefit to much of Europe. Allow me to explain this startling assertion.

Had there been no Russian Revolution in 1917, Russia would have been, without a doubt, one of the principal victors of World War I. We know what this would have meant. We are not reduced to speculations about it. It is all there in the Tsarist diplomatic documents of the period and in the French and British archives. What the Russian foreign ministers (and generals) wanted, and what their French and British allies were constrained to agree to, during World War I was: an Eastern Europe dominated by Russia, a Western Europe dominated by France and Britain, and a weak and divided Germany in the middle—altogether not very different from what Stalin, Bulganin, Khrushchev, Brezhnev, etc., wanted.

The Bolshevik Revolution (and also the liberal revolution that preceded it) were catastrophes for Russia. They resulted in millions of dead, in a brutal and barbarous civil war, and in a setback in the economic, social, and financial development of Russia—conditions from which Mr. Gorbachev is even now trying, against many difficulties, to extricate his country. It also led to a diminution of the old Russian Empire, to a one to two hundred miles eastward retreat of its frontiers. Unlike his successor Stalin, Lenin was not much of a statesman. He and his cohorts contributed, indirectly, to the independence of five European nations west of Russia, and directly to a retreat of the Russian imperial frontiers in Eastern Europe—the exact condition that Stalin and Molotov chose to restore in 1939-1940 and in 1944-1945.

There was another reason, too, why the communist revolution and regime in Russia proved to be a boon to Eastern Europe. In 1917, like today, the cultural and political prestige of Russia in Eastern Europe was so low that the very association of communism with Russia made the former overwhelmingly unpopular in most of Eastern Europe. Had the first successful communist revolution occurred in France or Germany instead of Russia, its imitative impact all over Europe would have been immeasurably greater.

It was thus that—unlike the French or the American or, later, the fascist or Nazi revolutions—communism (except with a small minority of intellectuals and committed revolutionaries) was not able to mount a successful revolution, establish itself in power anywhere in the world, and especially not in Europe. That condition lasted for about twenty-seven years—until, in Eastern Europe, communist or pro-communist regimes did eventually come into existence, but solely because of the predominance of Russian military power in that region. (In this respect not even Yugoslavia or Albania provide exceptions: had the British army "liberated" them in 1944 or 1945, the ensuing regimes would not have been wholly communist).

On the larger scale of history, in the twentieth century the importance of Eastern Europe became predominant—not just for Europe but for world history at large. By the early twentieth century these new Eastern European states were not altogether artificial creations. They were—as others in the Western world—states whose framework (including their frontiers) was often faulty but it was nonetheless a framework filled up by the content of their nations. Their nationalism had both positive and negative features and consequences—as indeed nationalism has had almost everywhere; *nationalism* (and not communism or fascism) remains the political ideology and phenomenon of the twentieth century. But this led to the two world wars; and, indirectly, the cold war. For it was in *Eastern Europe* (not in Western Europe) where World War I broke out; it was in *Eastern Europe* that the inadequacy of the peace treaties, including the breaking up of the Austro-Hungarian monarchy, led to unsettled political conditions that were later overridden by German power; it was in *Eastern Europe* that World War II broke out; it was in *Eastern Europe* that its most decisive battles (between Germans and Russians) were being fought; and, finally, it was in *Eastern Europe*—or, rather, because of *Eastern Europe* —that forty years ago the cold war developed between the United States and the Soviet Union.

This requires explanation or, rather, correction of a prevalent myth (perhaps especially in Washington). This myth consists of the belief that the main historical struggle in the twentieth century has been that between communism and capitalism (or call it communism and democracy), incarnated, respectively, by the Soviet Union and the United States. Yet during both of the world wars in the twentieth century, the American and the Russian empires were allies. The communist revolution in 1917 had nothing to do with the outcome of World War I. The competition between communism and capitalism had nothing to do with the outbreak of World War II (when, incidentally, or not so incidentally, communism and democracy were forced to become allies to defeat the most powerful incarnation of extreme nationalism, the German Third Reich; for neither the Western democracies nor the Soviet Union could accomplish that alone). The struggle between communism and capitalism had relatively little to do with the origins of the "cold war" either. That grew out of the division of Europe at the end of the war or, rather, out of a mutual misunderstanding of what that division meant. From 1945 to 1947 the government of the United States came to believe that, having communized Eastern Europe, the Soviet Union was ready to spread communism into Western Europe, which was not the case. Conversely, Stalin believed that, after having established dominion over Western and Southern Europe, the Americans were ready to challenge the Soviet dominion over Eastern Europe, which was also not the case.

Because of the brutal Soviet subjugation of Eastern Europe, the Marshall Plan, NATO, and the American assumption of energetic leadership in Atlantic and Mediterranean Europe took place. There were other conflicts between the United States and the Soviet Union at the time—in Iran, North Korea, and perhaps in China—but none compared in importance to the then ominous European scene. Had it not been for the Soviet imposition of terroristic communist regimes in Eastern Europe, the cold war would not have taken place—at least, not in the form, and not with the consequences, that we have come to know.

We have seen that for centuries Eastern Europe was largely divided between the Germanic and the Russian empires. After World War I, both of these empires retreated (the Russian one further than the German one). The so-called independence of a dozen Eastern European states was not enough for a stable balance. Sooner or later one of their enormous neighbor empires would rise again. It happened to be Germany, under Hitler. And when Germany was defeated, the vacuum would be filled by the Russians. From that moment on, the independence of Eastern Europe could be safeguarded only by determined and daring efforts on the part of the Western democracies. But that was not to be. We know already that between the two wars France, with all of her direct interests at stake, was not capable (and, in times of crisis, not even willing) to keep the Germans out of Eastern Europe at the cost of war. Only one step further and a strong national tradition further removed from Eastern Europe, the British policy was not much different. As long as the British government was —not—convinced that Hitler wished to dominate most of Europe, it would not commit itself to oppose Germany in the east. In 1940, under the leadership of their savior Churchill, the British defied Hitler; they would not make peace with him by accepting a German domination of Europe in exchange for the German acceptance of an intact British Empire. But Eastern Europe, or most of Eastern Europe, was another story. As early as the summer of 1940 (when the Stalin-Hitler Pact was still in effect) British documents indicate that their policy was fairly clear: half of Europe was better than none. If the alternative to a complete German domination of Europe was a Russian domination of the eastern half of Europe, so be it.

Churchill *knew* that he could not prevent Stalin from dominating most of Eastern Europe at the end of the war. But he also knew that a Russian domination would be the source of grave troubles to come. He tried to prevent some of it (not all of it) first attempting by to establish an Anglo-American presence in the Balkans near the end of the war; second, by a *quid-pro-quo* geographical bargaining with Stalin. But the Americans would not go along with Churchill. This is why the division of Europe (and of Germany) occurred *exactly* on the temporary demarcation lines along which Anglo-American and Russian armies would establish themselves in 1945. This is how Stalin correctly interpreted the Yalta verbiage about Liberated Europe in 1945. What was ours was ours; what was theirs was theirs. He told the Yugoslav communists on a visit: "It cannot be otherwise." It wasn't.

The United States government was hardly interested in Eastern Europe. What it hoped for was some kind of formula: the existence of pro-Russian, but not wholly pro-communist, governments in the Russian sphere of Europe, including Poland. Stalin did not want that. He knew the unpopularity of communism, and that such governmental set-ups would lead to a diminution of his control, fairly soon after the return of Soviet troops to the frontiers of the USSR. So the cold war began, and the course of the mighty American ship of state changed decisively after 1945 from exaggerated hopes to exaggerated fears about the ambitions of the Soviet Union. Yet, all exaggerations about communism notwithstanding, the Washington solution was a compromise. In its own way the American view was not that different from the British view. Half of Europe was better than none. NATO, the Marshall Plan, the American presence, the defense of West Berlin, the NSC directives, etc., were committed to the defense of Western Europe. All of the obsession with communism and the propaganda of "liberation" or "rollback" notwithstanding, the United States government—neither under President Truman nor under the latecoming ideological anti-communist, President Eisenhower—did not challenge the Soviet domination of Eastern Europe. Let me repeat: half of Europe was better than none.

Perhaps we should not blame the United States. But then again, perhaps we should, because the implementation of that policy (or non-policy) was often deceiving, dangerous, and, especially during the Dulles years, dishonest. But in any event,

Eastern Europe was (and still is) very far from the United States. For the United States to engage in the "liberation" of Eastern Europe would have entailed risks and dangers for the American people which were (and are) beyond its proper national interests and province—not to speak of those unexpected problems and difficulties that a permanent American predominance and presence in Eastern European affairs could mean.

The year 1956 was a turning-point in the history of Eastern Europe not only because of the Polish and Hungarian revolutions and not only because that year may have marked a deep crisis in Russia's Eastern European dominion. It was then that—notwithstanding the extreme American reaction to the Russian suppression of the Hungarian revolution—the Soviet government recognized the essence of the American policy regarding Eastern Europe: the American unwillingness to challenge or change the division of Europe either through force or through a diplomatic bargain that would lead to certain negotiated withdrawals.

In any event, what Winston Churchill told General De Gaulle in Paris in November 1944 (a statement included in the memoirs of De Gaulle but not of Churchill) was coming true. De Gaulle had been astounded at the American lack of policy regarding the growing Russian presence in Eastern Europe, whereupon Churchill answered that this was so; that the Russians had developed a voracious appetite for the states of Eastern Europe; but, in Churchill's words, "after the meal comes the digestion period." By 1956 at the latest, and for the past three decades or more, it has become increasingly evident that the Russians could not and cannot "digest" Eastern Europe—principally because of the established nationalities among its peoples.

As early as 1952 (when Stalin was still alive) the Russians indicated a possible willingness to withdraw from some parts of Eastern Europe (at that time this may have involved Eastern Germany) in exchange for an American withdrawal from a correspondingly important region or state. In 1953, when Stalin was gone, the new Russian leadership tried again;

but there was no American response. In 1955 the Austrian State Treaty brought about such a mutual withdrawal—despite American initial worries about it. But by 1961 (in this respect the erection of the Berlin Wall was a significant event for Eastern Europe too) it became more and more evident that a mutually arrangeable Russian-American withdrawal from Europe was not in the cards—because of the Russian knowledge that the Americans were not dissatisfied with the existing division of Europe (including that of Germany or even of Berlin).

What has happened in the last twenty-five years, however, is that on another level a Russian and an American withdrawal has been taking place. While in Germany (and elsewhere in Western Europe) the American military, political, cultural, financial, and economic influence has been weakening, the Russian influence in Eastern Europe has been weakening, too. I need not provide evidence here. Who would have believed, even ten years ago, that in Poland, a state so crucial for the Russians, the Soviets would feel compelled to tolerate the existence of a veritable national opposition movement, including the presence of a national non-communist, if not anti-communist, hero, Lech Walesa? This is one example of a general development that has by no means been reversed, or halted, during these years of the Gorbachev regime in Moscow. To the contrary! We now have regimes in Eastern Europe that feel threatened not by Russian rigor, but by the sentiments and examples of Russian liberalism wafting from Moscow.

History is full of ironies. We have seen that the wishful thinking of the State Department in 1945—to see pro-Russian but not necessarily Sovietized governments in Eastern Europe—was then largely devoid of meaning and of hope. Yet this is exactly what took place in Finland in 1945 and after—in a country with which the Soviet Union enjoys excellent and safe relations. On certain levels of culture and commerce (though not yet in political leadership) a certain "Finlandization" has already taken place in Hungary or in Poland—*mutatis mutandis*, with different local particularities, of course. It is conceivable, though not yet probable, that some day a leader in Moscow will recognize that the Soviet Union's own interests are safeguarded better by border states governed like an orderly Finland, rather than by having to fear uprisings against unpopular communist regimes that require painful Soviet intervention.

What is more than probable, indeed evident, is the recognition, by the leaders of the Soviet Union, of the grave and incorrigible shortcomings of the communist philosophy and the communist administration of the economy and culture of entire nations. That recognition does not mean the official denial of communism—after all, *that* remains the only legitimization of existing governments. It may mean, however, the emergence of new political structures, which I (although I am speaking as a historian who abjures prophecy) believe may be something other than multi-party ones. In this respect perhaps the people of Poland have been acting as pioneers. The main question for the future of Eastern Europe may involve the prospects of Germany. There are signs that in different fields—industry, economy, commerce, tourism, and even culture—German influences have begun to replace American ones in many states of Eastern Europe. Some day political consequences will ensue—especially if the Germans take their destiny into their own hands and bring about a new kind of German unity. Perhaps this is why one of the more interesting items in Gorbachev's Eastern European policy has already emerged: his proposal of closer cooperation between Austria, Czechoslovakia, and Hungary. Another irony of history: this is not entirely different from Churchill's Danubian confederation ideas of 1943, which were rejected not only by Stalin but also by Roosevelt.

In any event, the history of Eastern Europe during the last forty years provides clear evidence that nationality and nationalism cannot be wished away; that the predictions of world-famous thinkers and political prophets have not come about; that the future is not necessarily with larger and larger units but with national states, no matter how small; and that civilization and culture, resting on language, are far more important and decisive than economics. Consider only the acute problems of the Hungarian minority in Transylvania, or the even more acute and dangerous nationality problems in a Yugoslavia that was reunited in 1945 by a communist chieftain.

In any event, regarding America, the peoples of Eastern Europe must learn something that the neo-conservatives (as distinct from real patriots and conservatives) in Washington have yet to learn: that their best prospects lie not with sharpening but with mellowing, not with worsening but with improving relations between the United States and the Soviet Union. That is not an Absolute Law of History, because such things do not exist; but it is certainly true of the present, as it has been true for quite a number of years past.

The Russian presence—not only digestive capacity—in Eastern Europe will diminish further. Meanwhile it is not the business of the United States to "liberate" Eastern Europe. It is not the business of the Germans. It is the business of the Eastern European peoples themselves. Some of them are at it, in different ways, and some are perhaps closer than we, or the Russians, are inclined to think.

EIGHT

TO END
AN EMPIRE
WESTERN DILEMMAS IN
EASTERN EUROPE

Bennett Kovrig

The geopolitical permanence of the Soviet empire in Eastern Europe has been occasionally challenged by revolution, but the outcome was always the restoration of communist control and Soviet domination. For the West, torn between a principled wish for the national self-determination of the Kremlin's reluctant subjects, and a fear of the incalculable consequences of turbulence in the East, the promotion of desirable change in that region remains an interest in search of a policy. Eastern Europe does not rank high in the priorities of the West's chancelleries apart from Bonn's compulsive concern with the other Germany. Yet neither the majority of East Europeans nor, at least in principle, the West is satisfied with this political legacy of World War II and of the Cold War. Do the signs of a thaw in East-West relations foreshadow new opportunities for overcoming the division of Europe? The question has acquired fresh urgency, though concrete answers are, as ever, elusive.

Gorbachev's evocation of a "common European home" is commonly interpreted in the West as yet another siren song of detente designed to seduce NATO's European members away from the Atlantic partnership. For most East Europeans, on the other hand, it conjures up the hope of reintegration into a liberal and democratic Europe. Does the prospect of Eastern Europe's "Finlandization" pale beside the danger of the "Finlandization" of Western Europe? Such issues of symmetry and comparative advantage deserve objective recalculation in the era of *perestroika*. The impetus given to economic and political reform in Eastern Europe by Gorbachev represents one important dimension of the current process of change. The other is his "new political thinking" in foreign policy, which addresses both intra-bloc and East-West relations.

"The entire framework of political relations between the socialist countries must be strictly based on absolute independence," declares Gorbachev, although the principle has been asserted and flouted as well by his predecessors. He follows up the principle with the conviction that "the socialist community will be successful only if every party and state cares for both its own and common interests, if it respects its friends and allies, heeds their interests and pays attention to the experience of others."[1] The point where bloc solidarity (read: Soviet interest) overrides independence is as unclear as ever, but "new thinking" implies at least a more permissive attitude towards reform in Eastern Europe. Also, by implication, the Brezhnev Doctrine has been laid to rest, with Soviet foreign ministry spokesman Gennady Gerasimov being quoted as agreeing that the time is past when the Soviet Union would intervene militarily in Eastern Europe in the name of socialism.[2]

Gorbachev's multiple proposals for the control and reduction of arms have reopened the old debate about West European security and the American military commitment. In the Gorbachevian canon, "armaments should be reduced to the level of reasonable sufficiency, that is, a level necessary for strictly defensive purposes."[3] Domestic economic priorities probably inspire the current reformulation of the ideological underpinnings of Soviet foreign policy. The director of the Institute of World Economics and International

Relations, Yevgeny Primakov, recently offered a sample of the "new political thinking" according to which capitalism and imperialism do not necessarily spawn militarism—the West may be less of a threat to the Soviet Union than hitherto assumed, and therefore the prospects for East-West cooperation and lower Soviet defense expenditures are brighter.[4] Such ideological gyrations are commonly dismissed in the West as exercises in deception, but the possibility cannot be ruled out that in the present circumstances they represent the obligatory doctrinal rationalization of an authentic shift in Soviet tactics and, perhaps, strategy.

Anticipation of significant change in the Soviet system can easily be ridiculed as the triumph of hope over experience. Nevertheless, Gorbachev's mainly verbal revolution has progressed far enough that the West is compelled to reexamine its basic assumptions about not only the Soviet Union but also the Soviet-East European nexus. The strategy and tactics of the Western powers regarding Eastern Europe hang in the balance. Europe's division may be universally deplored, but the institutionalization of the status quo on both sides has served incidentally to inhibit the political imagination and will to change. Disappointment breeds prudence, and the record of East-West diplomacy and of East European popular challenges to Soviet hegemony allows little optimism regarding the possibilities of peaceful change. Yet the idea that it is time for a prudent reconsideration of existing assumptions about the Soviet world may be gaining ground. Indeed, the West would be remiss if it did not exploit the opportunities offered by Gorbachev's disposition to address the flaws in the Soviet system, domestic and imperial.

Western attitudes on these questions are in a state of flux. At a recent lecture in Berlin, the father of containment, George Kennan, reiterated his gloomy observation that the two superpowers are "immersed in a sterile and tragic long-range military rivalry—a rivalry predicated on the existence of Europe's divided condition and not conducive to the exploration of possibilities for its removal." He exhorted the Europeans to "discover the paths of escape" from this deadlock.[5] Zbigniew Brzezinski, who for decades has helped to shape American policy towards the East, anticipates a weakening of Soviet control over Eastern Europe and recommends negotiation toward a new political and security regime for Central Europe, involving arms control and confidence-building measures as well as the mutual thinning of conventional forces and a tank-free zone. Such a process, he argues, could "help to end the artificial division of Europe, thereby diluting Soviet control and diminishing the direct Soviet conventional threat to the free countries of Western Europe."[6]

Such informed speculation confirms certain fixed propositions regarding Western policies towards Eastern Europe. These are that significant change in the status of the latter is largely dependent on broader security considerations, and that effective redefinition of the conditions of security is dependent in turn on a thus far elusive coincidence of will and interest on the part of the two superpowers as well as their major European allies. Geopolitical realities can always be cited in defense of the status quo, but it must not be forgotten that these "realities" arise at least in part from historical choices. It may be salutary to review the record of Western approaches to Eastern Europe before returning to the current scope for change and choice.

The West's reluctance to accept the Sovietization of Eastern Europe derives in large measure from wartime proclamations by the allies, notably the Atlantic Charter and the Yalta Declaration on Liberated Europe, which promised democracy and self-determination. The geopolitical "realities" of postwar Europe were as much the consequence of allied military strategy as of the fortunes of war. The inconsistency between political promise and military strategy was mainly of American origin, and by the time of the Yalta conference little scope remained for remedy. Greater effort might have been expended by Roosevelt and Churchill to salvage genuine democracy in Poland, but the enduring myth of a sellout of Eastern Europe at Yalta does little to clarify the causes of Europe's division.

Western approaches to the problem of Eastern Europe in the Cold War era had two key determinants. The first was the ideological and strategic resolve of the United States to meet and challenge Soviet expansion in Europe. The second was the decision to consolidate the German Federal Republic as a member of the Western alliance and, at the same time, to retain the goal of German reunification.

The first postwar priority was to assure the economic and democratic revival of Western Europe, and the Sovietization of the Eastern half of the continent met with only powerless remonstrances on the part of Americans and Europeans. Both sides probably overestimated the other's aggressive intentions and acted accordingly. The founding conference of the Cominform had set the agenda for the accelerated consolidation of communist power in the East, while in the West the Truman Doctrine, the Marshall Plan, and the Vandenberg Resolution followed the logic of Washington's new policy of containment. The latter proclaimed the fundamental incompatibility between the philosophy and practice of Marxism-Leninism and liberal democratic values and advocated the effective isolation of the Soviet system. Containment of the opponent's revolutionary and expansionist impulse would, it was argued by George Kennan, eventually lead to its internal collapse. In the meantime, Washington refused to accept the legitimacy of the new order in Eastern Europe.

Inevitably, the twin processes of regional consolidation reinforced each other in a zero-sum game where each side regarded the opponent's moves as threatening vital interests. Thus Stalin's 1952 overture regarding the future of Germany was dismissed as a spoiling tactic, and when a year later, following the dictator's death, Churchill agitated for a last attempt at negotiation with the Russians on the division of Europe, his colleagues and American allies quickly killed the idea. The principle and practice of containment virtually ruled out the possibility of change by negotiation in the status of Eastern Europe, and the brutal Stalinization of the region left little doubt regarding the Soviet Union's determination to safeguard its western approaches. The already remote prospect of change by compromise was eliminated in 1954 by the incorporation of West Germany into the Western military alliance. Bonn's claim to represent all Germans was endorsed by her allies, as was the goal of a reunited democratic Germany, and the entrenchment of these principles effectively froze the division of Europe.

With regard to Eastern Europe, Washington took the lead in imposing punitive diplomatic and economic measures that its more pragmatic European allies followed half-heartedly or not at all. The essentially defensive thrust of containment was soon modified, so that by the end of 1949 the NSC 58/2 report would recommend offensive tactics to reduce or eliminate Soviet influence in Eastern Europe. Gradualism and differentiation, slogans that came to denote later versions of U.S. policy, were in fact already applied. The top priority was the detachment of East European regimes from Moscow's control, and Titoism was a palatable model. Indeed, American aid and patronage was instrumental in sheltering Tito from Stalin's wrath. At the other extreme from this evolutionary approach lay the attempt to overthrow the Albanian regime by infiltrating guerrillas, a covert Anglo-American operation which Kim Philby's treason turned into a bloody fiasco. In between lay the tactics of psychological warfare, with such instruments as Radio Free Europe and balloon campaigns, and of cloak and dagger operations to exacerbate the anti-Tito hysteria in Stalin's domain. These measures aimed as much at weakening the enemy as at liberating Stalin's East European subjects.

If Western policy helped to preserve Yugoslavia's precarious independence, its more offensive tactics brought little tangible result. The rhetoric of rollback and liberation, voiced principally by John Foster Dulles during the 1952 election campaign, alarmed America's allies as well as the enemy regimes and revived the hopes of many oppressed East Europeans. The substance of policy changed little, and the quick repression of the East German revolt in June 1953 made the promise of liberation sound hollow indeed. Psychological warfare and the encouragement of Titoism were only accentuated when Stalin's successors began to pay lip service to peaceful coexistence and the possibility of several roads to socialism. However, in 1956 when Khrushchev's de-Stalinization campaign unleashed a wave of unrest in Eastern Europe, the West's impotence was dramatically revealed.

The Hungarian revolution erupted as Britain, France, and Israel were putting the final touches to the Suez operation plan. That they proceeded with the intervention at the moment when the division of Europe was finally challenged reflects a degree of cynicism unjustified by either foresight or hindsight. Suez made it easier for a disoriented Soviet leadership to resort to savage retaliation, as did Washington's professions of benevolent disinterest. The Hungarians, of course, had reached well beyond Titoism by restoring a multiparty government as well as proclaiming their neutrality. Nevertheless, the suspicion lingers that a divided West and an overly prudent Eisenhower let a historic moment pass without fully testing its possibilities. The concurrent and more peaceful revolution in Poland offered momentary comfort to the West, and it was reinforced by some American aid, but Gomulka outlived his promise, and Eastern Europe settled back into uneasy normalcy.

Shorn of the extravagant language of rollback and liberation, Washington's approach to Eastern Europe retained both its ultimate objective and its essentially gradualist and differentiated tactics. The terms "peaceful engagement" and "bridge-building" (conceived by Brzezinski) symbolized the Kennedy and Johnson administrations' quest for selective rapprochement and a controlled weaning of the East European regimes from Moscow's embrace. The operational management of the policy remained constrained by America's limited leverage and by the reluctance of domestic public opinion to condone normal relations with communist regimes. President Johnson's attempts to liberalize trade with the East foundered on the shoals of congressional opposition. Increasingly absorbed by Vietnam, Washington lost interest in the intractable problem of Eastern Europe.

As America's interest waned, so waxed that of some Western European countries. The foreign policy orientations of the North Americans and of the West Europeans regarding Eastern Europe historically were influenced by different domestic factors and foreign interests. Waves of East European immigrants to the United States and Canada gave rise to a political constituency that impelled the governments to maintain a concern for developments in their countries of origin. Washington had espoused the cause of national self-determination in Eastern Europe already in the 19th century. Kossuth, and later Paderewski and Masaryk, sought American help. Woodrow Wilson's Fourteen Points foreshadowed the Declaration on Liberated Europe. But America had little commercial or, until 1948, strategic interest in Eastern Europe. The West Europeans, on the other hand, have pursued economic and security interests in the East without the encumbrance of domestic lobbies or of broader ideological considerations. After World War II, they adjusted to the new constraints on trade with the East and enrolled willingly in the U.S.-led alliance but did not fully share America's moral outrage at the fate of the East Europeans. They lacked America's sense of guilt and obligation and the ideological certainty underlying its idealism and missionary zeal. In the wake of the defeat of Nazism, many Europeans possessed a rosy view of Marxism and of the extension of its Stalinist variant to Eastern Europe.

In any case, West Germany was the ally with the greatest historical and potential interest in Eastern Europe, and for Bonn the issues of Germany's borders and reunification were predominant. Although diplomatic relations with the Soviet Union were established in 1955, the Hallstein Doctrine served to prevent both international recognition of the German Democratic Republic and the normalization of Bonn's relations with the other East European states. Bonn's reluctance to formally accept the postwar frontiers of the German lands further reduced its Eastern options. These policies ultimately limited the scope of the entire Western alliance for negotiating detente and inducing evolutionary change in the East.

The building of the Berlin Wall in August 1961 confirmed, both symbolically and materially, the permanence of Germany's division, and the Cuban missile crisis the following year ushered in a new era in superpower relations. Bonn tried to develop economic relations with the other East European states, partly in the hope that this would reinforce the polycentric tendencies exemplified by Romania's resistance to CMEA integration and flirtation with China. But as Washington inclined more and more to explore the possibilities of detente, some basic tenets of West Germany's Eastern policy necessarily came under review. The Kiesinger-Brandt coalition gingerly took the first steps in this direction in 1966 with a new *Ostpolitik* that decoupled detente from reunification and watered down the Hallstein Doctrine.[7] Only Romania broke ranks by establishing diplomatic relations in 1967 with Bonn. Until the West Germans made further concessions to Soviet and East European sensibilities, there could be little progress in bridge-building.

A more voluntaristic experiment in detente was that of Charles de Gaulle, who sought escape from the perceived threat of superpower condominium in the vision of a Europe of sovereign nations from the Atlantic to the Urals. France, therefore, was to loosen its links to the Western military alliance not only to reassert its own independence but also to encourage a similar process of self-assertion in the East. According to the logic of this strategy, the decline of American influence in the western half of the continent would induce the Soviet Union to permit, and the East European regimes to pursue, greater national autonomy. De Gaulle's visits to the Soviet Union (1966) and to Poland (1967) and Romania (1968) brought no tangible results, and the Warsaw Pact's invasion of Czechoslovakia dispelled Gaullist illusions regarding the symmetry of alliances East and West. The dynamics of West European integration and the irreducible conditions of Soviet security overrode his somewhat anachronistic and romantic vision of a new European order.

As the Hungarian revolution had vividly shown, liberal democracy and full national autonomy were ardently desired by most East Europeans but utterly beyond their reach. The Brezhnev doctrine confirmed that the far more modest objective of "socialism with a human face," introduced in Czechoslovakia through a party-led revolution from above, was also regarded by the imperial power as a threat to the integrity of the "socialist commonwealth." The West's growing detachment and fatalism were revealed in its reaction to the invasion, which ranged from "a traffic accident on the road to detente" (Michel Debre) to the short-lived profession of outrage by a Johnson administration intent on moving ahead with SALT and other avenues of detente. Gradual change in Eastern Europe remained an important objective, but none of the West's chancelleries could devise a contingency plan for deterring the Soviet Union from intervening in its sphere of dominance.

The concept of "European security," like the slogan of "peace," had been appropriated by Soviet diplomacy in the postwar period, and in 1969 the Warsaw Pact revived its periodic campaign for a European security conference. The Soviet Union's objectives remained a symbolic legitimization of the division of Europe, a weakening of the Western alliance and particularly of the American connection, and the acquisition of technological and economic benefits from the West.[8] The initiative was welcomed by Willy Brandt's new government, which was disposed to pursue an active *Ostpolitik* less encumbered by talk of reunification. The West Europeans' greater enthusiasm for detente was accommodated by Kissinger's strategy of linkages to other Western desiderata, notably normalization of the status of Berlin and talks on the reduction of conventional military forces.

Over the next three years a flurry of negotiations broke the log-jam. West Germany concluded treaties with the Soviet Union (August 20, 1970) and Poland (December 7, 1970) that amounted to non-aggression pacts and acceptance of the territorial status quo. On December 21, 1971 the two Germanys signed the Basic Treaty, which provided for diplomatic relations and easier human contacts; Bonn's constitutional attachment to the "one German nation" concept required that relations be kept below the ambassadorial level. West Berlin's links to the West were reaffirmed in the four-power agreement of December 3, 1971. The SALT I treaty was another notable display of detente, and Washington was keen to win the Kremlin's help in winding down the Vietnam war and its assent to talks of mutual and balanced force reductions. The European security conference was therefore used as a bargaining counter in the Kissingerian linkage strategy; as Helmut Sonnenfeldt recalls, "we sold it for the German-Soviet treaty, we sold it for the Berlin Agreement, and we sold it again for MBFR."[9] It was therefore with a mixed bag of approaches and expectations that the Western powers entered into the Conference on Security and Cooperation in Europe, which was convened in July 1973. The settlement of the German problem opened the way for new diplomatic explorations, but few anticipated that the CSCE would turn into a permanent fixture of East-West relations and serve to unify and reinvigorate Western approaches to Eastern Europe.

The basic continuity in the American approach to the problem was maintained by the Nixon, Ford, Carter, and Reagan administrations. The encouragement of domestic liberalization and foreign policy autonomy in Eastern Europe by the selective normalization of political and commercial relations came to be known as the policy of differentiation, and it found official formulation in 1973 in a National Security Council Decision Memorandum.[10] The diplomacy of the commitment to promote gradual change subsumed disavowal of any threat to legitimate Soviet security interests. Differentiation therefore required a delicate reconciliation of American popular abhorrence (shared also by the majority of East Europeans) of any hint that Soviet hegemony in Eastern Europe was officially condoned, of the sensibilities of the East European regimes trying to balance their needs for Soviet approval and Western trade, and the Soviets' chronic fear of disintegrative tendencies in their empire. Illustrative of the risks was the mythical "Sonnenfeldt Doctrine" which allegedly conceded Eastern Europe to Soviet dominance. Sonnenfeldt, in fact, had simply noted in a briefing of American diplomats in December 1975 that the differentiated promotion of national autonomy had to take into account the "context of a strong Soviet geopolitical influence." Two columnists drew more alarming conclusions, and the damage was done.[11] It was a salutary reminder to American leaders that terms like "sphere of influence," "sphere of dominance," and "organic relationship" (employed by Sonnenfeldt) were politically too provocative to be applied to the reality of Soviet power in Eastern Europe.

Presidential visits to Romania, Yugoslavia, and Poland highlighted the Nixon administration's conduct of differentiation, and Carter's National Security Adviser, Zbigniew Brzezinski, pursued the logic of his earlier analyses in urging Western efforts to draw the two halves of Europe closer together. The Carter administration's emphasis on human rights helped to focus Western approaches in the CSCE process, and it was ideologically redefined by the White House under Reagan. The latter was more outspoken than some of his predecessors in evoking the old Yalta myth and rejecting any notion of permanent spheres of influence, but the operational policy remained that of differentiation. There was reportedly some debate in the administration on the desirability of raising the ante for American favors, of making the latter dependent on both (rather than either) domestic reform and voluntaristic foreign policy, but the established pattern was not altered.[12] The symbolic accolade of high-level visits was granted with some frequency to the relatively more congenial East European regimes. These, apart from Nixon's, included visits by Ford to Poland, Romania, and Yugoslavia in 1975, by Carter to Poland in 1977 and by Secretary of State Vance to Hungary in 1978, and by Vice-President Bush to Yugoslavia, Romania, and Hungary in 1983.

The limited capacity of the United States to affect East European developments was once again displayed in the Solidarity crisis. Encouragement of the apparently reform-minded Gierek regime in the 1970s took the form of liberal

Western credits. The largesse was unconditional, but it was not effectively applied to the modernization of industry and did not spur the much overdue structural reform of the economy. Washington was caught unprepared by the rapid transformation of a local strike in Gdansk into a political mass movement that challenged the policies and ultimately the very legitimacy of the regime.[13] The Carter administration, in its last days, toyed with the idea of a well-coordinated international economic rescue package that would have been tied to conditions of economic reform and a legitimization of Solidarity's status within some new social contract with the regime. The scheme was fraught with uncertainty as to its organization and acceptability in Warsaw and Moscow.

The incoming Reagan administration grappled with the Polish dilemma, some advisers arguing against any aid that would lighten the costs of empire for the Soviet Union. The principal American objective became to delay and mitigate a Soviet intervention that was considered inevitable. Indeed, the Soviet Union came close to military intervention as early as December 1980 and again the following spring, and in the meantime plans for the alternative of martial law were already being drawn up. On both occasions, strong warnings from Washington and its allies were instrumental (but perhaps not the decisive factors) in deterring Soviet action. The advocates of economic aid continued to press their case, but the possibility of a domestic political solution to the Polish crisis was probably negligible in light of what is now known about Soviet pressures and demands.

Washington apparently had some advance notice from a Polish military source about the imposition of martial law in December 1981, but the allies had no contingency plan for responding to this eventuality. The United States retaliated with economic sanctions that eventually included suspension of most-favored-nation tariff status and tried to punish the Soviet Union for its decisive role. In the latter case, the sanctions backfired, for the European allies failed to go along with American attempts to scuttle Western participation in the Urengoi gas pipeline project. The result was a display of allied disunity only partially redeemed by the Western boycott of the Moscow Olympics. In the case of Poland, the consolidation of the Jaruzelski regime, its amnesties and relative tolerance of unofficial pluralism eventually led Washington to abandon punitive measures. In 1986 the United States allowed Poland to join the IMF and the World Bank. The following year, the Senate approved an "American Aid to Poland Act" sponsored by Senator Kennedy after a visit to Poland. The Act anticipated normalization of relations and mandated modest funding for a variety of privately-administered projects, including aid for Polish independent farmers via the Roman Catholic Church. George Bush's visit to Poland in 1987 included a well-publicized interview with Lech Walesa. It was a gesture that served not only electoral interests back home but also as a demonstration of American ambivalence regarding the legitimacy of the Jaruzelski regime.

The policy of differentiation, predicated on the manageability of evolutionary change, offered no prescription for American or Western response to a political crisis in Eastern Europe. Avoidance of such a crisis depended almost entirely on the ability of domestic forces to forge a compromise acceptable to the Soviet Union. The popular appeal and thrust of the Solidarity movement would have ruled out Soviet acquiescence even if the Polish ruling party had agreed to share its power. In such circumstances the West could do no more than offer aid and cautionary advice. The dismal conclusion is that neither a "Marshall Plan for Poland" nor tougher language could have altered the outcome. The appropriateness of the subsequent American sanctions can be debated, but at least initially many Poles welcomed the diplomatic isolation of a regime that had brutally dispelled their dream of self-determination.

Even in the absence of political crisis, American policy toward Eastern Europe has suffered from lack of leverage. Credits and trade did grow substantially in the 1970s, but the U.S. share of Western trade with Eastern Europe (which of course conducts most of its trade within Comecon) reached only 9 percent of exports and 5.9 percent of imports. The shares were somewhat greater for Poland and Romania, two countries that enjoyed MFN tariff status along with Hungary. The Jackson-Vanik and Stevenson amendments add further impediment to U.S. trade with the East by making MFN and credit guarantees dependent on liberal emigration policies. The best illustrative case is that of Romania, whose independent posture in foreign policy in the 1960s was rewarded with MFN. Fear of American displeasure did impel the Ceausescu regime to marginally relax restrictions on emigration, but its appallingly bad record on human rights drove the 1987 Congress to demand withdrawal of MFN. The Reagan administration had been defending Romania's MFN status in the spirit of differentiation with the argument that positive performance in either foreign or domestic policy was sufficient to win U.S. favor, but preferential tariff status for the most Stalinist dictatorship in Eastern Europe has become politically unpalatable.

While all the East European states seek access to American markets and technology, the fact is that most of their need for Western credits and goods has been met by the West Europeans. The latter are only marginally constrained by the restriction on high-tech exports administered by the allied agency Cocom and have no political inhibitions in expanding their commercial contacts with the East. For the United States, there are more symbolic instruments for the pursuit of its interests in Eastern Europe. Some of these are declaratory and serve domestic political purposes as well, notably the traditional annual proclamation of Captive Nations Week and the recent Congressional designation of Helsinki Human Rights Day and of days commemorating the independence of the Baltic states. On such occasions, American presidents do not shrink from branding the East European governments "Soviet-dominated." There remains a strong and perhaps unique strain of idealism in American foreign policy, and if its emanations occasionally seem to contradict the prescriptions of Realpolitik, it has inspired and reinforced the contemporary international concern for human rights.

America's political engagement in Eastern Europe is most striking in the field of communication, where the Voice of America and Radio Free Europe have been active ever since the onset of the Cold War. The former is the purveyor of American policies and culture, while the latter styles itself a "surrogate home service" for the East Europeans. RFE, which used to be financed by the CIA and is now funded by Congress through the intermediary of the Board for International Broadcasting, has an audience of over 30 million and provides essential competition for the state-controlled media. Once an agent of psychological warfare, RFE is now a professional source of news and commentary that fills a gap and is consistent with the Helsinki-endorsed principle of free access to information. None of the East European regimes subscribes fully in practice to this principle, and currently Poland, Czechoslovakia, and Bulgaria resort to jamming. Probably no other instrument of peaceful engagement is as cost-effective as broadcasting in nurturing the general awareness and Western orientation of the East European populations. Another American initiative is the National Endowment for Democracy, created by Congress in 1983 to fund organizations that aid democratic forces worldwide. With regard to Eastern Europe, funding from this source has aided labor support for Solidarity as well as some emigre intellectual endeavors.

Since the end of the 1960s West Germany has reemerged as the most active Central European power, expanding contacts with the East while retaining its key economic and military position in the Western alliance. Bonn and the "German Problem" for many years impeded progress on detente, but with the new *Ostpolitik* West Germany became the most committed promoter of detente and of peaceful engagement without differentiation. Its history and geopolitical position make such an orientation both perfectly natural and, for friend and foe alike, somewhat suspect. Fears of German neutralism in the West and of German economic and political influence in the East require a judiciously balanced application of *Ostpolitik,* ideally in the relaxed atmosphere of East-West detente. A stable relationship with Moscow and an undiscriminating political and economic rapprochement with the East European states sum up Bonn's approach. The strategy anticipates that the combination of a secure environment and progressively more intense economic and cultural interaction will induce Western-oriented liberalization in Eastern Europe. *Ostpolitik* is similar in spirit to peaceful engagement and bridge-building but benefits from West Germany's proximity, greater leverage, and willingness to forego public criticism of the East European regimes' political ways.

The focal point of Bonn's interest remains East Germany, and the latter has exacted a high price for its periodic concessions on such issues as intra-German travel. East German exports have duty-free access to West Germany (and therefore to the EEC), and the latter provides generous credit facilities (the "swing"). Bonn has also paid considerable sums in ransom for the release of thousands of political prisoners. Bilateral detente has its limits, and when in 1984 Bonn and East Berlin tried to ignore the cooling in superpower relations, a planned visit by Honecker was countermanded by Moscow. Three years later, with detente on the mend, Honecker finally made his historic visit to the state whose constitution denies his country's sovereign status.

Bonn's economic engagement with the East led to a rapid and profitable growth in trade that puts West Germany far ahead as Eastern Europe's principal Western trading partner and source of technology and credits. Although this engagement is driven in part by a long-term political objective, Bonn has been content to cultivate orderly relations and to pursue such minor linkages as the creation of West German cultural institutes in Eastern capitals. Instead of differentiation, Bonn opted for "synchronization," which eschews any notion of reward and punishment and tailors *Ostpolitik* to the requisites of Soviet tolerance and East European stability.[14] It is therefore not surprising that West Germany did not dramatize the Polish crisis and was no more willing than its EEC partners to follow Washington's lead in imposing economic sanctions on either Poland or the Soviet Union.

This *Ostpolitik* may have been consummate *Realpolitik*, but it set the West Germans apart from many of their allies, notably the Americans, the French, and the British, all of whom incline to a politically more active policy with regard to human rights and reform in Eastern Europe and are less inhibited about criticizing the Soviet Union's self-arrogated *droit de régard* over the region. By 1987 Bonn's *Ostpolitik* began to show greater activism and differentiation, for essentially political decisions were taken to aid the faltering Hungarian economic reform (and indirectly reinforce Gorbachev's *perestroika*) and to put pressure on the ever more oppressive Ceausescu regime.

The belated abandonment of Marxism by most West European socialists and intellectuals has gone hand in hand with a sharper perception of the fundamental incompatibility between democratic pluralism and human rights, and Soviet-style totalitarianism. This altered mood has informed the approaches of several Western allies to bilateral and multilateral contacts with Eastern Europe.

In France, the Gaullist tendency of pursuing a somewhat independent line on alliance commitments and detente has receded, partly because of changes in the domestic political mood and partly because it overestimated the possibility of greater national autonomy in Eastern Europe. While De Gaulle saw promise in Romania's foreign policy maneuvers, the Hungarian model of gradual liberalization aroused greater sympathy in the Mitterrand era. Trade with the Soviet Union has grown far more than with Eastern Europe, reinforcing the concentration on Moscow in France's Eastern policy. With regard to Eastern Europe, that policy is distinguished from *Ostpolitik* by its greater stress on human rights and cultural communication, by a pan-European vision that addresses the societies rather than the regimes in the East. This stress inspired France's approach to the CSCE process, where she played a leading role in the development of the Basket III concept.[15] But France, like the other European al-

lies, reacted fatalistically to the Polish crisis and President
Mitterrand was the first to break ranks by receiving General
Jaruzelski's visit in December 1985. Such mixed tendencies
take the place of coherent policy in France's approach to
Eastern Europe.

Britain's interest in the region is even more marginal than
that of France, although the Thatcher government has pursued diplomatic contacts with greater vigor than its predecessors. The British approach has been more differentiated (and
somewhat more favorable to sanctions against Poland) than
that of the other Europeans, but London, like Paris, lacks the
incentive to develop a distinct East European policy. On the
whole, the Europeans are disposed to promote their commercial interests in the East with state guarantees and without the
political conditions that obtain in Washington. At least in the
Catholic parts of Eastern Europe, the political influence of a
Polish pope (manifested most vividly in his visits to Poland)
is more tangible than that of the Western powers.

The Western powers originally approached the European
security conference with some diffidence, anticipating that its
principal purpose and outcome would be a Soviet propaganda coup enshrining the status quo and weakening the
alliance's perception of threat. Instead, the CSCE turned into
a permanent fixture on the international diplomatic agenda,
and one that has on balance worked to the advantage of
Western interests. The Helsinki process has helped the West
to coordinate its policies and the East European regimes to
test the limits of their autonomy in foreign affairs. It institutionalized a multilateral dialogue in which the smaller powers,
East and West, could not only make themselves heard but also
help to redefine the conditions and objectives of European
security.

That the Helsinki Final Act legitimized the territorial
status quo proved to be of little consequence, for it left open
the possibility of peaceful change, and the German treaties
had already settled the more controversial issues. Nor did this
principle materially alter the legalistic rationale and political
reality of Soviet dominance over Eastern Europe. Basket II,

encompassing economic and scientific cooperation, enjoyed high priority for the Soviet Union, but reviews of its implementation have been low-keyed and not particularly productive.

The Final Act and the ensuing review process did, however, facilitate progress in the areas of military security (Basket I) and humanitarian issues (Basket III). Confidence-building measures, expanded at the Stockholm conference in 1986, served to reduce the possibility of surprise attack. Articles 15 and 16 of the Stockholm Agreement commit the signatories to refrain from the threat or use of force against any state, allied or not. One would like to think that this nominal abrogation of the Brezhnev Doctrine could serve as a marginal deterrent to Soviet intervention in an East European crisis. The current Vienna review conference may yet produce agreement on new negotiations, with more participants than at the dilatory MBFR talks, aiming at the reduction of conventional forces from the Atlantic to the Urals. Allowing for the risks to Western solidarity and the technical complexities of balance and verification, this process could nevertheless enhance the East European regimes' sense of autonomy and need for domestic legitimacy by reducing the Soviet military presence.

It is in the area of human rights that the CSCE process has been of greatest service, by inspiring the West to develop a comprehensive strategy and dissenters in the East to exploit international concern. The Final Act's Principle VII (which proclaims human rights including the freedom of thought, conscience, religion, and belief) and Basket III (calling for unimpeded human contact and flow of information and for cooperation in culture and education) struck at the heart of the Soviet system, and the Western powers, led by the United States, lost no opportunity to draw attention to flagrant violations in the East. Each follow-up meeting has turned into a public embarrassment for the Soviet Union and, to a lesser extent, for the more repressive East European regimes such as Romania and Czechoslovakia.

The tangible results of the West's human rights offensive in the CSCE process have been mainly psychological, with only modest progress being made in inducing liberalization in the East. The Prague regime has not been deterred from persecuting the Charter 77 dissenters, nor the Romanian and the Bulgarian authorities from discriminating against their Hungarian and Turkish minorities. Yet the cause of human rights has galvanized not only Western governments but also countless individuals and private groups on both sides of the great divide, and the impact of derivative events such as the Budapest Cultural Forum is far from negligible. Such consciousness-raising can exert a salutary influence on communist regimes seeking domestic support. Significantly, even this ideologically controversial process can generate East-West cooperation, as illustrated by a proposal in Vienna on the rights of national minorities which was co-sponsored by Canada and Hungary.

Western participants at Vienna have been pressing for progress on freedom to travel and emigrate, family reunification, the liberation of political prisoners, the abandonment of radio jamming, freedom of religion, and the right of workers to form free trade unions. They have taken the process a step further by proposing a permanent mechanism for monitoring the implementation of human rights agreements. Such pressures test the limits of *glasnost'*, as will the West's handling of the Soviet proposal to host a special meeting on human rights in Moscow.

The engagement of Eastern Europe proceeds in other multilateral settings. Although the European Community and Comecon (the Council for Mutual Economic Assistance, by its official title) are far from symmetrical in structure, negotiations are under way to establish relations between them. Such an accord would not in itself alter the division of Europe, but it could symbolically reinforce the pan-European idea and possibly facilitate a greater degree of economic interaction.[16] The American policy of differentiation governs the admission of East European countries to such international economic institutions as the General Agreement on Tariffs and Trade, the International Monetary Fund, and the World Bank. Membership in the IMF and the World Bank, currently enjoyed by Hungary, Poland, and Romania (as well as Yugoslavia), should theoretically induce market-oriented reforms in economic structure and trade and exchange practices. The premise of peaceful engagement, shared to varying degrees by the Western powers, is that a growing web of interdependence will promote liberalization and a loosening of imperial bonds and obligations in Eastern Europe. The evolving circumstances and diversity of that region offer neither proof nor refutation of this intrinsically logical proposition or of its differentiation variant. Evolutionary approaches are never easy to appraise, and in the case of Eastern Europe their impact is ultimately governed by the attitude of the imperial power.

The ultimate Western objective, shared by most East Europeans, remains valid and imperative: a liberal democratic Eastern Europe integrated into a secure European community of nations. It is also axiomatic that such an outcome must be compatible with Russia's legitimate security interests. Most of the West's hypothetical options for dealing with the problem are demonstrably unrealistic. The will and the means are lacking for an aggressive "rollback" approach, and it would in any case carry impossible risks for all concerned. Tactics of active destabilization would be based on the false premise that serious crises in the East enhance Western security; instead, they tend to inhibit reform and justify conservative retrenchment. Punitive, positive sanctions such as trade embargoes and boycotts do not generally produce the desired results in the target country even if they have a cathartic function back home. Finally, the option of benign neglect is not consistent with the West's sense of moral and humanitarian obligation or with its security interests.

There remains the broad evolutionary approach that the West has been pursuing for many years, an approach designed to foster domestic transformation and the loosening of the imperial grip in Eastern Europe. This is the strategy that should be invigorated and coordinated by the Western powers in response to the Gorbachev revolution. Coordination is essential, and not only in crises, although given the diversity of bilateral links and interests it can only take the form of what has been called "flexible harmonization."[17] But the major Western allies must pursue a clear and common purpose if their Eastern approaches are to bear fruit.

In the security sphere, full advantage should be taken of Soviet willingness to reduce conventional military forces as an opportunity to weaken the Warsaw Pact's capability for domestic intimidation and police action. While neither such reductions nor additional international agreements and security guarantees can exclude the possibility of Soviet intervention, a more secure climate for autonomous reform experiments could be nurtured without significant risk to the Western half of the continent.

There are, of course, no simple equations for balancing the multiple interests of East and West in European security and disarmament. Even if the primary goal of both sides can be taken as the preservation of a credible deterrent, there remain asymmetries with regard to Eastern Europe, where the Soviet Union will never surrender its predominant interest. The Soviet objective of denuclearizing Central Europe was partially achieved in the INF treaty, which includes the removal of a few missile sites from East Germany and Czechoslovakia. Both alliances appear intent on negotiating the further elimination of battlefield nuclear weapons. But from the perspective of Soviet security, the strategic utility and necessity of the buffer zone offered by the East European landmass is only increased by denuclearization. The crucial question, then, is whether the Soviet Union is prepared to negotiate substantial reduction in the conventional military capability of the Warsaw Pact.

Given the Warsaw Pact's conventional superiority in Europe, notably in tanks and artillery, any negotiated reduction acceptable to the West would have to be asymmetrical. The Kremlin's new official line is that "the Warsaw Pact member states are prepared to adhere to the ceilings of sufficiency necessary for defense and to resolve the problem of asymmetries and imbalances on individual types of weapons through reducing the potential of the one who appears to be ahead."[18] Such concessions of principle should facilitate the launching of a new series of talks on conventional force reductions. The West, in the interest of its own security, will have to aim at equal levels of military manpower and weapons groups, such as tanks, and at stringent verification procedures.

The foreseeably long and arduous negotiations will stand a better chance of success if both sides address the East European factor. For the West, this means acknowledging the Soviet Union's special security interest in the region and offering guarantees that this interest will not be challenged. It will also have to reconsider the balance of American and allied conventional forces in Europe, in other words, the Europeanization of NATO's conventional defense. The Soviet Union, in turn, would have to concede the substantial reduction if not elimination of its military presence in Eastern Europe and the reformulation of its political *droît de régard* in the region by a categorical renunciation of the Brezhnev doctrine. Ultimately, as Walt Rostow observed, "the U.S.S.R. would have to decide to accept a balance of power rather than a hegemonic solution to its legitimate security interest in Eastern Europe; that is, a solution guaranteeing that no other major power dominates Eastern Europe, rather than Soviet domination of the region."[19] The chances of such an outcome are incalculable, but then five years ago the Gorbachev revolution was inconceivable.

If Eastern Europe's political emancipation from imperial rule will be a slow process only marginally susceptible to Western influence, its economic modernization faces almost equally formidable obstacles. The Soviet economic model is a historic failure, and none of the East European variants and marginal market-oriented reforms have prevented the relative decline of the region's economies. Foreign debt is rising again, productivity is stagnating, the technological gap is growing, and competitiveness in world markets is falling. The OECD reports that almost half of the export products of the six

Eastern European countries that were competitive on world markets in 1980 were no longer competitive in 1985. (Singapore exports 20 percent more machinery to the West than all of Eastern Europe.)[20] The common response of the regimes is to impose austerity measures and reduce capital and other imports. Most economists even in the East now acknowledge that only a determined shift to the market economy can halt the region's decline, but such a shift carries significant ideological cost and political risks for the ruling parties.

The West derives neither political nor economic advantage from the region's drift into third-world penury, and it does not possess the leverage to effect radical improvement. The experience of the 1970s showed that liberal foreign credits disappear unproductively in the bottomless pit of socialist mismanagement. State-guaranteed loans and trade preferences therefore should be linked to the degree of structural reform and marketization that the individual East European regime is prepared to implement. Western trade and diplomatic concessions should still be differentiated on the basis of domestic liberalization, but less so in regard to superficial variations in foreign policy. In general, financial and commercial relations are best conducted according to sound business principles and IMF and GATT standards if the East European economies are to be effectively integrated into the world market. For the unfortunate victims of socialist economics, such a painful adjustment is the only alternative to stagnation.

The West should also test the limits of *glasnost'* and other tendencies toward liberalization by increasing the pressure, in the CSCE and other venues, on behalf of human rights, free communications (including an end to all broadcast jamming), and other Helsinki principles as well as for civil rights and institutionalized pluralism in Eastern Europe. The people of that region are spiritually part of the West and its natural allies. The prospects for desirable evolutionary change are better than ever, making a concerted Western strategy towards Eastern Europe well worth the effort.

NOTES

1. Mikhail Gorbachev, *Perestroika: New Thinking for Our Country and the World* (New York:Harper & Row, 1987), p. 165.
2. Reuter, December 4, 1987.
3. Gorbachev, *op. cit.*, p. 204.
4. *Christian Science Monitor,* July 16, 1987, and *Pravda*, July 10, 1987.
5. Quoted by William Pfaff in the *International Herald Tribune*, July 2, 1987.
6. *Washington Post,* June 7, 1987.
7. See Josef Joffe, "The View From Bonn," in Lincoln Gordon et al., *Eroding Empire: Western Relations with Eastern Europe* (Washington: Brookings Institution, 1987), pp. 138-45.
8. See Bennett Kovrig, " 'European Security' in East-West Relations: The History of a Diplomatic Encounter," in Robert Spencer, ed., *Canada and the Conference on Security and Co-operation in Europe* (Toronto: Center for International Studies, 1984).
9. *Time*, August 4, 1975, p. 22.
10. Raymond Garthoff, *Détente and Confrontation: American-Soviet Relations from Nixon to Reagan* (Washington: Brookings Institution, 1985), p. 322.
11. See the Evans-Novak column, *Washington Post* March 22, 1976, and the official summary, *New York Times* April 6, 1976, cited in Gordon, *op. cit.*, pp. 80-81.
12. See Garthoff, *op. cit.*, p. 338.
13. See the excellent summary of U.S. responses to the Polish crisis in Gordon, *op. cit.*, pp. 118-27.
14. See Joffe, *loc. cit.*, pp. 161-64.
15. Pierre Hassner, "The View from Paris," in Gordon, *op. cit.,* p. 198.
16. Robert M. Cutler, "Harmonizing EEC-CMEA Relations: Never the Twain Shall Meet?" *International Affairs*, Vol. 63, No. 2 (Spring 1987), pp. 268-70.

17. Gordon, *op. cit.*,p. 322.
18. *Pravda*, December 19, 1987.
19. W. W. Rostow, "On Ending the Cold War," *Foreign Affairs*, Vol. 65, No. 4 (Spring 1987), p. 848. The case has been made most cogently and consistently over the years by Brzezinski, and it was recently echoed by the former U.S. ambassador to Prague, William H. Luers, "The U.S. and Eastern Europe," *Foreign Affairs*, Vol. 65, No. 5 (Summer 1987), p. 991. The Western view of the problems with conventional force reductions is outlined by David S. Yost, "Beyond MBFR: The Atlantic to the Urals Gambit," *Orbis*, Vol. 31, No. 1 (Spring 1987), pp. 99-134.
20. *New York Times*, December 20, 1987.

WAITING FOR GODOT

EASTERN EUROPE BETWEEN STAGNATION AND REFORM

Ivan Volgyes

O n the eighth day of December, 1987, amid pomp and circumstance, glitter and sparkle, Mikhail Sergeevich Gorbachev, the General Secretary of the Communist Party of the Soviet Union, came calling upon the President of the United States. Bearing the gift of an agreement to remove intermediate range nuclear weapons from Soviet arsenals, the well-dressed and stylish General Secretary also brought with him several things that attracted the attention of the media. In order of significance these were: a ZIL limousine whose weight was estimated as greater than that of the President's Cadillac, a wardrobe the value of which was estimated as considerably less than that of the President's, and a wife whose weight—for the first time in the history of the Soviet state—was significantly less than that of the General Secretary himself.

Unobserved in the process of negotiating—about both truly significant and weighty matters regarding nuclear survival and insignificant trivia not worthy of observance—was the impact that the lessening of tension between the USSR and the United States had upon the troubled region we call Eastern Europe[1] For the fact remained that in an era of lessening tension between the superpowers, new opportunities appeared to open up for the communist states of the region to fashion a future acceptable, on the one hand, to the dominant communist superpower—the USSR—and on the other hand would offer far greater benefits to the citizens of these states. Unhampered by communist cold war rhetoric, a window of reform was opened for Eastern Europe.[2]

That the states of Eastern Europe needed breathing space has been clear to the more thoughtful observers of the region for quite some time. Impacted by economic, social, and political malaise, uncertain of direction or goal, these states exist today between two worlds. On the one hand, they still live in the "traditional world" we have been accustomed to calling "the communist system." On the other hand, being fully aware of the "modern world" at their Western doorstep, they also appear to have wanted to take advantage of the technological-commercial wonder that has so dramatically transformed the non-communist states of Europe, the United States, Canada, and much of non-communist Asia during the last decade.

This chapter attempts to describe the tension and stress facing Eastern Europe as it grapples with the questions: "Where do we go from here?" and "How do we get there?" In Part I we will describe the malaise of the "traditional" communist world. In Part II we will outline a possible "modern" world that can emerge from potential reforms. In Part III we will discuss the limits of change in Eastern Europe, and in the concluding Part IV we will project the dangers these societies will face as—or if—they attempt to modernize their systems, methods, and goals of operation.

THE MALAISE EXAMINED

As has been noted *ad nauseum* lately, the East European states, with the possible exception of the German Democratic

Republic, exhibit signs of grave illnesses. Like a badly bruised and mangled patient on the examination table, they appear, both to us and to their own leaders, to be in need of a cure. The questions they are asking are familiar to members of the "medical diagnostic community." They are simply: 1) "What is wrong with me, doctor?", 2) "What causes the disease?", 3) "How can the disease be cured?", and 4) "Can you cure it?"

The greatest complication to answering these questions lies in the fact that the patients posing the queries are of entirely different characters. On the sickbeds of Eastern Europe one finds a wide range of patients. They range from the most centralized, dictatorial and terror-based regime, Romania, all the way to the most decentralized, semi-market oriented, and relatively liberal regime, Hungary. Thus, the observer of the human condition in these states often tends to offer nation- or development-specific advice, which, of course, provides no diagnosis of the systematic malaise. And yet, it should be noted that we are dealing with a disease that is system-specific: while the extent of the illness and the extent of its impact differs from state to state, all of these countries are affected.

Parenthetically, we should note that the malaise observed is not only system specified, for the disease also affects around 140 of the world's nearly 170 states. And we are not sure that cures have actually been found even for the twenty or so states that are recuperating at the time of this writing. In fact, the malaise impacts highly negatively upon all quasi-developed states; brought on by the general crisis of the world economy, these states have been forced to face their own adaptation crisis as well. What is unique, however, for the so-called socialist states is that the adaptation ability of these systems is severely hampered both by the fact that systemic strictures cannot be altered, and by the fact of the artifical constraints imposed on their freedom of action by the dominant super-power of the region, the USSR.

It is relatively easy to define the symptoms of the malaise. Economically, all of these states are characterized by centralized economic mechanisms for large scale production and general distribution. These economies exhibit several attributes of "communist" economic practices, among which the most notable are (1) outmoded, centrally planned production practices; (2) constant scarcities; (3) artificiality of prices and wages; (4) internalism; and (5) backward technologies. Central planning and constant scarcities are especially limiting factors for any attempt at modernization, but the other elements also greatly inhibit change. While it would be relatively easy to write several papers on each of these characteristics, let us, briefly summarize these attributes of centrally planned, or "communist" East European economies.

Production practices in Eastern Europe are still concentrated on extensive, rather than intensive development, e.g., the growth of the economy through the utilization of additional raw material, manpower, or productive units. At a time when manpower was widely available, its continual addition to productive industries provided measurable growth. As labor resources became exhausted, increases in growth could no longer occur from the mere addition of labor units. Simultaneously, as these societies developed, the percentage of people employed in industrial production began to near the plateau of efficiency; by the late 1970s these two developments resulted in seemingly incurable stagnation.

Moreover, each and every one of these economies and policies were based upon the ever-present scarcity, both in production and distribution. If one had to describe communist systems, the best single description would be that these societies, by their nature, are involved in the continuous re-creation of scarcity.[3] The fact that this is endemic to the system cannot be denied; the result is a totally irrational demand within the productive and distributive forces that twists the whole question of value out of proportion to reality.

These problems are, in large measure, due to the fact that the socialist system was based ideologically on the premise that central planning will "rationalize" and, thus, replace the "imperfect" market. The fact that this has not and could not take place was also complicated by a consequent complete artificiality of the wage and price scales. Due to the original

egalitarian purpose of the wage-scale, and to the socio-politi-
cal-economic goal-orientations of the productive sources,
even today the best informed planner is at a loss for the real
costs of anything. Even the black-market, or secondary
economy in these states is distorted by this artificiality!
Moreover, the extent of subsidization of various products, industries, or economic activities today makes it impossible
even for the economic planners to know how much economically efficient subsidy should be given to any participant unit
in the national economy.

The concept of internalism, the orientation toward an internal market has been the inevitable result of early autarchy
and of the faulty integration mechanisms that have been
enshrined within the COMECON. Such internalism,
however, has rendered these economies totally immune to the
technological development that has taken place in the
Western economies during the last two decades. Consequently, markets for Eastern European products—mostly substandard in performance, bulk, appearance, packaging, sales,
after-sales service, etc. to similar Western products—in states
that are capable of paying hard-currency for their importation
cannot readily be found.

The backward technologies of these states are partially the
results of these forces, but are also partially caused by the
isolation of the "autarchic" communist economies from the
West, and the subsequent exclusion of the communist
economies by the West. These economies—with the possible
exception of that of the GDR, primarily by virtue of its participation in the intra-German market—have missed the com-
puter-chip revolution. Thus, today they cannot innovate.
They can only produce below the levels of formerly "underdeveloped" states of Taiwan, Singapore, or South Korea, to
name a few countries.

The economic illnesses of these states is coupled with a
malaise in these societies. Unparalleled growth in alcoholism,
suicide, heart-attacks, and divorce-rates during the last 10-15
years exists everywhere in Eastern Europe. The rate of growth
for such indicators of social illnesses are not only striking in

comparison with similar indices in Western societies, but even in comparison with similar rates from earlier times in the life of these states! The appalling housing shortages, the ever-shrinking availability of medical services at acceptable levels, the dreariness and the struggling, war-like attitudes coupled with the hopelessness of everyday life, of course, are contributors to these ills, but *their very existence* appears to be a "natural" characteristic of these societies.

Finally, these polities are divided far more clearly than any other political system of modern states between the ruler and ruled. The rulers, an ever narrower group of communist party/state elites, are separated from the people by a chasm that, at the present time, cannot be bridged. The holders of power are clearly rulers, but the people are simply the ruled, and not citizens. Their efficacy, if any, is minimal at best; where the regimes give them some choices, as in the case of the referenda in Poland in 1987, their answer to any proposition is a nihilistic "no!" It is the party that lead us into this mess, they seem to say, let them get us out of it. But, they also add: *ohne mich*!

While the symptoms, can be defined relatively easily, it should be repeated, that they exhibit an astounding degree of divergence in the region. It is clear, however, that to a frighteningly great extent, in all these societies, all of the above symptoms can be easily recognized. The question that must now be asked, however, is the cause of these symptoms, the cause of the disease—even if the name has yet to be attached to it.

Simply put, the cause of these diseases is the existence of the communist system. While one could make apologies, none of the apologies serve as meaningful causal explanations. Thus, to blame the present disease on the "traditional backwardness of the region" does not explain the contemporary existence of these ills in light of the interwar economic, social, or political health of Czechoslovakia, or explain the far more positive developments that have taken place in such diverse parts of the world as Spain, Finland, or for instance, Singapore. And, to blame the present disease on "the underdeveloped socio-educational level of the citizenry" makes little sense when we compare the growth of political efficacy in relatively brief periods of time, in South Korea, or Spain. No, the causative sources of these ills, is the existence of the communist system.

The Stalinist emphasis on central planning and the primacy of heavy industrial production simply cannot be bent enough to fulfill the dynamically changing demands of a modern economic system when the Marxist negation of the necessity of the market is de-legitimizing this most important attribute of modern economy. The Leninist emphasis on an ideologically equitable pay-scale clearly abolished individual and firm incentives. The Stalinist autarchy separated these states and their economies from the rest of the rapidly developing world. The social benefits given to everyone kept such benefits at artificially high levels that were not warranted by adequate productivity improvements while internally creating an attitude among the citizenry that can only be characterized as *bellum omnium contra omnis*. Under such circumstances, the stress and the internecine daily warfare over scarce commodities were bound to create the results we are witnessing. And finally, the Leninist concept of the "vanguard," and the Stalinist concept of the exclusive, "leading role of the party," socialized people to not regard the party positively, nor feel themselves citizens in their states. I would like to reiterate that these developments were not forced upon the communist states by the West; they came from the Soviet Union, and from the ruling, communist elites in these states.

Can these diseases, these ills, this systemic malaise be cured? There can be no doubt that some of the ills can, indeed, temporarily be cured. Thus, for example, the Hungarian reform that has been in existence since 1968 has provided a partical cure for some of the ills. It created a second economy and a second society, allowed the restrictions caused by central planning to be minimized, fiddled with the market, reduced consumer subsidies, and even permitted a bit more freedom and liberalization than customarily existed everywhere else in the region. And yet, it is in Hungary that we observe the culmination of these ills most clearly; even the newly introduced personal and added-value tax system is expected to provide a satisfactory cure for the malaise. But, personally, I would be surprised if even the most highly visible negative symptoms of the disease were severely reduced in that unfortunate land.

A cure of sorts clearly does exist for these ills; it is the removal of those restrictions that have hitherto characterized the systems and hindered the development of these systems in the first place. I am not suggesting the abolition of the communist system as a whole, for such is not a viable option under the present circumstances of world affairs. These states are clearly a part of the last empire in history, and they are likely to be political parts of the Soviet alliance system. But within these confines, one can expect to witness the emergence of a "new, more modern" communist world in Europe. While this world is yet to be born, a few outlines of its nature are slowly becoming visible.

THE NOT-SO-BRAVE NEW WORLD OF COMMUNIST EASTERN EUROPE

The new world—if it is, indeed, in the process of being born, and if it is to be viable in the modern era—will be a variety of "reform-communism." The term "reform," however, is used in contrast to "centrally planned," or "traditional/totalitarian" and does not connote a specific variety of "liberal reform." Thus, it is not used to allude to former models such as the 1956 October Revolution in Hungary, or the 1968 Prague Spring, or the liberalization in Poland in 1980-1981. Moreover, the "reformed-communism" that may emerge from these new processes will be differently "reformed" in each state, and within each state the extent of reforms will be differently manifest in the economic, political, and social spheres.

In the economic sphere today, Hungary remains the most liberal, followed by Poland—still uncertain about the direction of desired change, not to mention speed—and Bulgaria. The other states follow strict centralization, and there is only a hint of reform in the air. While Hungary is the most liberal, and Romania is the most "unreformed," their economies have the greatest problems. To be sure, these problems are different, and they pertain in different ways to the near modern economy of Hungary, and the still "backward" economy of Romania. But they are nevertheless common problems in that they stem from the inability of a ruling party to give up an idea bypassed by history!

The concept of the "socialist economy"—the concept that hinders advanced development—has six basic characteristics. They are: the principle of central planning; the exclusivity of socialist ownership; the importance of heavy industrial production; the central balance of wages and prices; the "autarchic" development pattern; and the integration of these economies with the USSR and with those of the other socialist states. While, naturally, other elements of the economy can also be emphasized, these six elements, in my interpretation, must be changed if a "reform-model" is to exist.

The principle of central planning has long been a key part of communist economic systems; prices, wages, the standard of living, and the production and distribution of goods and services are centrally planned without regards to market considerations. While theoretically it is supposed to be "rational," the truth is that central planning—which may be useful in the "take-off stage"—is generally useless for modern economies where production units must meet the demands of the market with great rapidity, exporting and importing according to swiftly changing production technologies. Planning these activities simply does not work. If these economies are to enter the modern era, central planning authority and practice must be severely reduced, greater opportunities must be given to local enterprises, and inefficiencies resulting from central planning must be eliminated.

The concept of exclusivity of socialist/state property, with its exclusive legal priorities and prerogatives, also must be altered. While the original ideological strictures regarding the evils of private productive property emanated from its well-documented abuses, noted by Marx and company, state/socialist property proved no less exploitative, but far less efficient. Supported by huge subsidies, producing inefficiently unproductive and overpriced merchandise, these units have no real "responsibility" for the manner in which they allocate their practices. They maintain their ideologically "higher" position *vis-à-vis* private property, and thereby discriminate against even the beneficial uses of such wealth. As a consequence, even in states where huge personal surpluses of private funds exist—generally true of scarcity plagued communist systems—they cannot be invested into ventures where "private property" is involved. For these systems to operate successfully, therefore, a primary requirement is the theoretical and practical diminution of the rights of socialist/state property, and a consequent recognition of rights extended to activities involving private property.

A reformed and successful communist economic system must take into account that the emphasis on heavy industrial production, so characteristic of extensive capitalist growth, and its belated statist (e.g. "Stalinist") alternative, especially as it was introduced in Eastern Europe as an imitation of the Soviet model—no longer suffices in a modern age, where tertiary sector, or light/consumer industry with its attendant, constant technological improvements, provide the spurs to intensive growth. Thus, obsolete factories that produce steel and more steel when demands for steel peaked long ago, cannot and should not be supported. The change to this production technology, however painful, must occur, as it has in the GDR. It must result—negatively—in the elimination of major subsidies to unproductive industries with long lines of non-competitive goods, and—positively—in reallocating the attendant surplus funds to tertiary sector and technology-intensive industrial production activities. But it will also create huge dysfunctions, such as unemployment, greater housing shortages, and a regional and sectoral "restructuring" of the manpower that will cause still further social problems. Nonetheless, without such a reform of the productive sector, no economic reform could succeed.

Also, the "market" will have to be reintroduced and accepted as a "normal part" of the system, with all its ramifications, especially the abolition of central control over wages and prices. It will not be a "pure" market, of course, for such things exist only in the fertile minds of "pure-economists." But, it will be a market where, by and large, prices and wages will be determined by the dynamic interplay of supply and demand, a market, in short, that will incorporate the productive elements of both state and secondary economies ("black-markets") of these countries. What will be different, however, from what exists today, for instance in Hungary, is that the state will no longer exploit the workers by paying artificially low wages—and, in turn, the workers cannot exploit the state by withholding their "normal" labor productivity. This too will require a transformation of mentality by both the elites and the subjects of the economy. However, without this transformation, I cannot imagine a modern economy coming into existence.

In addition, the prevailing "autarchic" economic development patterns—introduced in the 1950s, largely as a dual result of Soviet pressures and the Western embargo against "communist goods"—must end. In an age of global interdependence, relying on "oneself" for development, on a single system for research and advances, will not suffice, even if the existing system has largely resulted from the dysfunctions of the Soviet-dominated Council for Mutual Economic Assistance (COMECON). The member economies are small in size, too small, in fact, to produce breakthroughs in any but the smallest areas. Therefore, to rely on themselves, or on their COMECON partners, for advanced technological development is nonsense. A modern economy must be fully integrated with the advanced economies, with freely convertible currencies, choosing specializations carefully, taking advantage of "holes" in development and prevailing market practices, alert and open to change. Thus, "openness" to changes in development and rapid response to demands—a prerequisite to modernity—will accomplish two goals: it will end the autarchic patterns of development, and will also free management to pursue aggressive avenues and, hence to reap their success or pay for their failure.

And, finally, the reforms must result in the reintegration of these economies with the world economy, openness for trade and competition, and financial "convertibility." The attendant ills will be many; these states will first have to find out how backward they truly are, how difficult the adjustment will be, and how the double whammy of stagflation will, especially at the outset, decimate their efforts. *But there is no alternative to this element of modernization.* Economies that are tied, as are these economies to a large extent, to a single system that is itself trying to make changes, are economies at risk. The old and guaranteed supply network will be gone, as will be the ready markets for products below world standard. Questions of payment and the repayment of the huge loans will be raised and answered negatively; national bankruptcies will be the price to pay for the mistakes of the past. There will also be outlines of emerging change: joint ventures, technology import, and general modernization. Together they will create the basis of the modern economy, although the extent of the "reform" will vary according to the extent that these regimes give up the old-fashioned bases that led them to the current malaise.

I have not mentioned the question of "ownership" and "recapitalization of the commanding heights of the economy." In fact, ownership is a bugaboo that should not even be raised, lest it scare the "doctrinaire" away from experimentation. For ownership can be "public"—as are many successful municipal utilities in the West—or "private" with many stockholders. Neither of these must result in the much feared exploitation of man by man anymore than it results today in the exploitation of man by the state. Reprivatization on a small scale, indeed, has been the rule in many of these countries, starting with private agricultural ownership in Poland, and culminating in large private firms in Hungary today that employ, semi-legally, several hundred employees. What truly matters is not the fact of ownership, but the successful or unsuccessful management of the available resource.

Clouded as they are in relative uncertainty, the economic outlines of the reform, e.g. where it must go to create a modern system, are relatively clear when compared to the potential changes in the much more confusing political arena. Although there are available several reform "models" to ground our projections on more realistic bases, the potential political reforms will reflect a greater system-wide variance than those in the economic sphere. Moreover, resistance to political change will be more difficult to overcome, by even the most determined reformers. Simply put, in all of these countries power is exercised with missionary zeal by a narrow circle, a single party, and a single class. If that narrow group, its *nomenklatura* and coterie, continue to maintain the controls they have hitherto exercised, no reform can be achieved. The interests of that narrow group lie in maintaining stability, the *status quo*, and not in fostering change; the interests of change and modernity, *au contraire*, lie in this narrow group's demise.

Yet, there can be room for compromise in this respect. Hence, it is conceivable that the party withdraws, to a varied degree, from day-to-day management and confines itself to giving general directions or policies. Thus, one can see greater roles played by formal institutional structures, such as the Parliament or trade unions in Poland, and public or interest groups like the "government" in Hungary or the management apparat in Bulgaria. However limited that pluralization will be, it will slowly remove the party as a whole from being the source of change. Indirectly, it will allow the party to blame other institutions for the expected failures, rather than accepting the blame totally by itself.

Allowing dissent or the right to express different opinions about policies is not *eo ipso* the same as allowing dissenters to present alternative platforms. But dissent is a precondition of change, insofar as it leads to the correction of errors, the elimination of glaring inefficiences, the remedying of failures, and the projection of alternative methods. For dissent to be successfully harnessed by the "reform" leadership, it must be given "legitimacy" through recognition that the dissenters' motives are not hostile, and that they are not committing crimes stemming from "imperialist machinations." Thus, for the political reform to succeed, the party must surrender its right to be the sole source of wisdom. Its legitimacy, whatever remains today, would not be greatly diminished by such a concession and surely chances for the survival of the socialist system would be greatly enhanced. Lastly, in the political realm, having a younger, "reform" leadership would be the absolute *sine qua non* of a "modern" system. Currently, Eastern Europe is ruled by gerontocrats: men whose average age is 73 whose average tenure is twenty years, and whose vision of the future is clouded by dread of loss of privilege and power should there be any change. That they are incapable of organizing their societies for the great task of modernization is clear to most observers. The mind-set of the revolutionary trying to seize power, of the dictator mobilizing his people, of the autocrat instilling order, is not suitable for the reformer who must grapple with the challenges of destabilization that any reform will bring about. Maintaining power while undertaking reforms is a task these gerontocrats cannot comprehend, let alone undertake. Thus, for any regime to undertake reform it must be led by new elites; the sign "under new management" must be prominently displayed.

The signs of successful modernization will be evident in the improvement of the general health of society at a latter phase of the reform. In this area the negative consequences of the changes from the old to the new system will be most visible, most detrimental, and most undesirable. Unemployment and inflation will thrust a large number of people into abject poverty; the fact that already 40 percent of the people in Hungary today earn below the so-called minimum, bodes ill for all reform societies. The already high suicide, divorce, alcoholism, morbidity, and mortality figures will continue to rise. The pressures of re-adapting a society to competition will cause further heart attacks among the middle-aged, and will cause increases in the already high numbers of nervous disorders in societies that regularly live on Valium.

However, socializing everything has brought no earthly paradise, but perhaps the sobering effects of opportunities to excel may encourage the citizens to act as citizens. While it will be a difficult transformation, the re-emergent entrepreneur, or the industrious worker, and the technical intelligentsia can and may become the basis of transformation and reform. If the emerging trends are correct, the pattern of reform in Hungary and Poland, and even the successes of East Germany, seem to indicate optimism in this regard.

THE LIMITS OF CHANGE

While prognostications about the future may be tinged by wishful thinking, we should remind ourselves of the Bismarckian maxim *Die Politik ist das Kunst des Möglichen*. Our analysis of the realistic potentialities of change should be, therefore, based on a clear delineation of the limits of such change. We should suggest broad outlines of the alterations expected to occur within the next decade in Eastern Europe.

First, the changes will be within-the-system, rather than alterations in the basic system. However fundamental they may be, short of a total collapse of the Soviet empire, in which case these regimes would disappear immediately, these changes will be phrased in ideologically acceptable terms, such as the "adaptation of communism to modern times," and framed within the context of quantitative improvements of the system. Thus, an expectation that "socialism" or the "communist system" will be replaced by "democracy" or some pseudonym thereof, does not have a firm basis in reality.

Second, these changes will be limited by the extent of institutional adaptation. Consequently, certain institutions are likely to remain as frameworks within which these alterations may be accommodated. In the economy the "institution" of public property, as the mainstay of property relations, will not be replaced by re-privatization, or at least not altered as a theoretical achievement of "socialism." Within the limitation of that framework, however, private productive property on a scale from private factories like those once operating on the East German model, to small farms operating on the Polish model, can easily be accommodated. For example, the rights of private productive property ownership may be extended from holding shares in modern stock-companies through an active "state/public" bond-market, all the way to ownership in various sized private firms, including the "traditional" cooperatives. Private, non-productive property, of course, already has practically no limitation—houses or apartments, personal luxury goods, etc. The trick for the system will be to channel the huge untapped financial surpluses that have accumulated in the banks of the region—largely as a result of the constant scarcity of consumer goods—into areas of investment. Thus, any thoughtful reform will rely on these local and easily available resources in its efforts to infuse funds into the necessary economic *"perestroika."* And the best means seem to be the combination of the "traditional socialist" concept of property with a renewed emphasis on private productive property *cum* investment interests.

Third, the central function of "planning" will likely be continued as an ideological parameter of the "system." But the term "planning" already covers a variety of sins from simple indexing to the detailed planning for the production, pricing, and distribution of every imaginable good. The authorities can either continue detailed and total supervision of all economic functions, or, by loosening control over allocations, they can permit near-total decentralization. Ending subsidies, giving a significant amount of play to the market, terminating the internalism and the overwhelmingly pro-CEMA orientation, and even establishing "joint-stock companies" with modern, "Western," technology-intensive firms—on both the domestic and the external trade levels of the economy—can be accommodated within the "socialist model." It depends upon whether the authorities are willing to change this largely bankrupt system.

Fourth, while the "sacred" concept of the "leading role of the party" (e.g., its desire to control everything, including the economy) will limit the potential for change, my formulation is broad enough to accommodate diverse experiments. Consequently, the party could lead, merely by providing broad principles, or by directing operations at every level. In other words, the principle of the leading role of the party, is a factor of minimal limitation. However, its application in practice, and the extent to which the party elite desires to retain control over its application, will determine the success of the changes in the economy.

Finally, in the economic sphere, the state could most easily encourage the development of what is loosely referred to as the "second economy," e.g., the system of relations and structures existing outside of the "planned" economy. The opportunities appear endless, for the second economy already exists in some form everywhere in the region (the extent of its operations differing from state to state). In a modern economy such secondary activities could not only supplant, but even replace the traditional and outmoded primary economic activities. The second (private, small scale) economy is more dynamic, more capable, and more flexible than its planned counterpart and thus more able to incorporate modern, consumer, technology- or export-oriented activities. While one would presumably need to attach the adjective "socialist" to the second economy, in order for it to be acceptable as an ideologically proper "formation," the operations of such a system can easily serve as the basis for the micro-modernization of the economic system.

Changes in the political structure of institutions will be even more tricky, and they too must be expressed in "within-the-system change" terms. In other words, care must be taken by the reformers not to pose an "alternative model" to that of the USSR, however much General Secretary Gorbachev caters to the notion of "divergent roads of development" in Eastern Europe.[4] During the "reform-era" the principle that apparently has to remain theoretically unchallenged is that of the leading role of the party. But, here too, there is a great deal of latitude. The concept is broad enough to accommodate everything from a theoretically "directive" party that merely provides vague or broad ideological outlines, to an activist party that involves itself with every small detail. In other words, the concept can retain ideological purity, while the party slowly melts away.

A second institutional limit to political change is the "socialist structure of the administrative system." Based on the "Soviets" and the by-now familiar "communist" institutions that permeate these systems, a framework is in place and its established structures are not likely to be altered. However, the communist party monopoly within these institutions can, clearly, be altered to accommodate reform. Thus, for instance, Parliaments—whether they are called the Sejm or the Grand National Assembly—can become vital bodies for the discussion of alternative policies and roles. The "governments"—as distinct from the theoretical guiding role of the single party— can respond to administrative tasks. We should note, again, parenthetically, that it would be easier and more legitimate for the governments to accept blame for prospective failures than for the omniscient, though no longer omnipotent, party.

A third institutional limit of political change also emanates from the theoretically monopolistic nature of the party. In the past, monopolization of the political spectrum has forced every other organ or group to fulfill subordinate or "transmission" functions and prevented effective pluralization of the input, feedback or output functions. Yet, it is possible to achieve greater pluralization, both institutional and grassroots, necessary for the functioning of modern systems. Open and alternative interest groups, "dissident" alternatives, or truly multi-person (as distinct from oppositional multi-party) elections could be accommodated within the existing system of "communist party supremacy."[5]

Finally, dramatic changes in the social structure could be introduced without destroying the "communist" base. A greater privatization, in fact, has already been taking place all over the region; as the money for social benefits becomes ever more scarce, these regimes withdraw from the maintenance of hitherto "free" social services. Thus, one sees the appearance and domination of the second society, characterized by Balkanized personalization of statist social systems, by personal contracts based on personalized contacts, and by an ever-decreasing reliance on the state for assistance with an individual's desired social and personal goals. The potential changes in this area are probably the greatest, for the options of the elite in providing benefits to the citizenry are limited by the unavailability of resources.

Let me make clear, however, that the chances for the success of institutional change are not only limited by institutional factors, but also by personal and personnel considerations as well. The systems in force are run by people who have built up a narrow power elite, with a *nomenklatura* with a vested interest in the *status quo*. This *nomeklatura* operates at all levels, from the top to the local party apparat, and affects (with all the coteries) about twenty to thirty percent of the populace. It includes the *apparatchiks* of the party and state, the individuals who receive their salaries and benefits for "administering" the system. But it includes many more, the economic white collar administrators, the trade union officials, the store-keepers, and the the gas station managers. However, the *apparatchiks*, like nearly everyone living under communist rule, play dual roles in society. On the one hand, they are subject to the benefits doled out by others, while, on the other hand, by virtue of their positions they are also "representatives" of the state, and, thus have "power" they can exercise. In a new system, where a premium is placed on performance and not "function," where one's "position" is determined by the interplay of accomplishment *cum* incentive, the position of these individuals and groups will be threatened. Thus, those who have hitherto been the greatest beneficiaries of the system, are likely to be the least interested in altering it. The personal displacement potential of these groups will be as much of a limiting factor in the modernization of these systems as the institutional obstacles referred to above.

Especially in the top elite, we can see an opposition to and hence a limit on modernizing change. The men are old and wish to live the remainder of their lives in the style to which they are now accustomed. They wish to give up neither power nor privileges, and, therefore, regard attempted change as a threat to their existence. Regardless of the costs to their states, they believe that the policies they have pursued ("Haven't they been successful to date?" they ask, for "after all, our system is still in existence") have been in the best interests of their country. With the possible exception of General Jaruzelski, none of these leaders are capable of undertaking the necessary reforms. Thus, the greatest limit to any potential reform lies first in the inability of the top political leaders to recognize the problems facing the East European states, and second, in the unwillingness *cum* inability of the leaders to do something about the malaise.

It has frequently been posited that the changes that can occur will depend upon the attitude of the USSR toward the ideals of reform. On the one hand, such assertions are indeed correct, for not only ultimately, but daily, by its every activity, the Soviet Union exercises an overwhelming influence on the region and on the regimes in power. The USSR, however, appears to vacillate in defining what it wishes to accomplish in the region. Sometimes, in its extreme isolationist mode it may wish to give up the Empire in disgust over those "troublesome East Europeans," while at other times it wishes to exploit them to the fullest for the benefit of this last colonial center of the world. Gorbachev himself appears to vacillate; between rethinking the 1968 invasion,[6] while engaging in unlimited *perestroika* and *glasnost'* at home on the one hand, and "strengthening integration" and merely engaging in largely cosmetic, "diluted change," on the other. Between these extremes are ample opportunities for reform and the East European elites cannot predict what the USSR will allow these regimes to actually accomplish. I believe that a large dose of skepticism, concerning the extent of change allowed these regimes, is well warranted.

On a different level, however, the Eastern European regimes are not merely stooges of the USSR. While they could be replaced at will by the USSR in a crisis situation, normally (for reasons too complex to elaborate here) the top leaders are treated by the Soviet elites as "legitimate rulers."

Conversely, these rulers actually believe they are legitimate elites, in charge of their nations' welfare and destiny, and are even deluded into thinking that they can and do decide what policies to undertake in their land. Most of these aged fossils think that Gorbachev does not realize the threat of instability stemming from reform, but even more importantly, most of them doubt that a young "upstart" like Gorbachev can possibly succeed. Should Gorbachev stress reforms at home and press reforms on the East European leaders, the septuagenarians feel that they can ignore the pressures; Gorbachev's visit to Budapest, East Berlin, Bucharest, and Prague illustrate this point, nothwithstanding Husak's replacement by Milos Jakes. Thus, while the USSR continues to exert dominant influence in the region, its ability to dictate policies is severely limited in non-crisis situations. Putting it differently, while the Soviet leaders can decide the limits of reforms in Eastern Europe, and while Gorbachev and Company do reserve a veto-power over the successors to the current leaders, their ability to shape and influence reforms in these systems is also constrained.

Parenthetically, it is worth mentioning that Gorbachev's reform attempts at home are also constrained by a force that is more extensive than simply "opposition by Ligachev" or by other party leaders. For, as Stephen Cohen argued in an article nearly ten years ago, "The real obstacle to reform in the Soviet Union is not this or that institution, group, faction, or leader, but the profound conservatism that seems to dominate them all, from the ordinary family to the Politburo, from local authorities to the state *nachal'stvo*."[7] Notwithstanding the powerful positions of some reformers in 1987 in the USSR, reforms in the Soviet Union have not even begun to crack the wall of conservatism. Thus, it would be silly for us (or for East European reformers, for that matter) to expect that Gorbachev will assert his influence for reforms abroad when he cannot even get his "reformist ways" instituted within the USSR. No, reforms in Eastern Europe must come from within, and the best hope for those regimes bent on reform is that the USSR stop interfering with ongoing processes of change.

CONCLUSION: THE DANGERS OF CHANGE

I have tried to demonstrate that the states of Eastern Europe are at a crossroad of change once again. As in the past, the choices facing the people and the leaders are serious and significant; the road to be travelled must be chosen with care. But the choices that will be made by the elites are more crucial than those made in the past. Today the options are more starkly outlined: either they engage in serious reform or their economies and policies will fall farther and farther behind those of the "post-modern" states of the world.

As I posited earlier, the causes of the malaise, are clearly systemic: they are due to the imposition upon them, and the continued operation by them, of the "communist" system. The malaise, thus, is both "homemade" and, not importable. It is not caused by imperialistic machinations, by spending unnecessary sums on the military, or by such forces as "the oil crisis in the West." And thus, the cure for the malaise also must be both systemic and introduced at home.

Of course, these states have often faced difficult choices, frequently involving serious consequences: freedom, independence versus enslavement, and territorial or national extinction. The countries were often wiped off the map, the people became subjects of foreign powers, their languages or cultures were driven underground, and the death of patriots, buried under rubble or in unmarked graves, in broken fields, or in destroyed cities were common occurrences. Extinction is not an immediate threat in the crisis these states are about to confront. At stake today, however, is the future of these people as part of the modern world, as well as their aspirations to live under a better and freer system. Muddling through is not an adequate response to the challenges of the next few decades; muddled stagnation means falling farther and farther behind, without hope of catching up with the West. Hence, the welfare of the people and the countries demands that signficiant reforms be undertaken.

Even if they were to begin fundamental reforms, these states would still face grave dangers, for expectations are raised unreasonably when reforms are underway. But this is now a matter of crisis-management rather than fundamental choice. The options for the regimes are no longer *whether* to have reforms, but the extent, speed, and direction of the projected changes. For the alternative to reform is not simply stagnation *cum* terror forever and ever. The alternative to reform now is revolution later, resulting in tragedies both for the people and for the regimes in power. Undertaking major reforms now, may save the system in its altered forms, and may prevent widespread tragedy.

The "cure" is relatively easy to discern: reform in order to enter the modern world. While the trappings of the ideological mumbo-jumbo some call "Marxism-Leninism" can perhaps be saved as an overlay that is truly irrelevant, the essence of the centralized, directed state and policy, must be modified to reach modernity. The question, thus, is not what to do, but rather whether the people of the region can trust their doctor, the party elite, to provide the much-needed cure. Unfortunately, for most of the region, a second opinion is not readily available, for their is no second doctor of their own choosing. Their contemporary leaders, whose ideology and trust in the operation of an outmoded system convinced them to choose this path, are, largely, responsible both for the malaise and the salvation of the patient.

And here, perhaps, there is a glimmer of hope in the fact that a generation of elderly leaders will enter the "communist nirvana" within the next decade. If they are followed by leaders who are more enlightened, more cognizant of the needs of a modernized system, less beholden to ideological tenets that have proven inapplicable and incorrect, and less restrictive in their philosophy, perhaps there is a possibility for the people of the region to live as citizens in states that a are part of the post-modern world. And if the USSR itself undertakes the same much-needed reforms, the chances for the success of reforms in Eastern Europe will be greatly strengthened.

NOTES

1. In this essay primary attention will be focused on the states of Bulgaria, Czechoslovakia, the German Democratic Republic, Hungary, Poland, and Romania. While the malaise also affects Yugoslavia and Albania, the special conditions affecting these two states are so divergent that generalization regarding them is even more difficult to make than in regards to the current European members of the Warsaw Pact.
2. See Gorbachev's speech in Prague, *Pravda*, April 11, 1987.
3. Janos Kornai, *A hiany* (Budapest: Kozgazdasagi es Jogi Kiado, 1980).
4. Gorbachev has tantalized reporters, East and West alike, with casual references to his conception of freedom for Eastern Europe, but it is still difficult to know what he thinks the limits of his "modified Brezhnev Doctrine" are. See *Pravda*, November 9, 1987.
5. To date, aside from the Hungarian case, only the Polish system tried to deal with "public groups." Even here, however, officials have maintained that only "socialist" associations that subscribe to the notion of "socialist pluralism," e.g., pluralism within the accepted "socialist framework" of one party rule, can become "legitimate" partners of the party. *Rzeczpospolita*, September 30, 1987.
6. See especially *The New York Times*, November 5 and 10, 1987, pp. 1 and 7.
7. Stephen Cohen, "The Friends and Foes of Change: Reformism and Conservatism in the Soviet Union," *Slavic Review*, June, 1979, p. 198.

CONTRIBUTORS

AUREL BRAUN was born in Romania and emigrated to Canada in 1961. Since receiving his Ph. D. from the London School of Economics, he has taught at the University of Toronto where he is an Associate Professor of Political Science, specializing in Eastern European politics, military affairs, and the Middle East. A prolific scholar, his most recent publication is titled *Soviet-East Europe Relations during the Gorbachev Era*, (Duke University Press, 1988).

NICHOLAS KITTRIE, the Edwin A. Mooers Scholar and Professor of Law at The American University, Washington, D.C., has travelled extensively and done research in the Soviet Union and Eastern Europe. Previously Counsel to the United States Senate Judiciary Committee, Dr. Kittrie serves as vice-chairman of the United Nations Alliance of Non-Governmental Organizations for Crime Control and Criminal Justice.

ANDRZEJ KORBONSKI was born in Poland and emigrated to the United States after World War II. He received his Ph. D. from Columbia University and has specialized in Eastern European politics, agrarian politics, and politics of modernization. He is a Professor of Political Science at UCLA and a co-director of the RAND-UCLA Center for Soviet and East European Affairs. His most recent book (edited with Frank Fukuyama) is titled *The Soviet Union and the Third World: The Last Three Decades* (Cornell University Press, 1987).

BENNETT KOVRIG was born in Hungary and emigrated to the United States following World War II. He received his Ph. D. from the London School of Economics and has been Professor of Political Science at the University of Toronto, specializing in Eastern European politics and American Foreign Policy. He is the author of scores of scholarly articles and five books, the most significant being *Communism in Hungary* (Hoover, 1979) and *The Myth of Liberation* (Johns Hopkins, 1973). Dr. Kovrig currently serves as the Director of Research for Radio Free Europe.

JOHN LUKACS emigrated to the United States in 1945. He is a Professor of History at Chestnut Hill College in Philadelphia and one of the most prolific historians of our time. His broad range of writings include such studies as *Philadelphia, Outgrowing Democracy*, and *A New History of the Cold War*. His newest volume is *Budapest, 1900* (Weidenfeld and Nicholson, 1988).

JAN PRYBYLA, a native of Poland, emigrated to the United States in the aftermath of World War II. He received a Ph. D. from National University in Ireland and since his graduation has specialized in the study of the Eastern European, Soviet, and Chinese economic systems. Dr. Pryblya is a Professor of Political Science at Penn State University. A prolific scholar, his most recent work is *Market and Plan Under Socialism: The Bird in the Cage* (Hoover, 1987).

ROBERT SHARLET was born in the United States and received his Ph. D. from Indiana University. A specialist in Soviet and East European law, human rights, and dissent, he is a Professor of Political Science at Union College and a Visiting Fellow at the Research Institute for International Change at Columbia University. In addition to his extensive publication activities, Dr. Sharlet also served as a senior analyst monitoring human rights abuses in the USSR and in Eastern Europe for Amnesty International.

OTTO ULC, a native of Plzen, Czechoslovakia is a graduate of Charles University Law School. After serving as a judge from 1953 to 1959, he came to the United States and received a Ph. D. from Columbia University. He is a Professor of Political Science at SUNY Binghamton, where he specializes in comparative politics, Eastern Europe, international relations and international law. A prolific writer in both Czech and English, he has written eleven volumes and scores of articles. His most significant scholarly volumes in English are The Politics of Czechoslovakia (Freeman, 1974), and The Judge in a Communist State (Ohio University Press, 1972).

IVAN VOLGYES is a senior faculty member and Professor of Political Science at the University of Nebraska at Lincoln. He is the author of numerous books and articles dealing with the Soviet Union and Eastern Europe. He is a frequent consultant to the Departments of State and Defense. Dr. Volgyes is a member of the editorial board of the quarterly journal on world affairs, ORBIS.

BIBLIOGRAPHY

AND SELECTED FURTHER READINGS

Ancsel, Eva. *The Dilemmas of Freedom.* Budapest: Akademiai Kiado, 1978.

Bender, Peter. *East Europe in Search of Security.* Baltimore, MD: Johns Hopkins University Press, 1972.

Berend, Ivan T., and Gyorgy Ranki, eds. *Underdevelopment and Economic Growth: Studies in Hungarian Social and Economic History.* Budapest: Akademiai Kiado, 1979.

Besemeres, John F. *Socialist Population Politics.* White Plains, NY: Sharpe, 1980.

Bornstein, Morris, Zvi Gitelman, and William Zimmerman, eds. *East-West Relations and the Future of Eastern Europe: Politics and Economics.* Winchester, MA: Allen & Unwin, 1981.

Braun, Aurel. *Ceausescu: The Problems of Power.* Toronto: Canadian Institute of International Affairs, 1979/80.

Bromke, Adam, and Terry Novak, eds. *The Communist States in the Era of Detente.* Oakville, Ont.: Mosaic Press, 1979.

Brown, J.F., *Eastern Europe and Communist Rule.* Durham, NC: Duke University Press, 1988.

Brown, James F. *Relations Between the Soviet Union and Its East European Allies: A Survey.* R-1742-PR. Santa Monica, CA: The Rand Corporation, 1975.

Brucan, Silviu. *World Socialism at the Crossroads: An Insider's View*. New York: Praeger, 1987.

Brzezinski, Zbigniew and Samuel P. Huntington. *Political Power: USA/USSR*. New York: The Viking Press, 1963.

Brzezinski, Zbigniew K. *The Soviet Bloc*. Cambridge, MA: Harvard University Press, 1960; rev. ed., New York: Praeger, 1961.

Burks, R.V. *The Dynamics of Communism in Eastern Europe*. Princeton: Princeton University Press, 1965.

Carrere d'Encausse, Hélène. *Big Brother: The Soviet Union and Soviet Europe*. New York: Holmes and Meier.

Colton, T.J.. *Commissars, Commanders, and Civilian Authority*. Cambridge, Mass: Harvard U.P., 1979.

Colton, Timothy J. *The Dilemma of Reform in the Soviet Union*. New York: Council on Foreign Relations, 1984.

Connor, Walter D. *Socialism, Politics, and Equality: Hierarchy and Change in Eastern Europe and the USSR*. New York: Columbia University Press, 1979.

Curry, Jane L., ed. *Dissent in Eastern Europe*. New York: Praeger, 1983.

Dawisha, Karen. *The Kremlin and the Prague Spring*. Berkeley: University of California Press, 1984.

Drachkovitch, Milorard M., ed. *East Central Europe: Yesterday, Today, Tomorrow*. Stanford, CA: Hoover Institution Press, 1982.

Erickson, John. "The Warsaw Pact: The Shape of Things to Come?" In *Soviet-East European Dilemmas: Coercion, Competition, and Consent*. edited by Karen Dawisha and Philip Hanson, 148-171. London: Allen & Unwin, 1981.

Fejto, Francois. *A History of the People's Democracies: Eastern Europe Since Stalin*. New York: Praeger, 1971.

Ferge, Zsuzsa. *A Society in the Making: Hungarian Social and Societal Policies, 1945-75.* White Plains, NY: Sharpe, 1980.

Fischer-Galati, Stephen, ed. *The Communist Parties of Eastern Europe.* New York: Columbia University Press, 1979.

Friedrich, Carl J. and Zbigniew A. Brzezinski. *Totalitarian Dictatorship and Autocracy.* New York: Praeger, 1962.

Garthoff, Raymond. *Détente and Confrontation: American-Soviet Relations from Nixon to Reagan.* Washington: Brookings Institution, 1985.

Gati, Charles, ed. *The International Politics of Eastern Europe.* New York: Praeger, 1976.

Gorbachev, Mikhail. *Perestroika: New Thinking for Our Country and the World.* New York:Harper & Row, 1987.

Grzybowski, Kazimierz. *The Socialist Commonwealth of Nations.* New Haven, CT: Yale University Press, 1964.

Hammond, Thomas T., ed. *The Anatomy of Communist Takeovers.* New Haven, CT: Yale University Press, 1975.

Haraszti, Miklos. *The Velvet Prison: Artists Under State Socialism.* transl. by Katalin and Stephen Landesmann with the help of Steve Wasserman. New York: The New Republic/Basic Books, 1987.

Held, Joseph, ed. *The Modernization of Agriculture: Rural Transformation in Hungary.* Boulder, CO: 1980.

Herspring, Dale R. and Ivan Volgyes. *Civil-Military Relations in Communist States.* Boulder, CO: Westview, 1979.

Hoehmann, Hans-Hermann, Michael C. Kaser, and Karl C. Thalheim, eds. *The New Economic Systems of Eastern Europe.* Berkeley, CA: University of California Press, 1976.

Holzman, Franklyn D. *International Trade Under Communism: Politics and Economics*. New York: Basic Books, 1976.

Huntington, Samuel P. and Clement H. Moore, eds. *Authoritarian Politics in Modern Society*. New York: Basic Books, 1970.

Ionescu, Ghita. *The Politics of the European Communist States*. New York: Praeger, 1967.

Jamgotch, Nish, Jr. *Soviet-East Euorpean Dialogue: International Relations of a New Type?* Stanford, CA: Stanford University Press, 1968.

Johnson, Chalmers ed. *Change in Communist Systems*. Stanford, CA: Stanford University Press, 1970.

Johnson, A. Ross, R. W. Dean, and Alex Alexiev. *East European Military Establishments: The Warsaw Pact Northern Tier*. Santa Monica, CA: Rand Corporation, 1980.

Jones Christopher D, *Soviet Influence in Eastern Europe: Political Autonomy and the Warsaw Pact*. New York: Praeger, 1981.

Joseph, Philip, ed. *Adaptability to New Technologies of the USSR and East European Countries*. Brussels: NATO Colloquium, 1985.

Kaser, Michael. *Comecon: Integration Problems of the Planned Economies,* 2nd ed. London: Oxford University Press, 1967.

Kertesz, Stephen P., ed. *East-Central Europe and the World: Developments in the Post-Stalin Era*. Notre Dame, IN: University of Notre Dame Press, 1962.

King, Robert R. *Minorities Unde.' Communism: Nationalities as a Source of Tension Among Balkan Communist States*. Cambridge, MA: Harvard University Press, 1973.

Korbonski, Andrzej. *The Politics of Socialist Agriculture in Poland: 1945-1960*. New York: Columbia, 1965.

Kovrig, Bennett. *Communism in Hungary: From Kun to Kadar*. Stanford, CA: Hoover Institution Press, 1979.

Kovrig, Bennett. *The Hungarian People's Republic*. Baltimore, MD: Johns Hopkins University Press, 1970.

Kovrig, Bennett. *The Myth of Liberation*. Baltimore, MD: Johns Hopkins University Press, 1973.

Kuhlman, James A. *The Foreign Policy of Eastern Europe*. Leyden, Neth.: Sijthoff, 1978.

Laszlo, Ervin, and Joel Kurtzman, eds. *Eastern Europe and the New International Economic Order*. Elmsford, NY: Pergamon Press, 1980.

Lendvai, Paul. *The Bureaucracy of Truth*. Boulder, CO: Westview, 1981.

Lendvai, Paul. *Anti-Semitism without Jews*. Garden City, NY: Doubleday, 1971.

Linden, Ronald H. *Bear and Foxes: The International Relations of East European States*. New York: Columbia University Press, 1979.

Lovendevski, Joni and Jean Woodall. *Politics and Society in Eastern Europe*. London: Macmillan Education, 1987.

Luttwak, Edward N. *The Paradoxical Logic of Strategy*. Berkeley: Institute of International Studies, 1987.

Malcher, George C. *Poland's Politicized Army: Communists in Uniform*. New York: Praeger, 1984.

Marer, Paul, and John Michael Montias. *East European Integration and East-West Trade*. Bloomington, IN: Indiana University Press, 1980.

Millar, T.B. *East-West Strategic Balance*. Winchester, MA: Allen & Unwin, 1981.

Morton, Henry W. and Rudolf L. Tokes, eds. *Soviet Politics and Society in the 1970s*. New York: The Free Press, 1974.

Nelson, Daniel N. *Soviet Allies*. Boulder, CO: Westview, 1984.

Nelson, Daniel N. *Alliance Behavior in the Warsaw Pact*. Boulder, CO: Westview Press 1986.

O'Connor, James. *The Meaning of Crisis: A Theoretical Introduction*. Oxford, UK: Basil Blackwell, 1987.

Pryblya, Jan *Issues in Socialist Econmic Modernization*. New York: Praeger, 1981.

Rakowska Harmstone, Teresa, et al. *Warsaw Pact: The Question of Cohesion*. Vol. 1, Ottawa: ORAE, 1984.

Rakowska-Harmstone, Teresa, and Andrew Gyorgy, eds. *Communism in East Europe*. Bloomington, IN: Indiana University Press, 1979.

Rosser, Richard F. *An Introduction to Soviet Foreign Policy*. Englewood, N.J.: Prentice-Hall, 1969.

Schopflin, George. *Eastern European Handbook*. London: St. Martin's Press, 1982.

Scott, W. Richard. *Organizations: Rational, Natural and Open Systems*. Englewood Cliffs, N.J.: Prentice-Hall, 1981.

Seton-Watson, Hugh. *The East European Revolution*. New York: Praeger, 1956.

Silnitsky, Frantisek, et al., eds. *Communism and Eastern Europe*. New York: Karz, 1979.

Skilling, H. Gordon. *The Governments of Communist East Europe*. New York: Crowell, 1966.

Staar, Richard F., *Communist Regimes in Eastern Europe*. 4th ed. Stanford, CA: Hoover, 1982.

Terry, Sarah M., ed. *Soviet Policy in Eastern Europe*. New Haven and London: Yale University Press, 1984.

Tokes, Rudolf L., ed. *Opposition in Eastern Europe*. Baltimore, MD: Johns Hopkins University Press, 1979.

Triska, Jan F., and Charles Gati, eds. *Blue Collar Workers in Eastern Europe*. Winchester, MA: Allen & Unwin, 1981.

Valenta, Jiri. *Soviet Intervention in Czechoslovakia, 1968: Anatomy of a Decision*. Baltimore: Johns Hopkins University Press, 1979.

Volgyes, Ivan. *Environmental Deterioration in the USSR and in Eastern Europe*. New York: Praeger, 1975.

Volgyes, Ivan, ed. *Comparative Political Socialization: Eastern Europe*. New York: Praeger, 1975.

Volgyes, Ivan. *Social Deviance in Eastern Europe*. Boulder, CO: Westview, 1978.

Volgyes, Ivan. *The Reliability of the East European Armies: The Southern Tier*. Chapel Hill, NC: Duke University Press, 1983.

Volgyes, Ivan. *The Government and Politics of Eastern Europe*. Lincoln, NE: Cliff Notes, 1979.

Volgyes, Ivan. *Politics in Eastern Europe*. Chicago: Dorsey Press, 1986.

Volgyes, Ivan, ed. *The Political Reliability of the Warsaw Pact Armies: The Southern Tier*. Durham, NC: Duke University Press, 1982.

White, Stephen, John Gardner, and George Schopflin. *Communist Political Systems: An Introduction*. London: Macmillan, 1982.

INDEX